Governing the Galleys: Jurisdiction, Justice, and Trade in the Squadrons of the Hispanic Monarchy (Sixteenth–Seventeenth Centuries)

Mediterranean Reconfigurations

INTERCULTURAL TRADE, COMMERCIAL LITIGATION, AND LEGAL PLURALISM

Series Editors

Wolfgang Kaiser (*Université Paris I, Panthéon-Sorbonne*)
Guillaume Calafat (*Université Paris I, Panthéon-Sorbonne*)

VOLUME 1

The titles published in this series are listed at *brill.com/cmed*

Governing the Galleys: Jurisdiction, Justice, and Trade in the Squadrons of the Hispanic Monarchy (Sixteenth–Seventeenth Centuries)

By

Manuel Lomas

Translated by

Consuelo López-Morillas

BRILL

LEIDEN | BOSTON

The Open Access publication of this book has been funded by the ERC.

Cover illustration: *The Voyage of the Cardinal Infante Ferdinand of Spain from Barcelona to Genoa in April 1633, with Neptune Calming the Tempest* by Peter Paul Rubens, 1635. Oil on panel, Harvard Art Museums/Fogg Museum, Alpheus Hyatt Purchasing Fund.

Library of Congress Cataloging-in-Publication Data

Names: Lomas Cortés, Manuel, author. | López-Morillas, Consuelo, translator.
Title: Governing the galleys : jurisdiction, justice, and trade in the squadrons of the hispanic monarchy (sixteenth–seventeenth centuries) / by Manuel Lomas ; translated by Consuelo López- Morillas.
Description: Leiden ; Boston : Brill, 2020. | Series: Mediterranean reconfigurations; vol. 1 | Includes bibliographical references and index.
Identifiers: LCCN 2019034667 (print) | LCCN 2019034668 (ebook) | ISBN 9789004381469 (hardback) | ISBN 9789004413290 (ebook)
Subjects: LCSH: Naval law–Spain–History–16th century. | Naval law–Spain–History–17th century. | Naval offenses–Law and legislation–Spain–History–16th century. | Naval offenses–Law and legislation–Spain–History–17th century. | Spain–History, Naval–16th century. | Spain–History, Naval–17th century.
Classification: LCC KKT3748.N38 L66 2020 (print) | LCC KKT3748.N38 (ebook) | DDC 387.5/44094609031–dc23
LC record available at https://lccn.loc.gov/2019034667
LC ebook record available at https://lccn.loc.gov/2019034668

Typeface for the Latin, Greek, and Cyrillic scripts: “Brill”. See and download: brill.com/brill-typeface.

ISSN 2494-8772
ISBN 978-90-04-38146-9 (hardback)
ISBN 978-90-04-41329-0 (e-book)

This book is printed on acid-free paper and produced in a sustainable manner.

Contents

Abbreviations, Coinage, Weights, and Measures VII

Introduction 1

1 **Galleys on the Coast!** 12
1 The Jurisdiction of the Galleys 13
1.1 *Continuity and Change under the Catholic Monarchs* 13
1.2 *Culmination of the Process: from Andrea Doria to Don John of Austria* 18
1.3 *The System in Its Maturity: from the Conquest of Portugal to the Thirty Years' War* 22
2 Galleys and Ports: Profiles of a Complex Relationship 25
2.1 *The Galleys: a Vehicle for Concord* 26
2.2 *"That Is Spain's Flagship, and This Is the Pope's Fortress"* 30
2.3 *Soldiers, Sailors, and Townspeople* 34
3 Between Naval Tradition and Military Innovation 39
3.1 *Galley Ordinances and Corsair Customs* 40
3.2 *Convergence with the Tradition of Military Privileges* 42
3.3 *Roman Law and Experience: the Introduction of Auditores into the Galleys* 45
3.4 *The Galleys' Jurisdictional Supremacy* 49

2 **Captures, Commerce, and Corruption** 59
1 Prizes, Embargoes, and the Audiencia de las Galeras 60
1.1 *Ship Capture and Its Benefits to Crews* 60
1.2 *Acquisition of Slaves* 64
1.3 *The Audiencia de las Galeras and Embargoes* 69
2 Cross-Cultural Trade and Control of Smuggling 80
2.1 *Between Religious War and Collaboration: the Action of Tunis, 1609* 81
2.2 *Profiles of a Cross-Cultural Trade: Ransoms* 85
2.3 *Purchase of North African Wheat and Control of Maritime Trade* 91

3 Legitimate Trade and Fraud in the Galleys 95
3.1 *Smuggling in the Galleys* 96
3.2 *The Visit of 1591* 103
3.3 *The Galleys of Spain and El Puerto de Santa María* 107

3 Resistance, Consensus, and Solidarity 119
1 Escapes and Mutinies 120
1.1 *Escapees* 120
1.2 *Mutineers* 125
2 Internal Justice, Mercy, and Solidarity in the Galleys 133
2.1 *The Captain General's Mediation and Mercy* 134
2.2 *Auditores, Inspectors, and Other Officials* 142
2.3 *Solidarity among Soldiers, Sailors, and Rowers* 146
3 Religious Belief 152
3.1 *Catholic Belief* 153
3.2 *Vice among the Crews* 157
3.3 *Captains General and the Inquisition* 160

Conclusion 168

Bibliography 173
Index 186

Abbreviations, Coinage, Weights, and Measures

ADM	Archivo Ducal de Medinaceli
AH	Archivo Histórico
PSM	Puerto de Santa María
ADP	Archivio Doria Pamphilj, Rome
AEESS	Archivo de la Embajada Española ante la Santa Sede [Spanish embassy to the Holy See]
AGS	Archivo General de Simancas
Estado	Section "Estado" [the state]
GyM	Section "Guerra y Marina" [army and navy]
CMC	Section "Contaduría Mayor de Cuentas" [accounts]
AHCB	Arxiu Històric de la Ciutat de Barcelona
AHN	Archivo Histórico Nacional
ASV	Archivio Segreto Vaticano, Vatican City
BNE	Biblioteca Nacional de España
Mss.	Section "Manuscritos"

Equivalencies

1 ducado = 11 reales
1 ducado = 375 maravedís

Weights in Castile

1 quintal = 4 arrobas
1 arroba = 25 libras
1 libra = 460 grams

Introduction

The study of galleys is no longer confined to the history of events, navigation, or tactics. The classic paradigm has gradually been transformed: essentially descriptive—of types of ships and their components, or of the number and composition of their crews—it also served nationalist ends. The affirmation of an epic, glorious past could legitimate a nation's identity and its role in building the political, legal, and cultural reality of the modern-day Mediterranean.[1]

This change in emphasis has come about slowly and has involved different analytical approaches. One of the earliest innovations highlighted the technical and logistical aspects of mobilizing the galleys. Fernand Braudel was the first to offer an overarching view of their costs, the challenges they presented, and their role in the decline of the great Mediterranean armadas, and his work formed the basis for later research.[2] Maurice Aymard, following Braudel's outline, proposed that technical changes in galley construction in the sixteenth century were linked to the evolution of Spain's foreign policy, principally, that an increase in the ships' size required greater human resources for operating them.[3] Shortly afterward, John F. Guilmartin built on Aymard's observation that the trend toward longer galleys affected their logistical impact and maneuverability, adding that other technological changes, such as the introduction of bronze artillery, contributed to the disappearance in the late sixteenth century of the large galley fleets that had previously dominated Mediterranean warfare.[4]

Guilmartin's thesis that galleys grew increasing inoperable, however, was revisited in its turn. Philip Williams maintained that for the Hispanic Monarchy, other pressures beside maintenance costs and technological changes (for example, an evolution in tactical priorities) must have affected the use of galleys in the seventeenth century. In recent years, this scholar has returned to a neglected but classic line of research: he proposes that the training of officers, access to intelligence, improved nautical technology, and strategies of navigation and combat can explain how, though large fleets had disappeared, galleys were not in decline in the early-seventeenth-century Mediterranean. They had

1 Rivero Rodríguez, *Batalla de Lepanto*, 9–17.
2 Braudel, *Méditerranée*, 2:578 ff.
3 Aymard, "Chiourmes."
4 Guilmartin, *Gunpowder and Galleys*, 253–73.

simply adapted to a form of fighting that was different and better suited to their efficiency and manageability, while maximizing their financial costs.[5]

Reliance on galleys in war has been persistently linked to an increase in costs to those who maintained them; according to this view, their use was one of the major challenges that drove the bureaucratic and fiscal development of the new Mediterranean monarchies of the sixteenth century. This line of research, initiated by Otto Hintze in the early twentieth century and continued by Jaume Vicens Vives, was defended by I.A.A. Thompson in the case of the Spanish war-fighting fleet. He stressed the enormous investment involved in creating and maintaining a fleet of galleys. Infrastructure had to be constructed even before the ships were built, and the costs of recruitment and provisioning increased steadily, a problem never well solved even after different models of management were tried.[6] Scholarly attention next turned to the land-based logistics of galley fleets, first studied in the case of Spain by René Quatrefages, continued by Carla Rahn Phillips and Carmen Sanz Ayán, and culminating (so far) in José Miguel Escribano Páez's recent work on the supply chain in Málaga. These publications have shown the importance of examining the role of the king's officers in each of the Crown's dominions and that of the businessmen who held the chief supply contracts; these men could be decisive in the success or failure of a fleet. A persistent question, important but not yet fully resolved, involves the economic and administrative costs to the Hispanic Monarchy of war in the Mediterranean compared to those of war on other better-known fronts.[7]

Another basic principle that interpreted the creation of permanent squadrons of galleys as an expression of centralized administration still prevails in the current debate. Many scholars have accepted Jan Glete's theory that these fleets appeared in parallel with the development of fiscal-military nation-states, those in which bureaucracy and the power to tax grew along with the needs of warfare, particularly the drive to control the sea and monopolize its violence.[8] In the case of the Hispanic Monarchy, it has been followed by Antonello Mattone, Giulio Fenicia, and Valentina Favarò to explain the development of maritime defenses in, respectively, the kingdoms of Sardinia, Naples, and Sicily in the second half of the sixteenth century.[9] Recently, Fabrizio Filioli

5 Williams, "Past and Present." His analysis is cited by Thompson, "Galeras," 115.
6 Hintze, "Organización militar"; Vicens Vives, "Estructura administrativa"; Thompson, *War and Government*, 163–273.
7 Quatrefages, "*Proveeduría*"; Phillips, *Seis galeones*, 42–54; Sanz Ayán, "Abastecimiento"; Escribano Páez, "Actores."
8 Glete, *War and the State*, 30–39.
9 Mattone, "Amministrazione," 514; Fenicia, *Regno di Napoli*, 199; Favarò, *Modernizzazione*, 161.

Uranio has applied it to the birth and evolution of the permanent squadron of papal galleys.[10]

A few years ago, Daniel Dessert wrote in similar terms of the increase in naval power under Louis XIV, although he viewed the royal role as more nuanced. In order to explain the limits, successes, and failures of that naval policy one had to consider, beside the king's initiative, the influence of several great families connected to the nautical world. Following the same line of thought but reaching back to the reign of Louis XIII, David Parrot noted that although the French monarchy strove for centralization, confusion resulted from the lack of a single centralized authority that controlled the military. Olivier Chaline has recently observed that agreements were indispensable if the complicated supplying of French ships were to be successfully carried out.[11]

The trend among historians, then, has been to broaden the number of both actors and analytical perspectives. Significantly, it is now possible to apply to France and Spain models from other contemporary navies that are not necessarily based on the decisive, continuous action of a government in the process of asserting its strength. Thomas A. Kirk and Claire Judde de Larivière have explained the bases of naval power in the republics of Venice and Genoa, respectively, in the sixteenth century in the light of the shifting balance between public benefit and private interest; we should bear their interpretations in mind as we study situations that were distant but by no means contradictory.[12] Guido Candiani, in fact, has demonstrated the influence of the Venetian system on Spanish naval organization, and the avenues for research do not end there.[13] We must not forget that throughout the sixteenth century and into the seventeenth, Spanish strategy in the Mediterranean—and its financial underpinning—was in the hands of a succession of leaders from the Genoese aristocracy, together with other families that soon became closely linked to them. In exploring alliances and explaining attitudes and decisions, we need to understand how those persons conceived the management of galley fleets.

Several recent research projects show the prominence of this last area of inquiry. Arturo Pacini, with his work on the relations between Andrea Doria's Genoa and Charles V; Rafael Vargas-Hidalgo, who edited a large volume of correspondence between Philip II and the Doria family; and Bastien Carpentier, a student of Gian Andrea Doria's client network, have each provided new understanding of the strategies of this leading Italian clan, which administered

10 Filioli Uranio, *Squadra navale.*

11 Dessert, *Royale*, 15–16; Parrot, *Richelieu's Army*, 390; Chaline, *Armées du Roi*, 10–14.

12 Kirk, *Genoa and the Sea*, 46–50; Judde de Larivière, *Naviguer*, 305–10.

13 Candiani, "Galere forzate."

many contracts of the Hispanic Monarchy's galleys in the sixteenth century.[14] Benoît Maréchaux has illuminated the Madrid connections of another Genoese family, the Centuriones, as that collaboration extended into the seventeenth century. Manuel Herrero Sánchez and Yasmina R. Ben Yessef Garfia have done likewise for the Spínolas and Serras, families who also contracted for galleys and provisions, perhaps less continuously and intensely but to an equally significant degree.[15]

These studies have sometimes delved more deeply into these families' social, as well as political, activities. Because some of their members were physically present on the ships and took part in their daily administration (the Dorias and Centuriones wrote many letters while on board), we are acquiring a new understanding of the social history of the leaders and officers who sailed on them.[16]

For a long time, one of the chief aims of historians in this field has been a complete social history of the men who lived and died on the galleys. It was born, as Benedetto Croce wrote, out of the natural human tendency to feel horror and indignation at the harshness of the past and its customs—as a way of not forgetting man's inhumanity to man.[17] Although research has since evolved toward less morbid and didactic ends, there is no doubt that when we imagine life in the galleys, we think first not of their officers or famous passengers but of the men chained to the rowing benches below.

One of the earliest essays on this question in Spain was that of Gregorio Marañón, who, drawing principally on literary texts, sought information on the diet and health of the crews.[18] The first studies based on archival documents, which came somewhat later, analyzed the composition and functions of the rowers. Francisco-Felipe Olesa Muñido provided the first systematic evidence for the Hispanic Monarchy. He tried to go beyond mere classification, but the types of documents he used limited his ability to analyze the crews' social status and their life aboard ship.[19] The line of research that he opened was not followed consistently, but Manuel Marchena Giménez has brought it up to date and, following Olesa Muñido's methods, has attempted to reconstruct the

14 Pacini, *Genova di Andrea Doria*; Vargas-Hidalgo, *Guerra y diplomacia*; Carpentier and Priotti, "Philippe II," 159–82.

15 Maréchaux, "Instituciones navales"; Ben Yessef Garfia, "Perfiles de nobleza"; Herrero Sánchez, "Red genovesa."

16 Lomas Cortés, "Las Galeras de España."

17 Croce, "Vita infernale," 83.

18 Marañón, "Vida en las galeras."

19 Olesa Muñido, *Galera en la navegación*, 155–69.

daily life of galley crews through a valuable archival collection of reports and ordinances.[20]

To explain the commonest research methodology in this field, however, we must turn to the work of Aymard. This French historian was among the first to bring New Social History to bear on the study of galleys, focusing on the acute need for larger numbers of rowers in the sixteenth-century Mediterranean. By combing through surviving registries and lists of crew members, he began to quantify, for a wide range of times and places, the three groups who made up the body of oarsmen, called in Spanish the *chusma* (a Genoese word, ultimately of Greek origin): slaves, convicts, and *buenaboyas*, or salaried freemen (from the Italian *buona voglia*, "free will"). By this method, we learned more about how men entered and left the galleys, the length of their service, the state of their health, and their mortality rate. All these had been very little known except in the Venetian case, which could not easily be applied to other contexts.

The next step was a series of investigations into the strong links between growth in the number of rowers in Mediterranean fleets and the widening range of crimes punishable by service in the galleys. For the Hispanic Monarchy, the basic study was that of José Luis de las Heras on punishment under the Hapsburgs, although more recently Manuel Martínez has taken up the theme with his work on men condemned to naval service in the eighteenth century.[21] As the latter acknowledges, however, the most complete study for the Mediterranean as a whole is that of André Zysberg on France from the late seventeenth to the mid-eighteenth centuries.[22]

At present, this line of research is well established and, without neglecting convicts, has turned toward examining types of enslaved rowers. This second theme was originally linked to interest in the financial management of the galleys. Once it was found that the purchase and maintenance of slaves was sometimes the ships' greatest expenditure, historians took a renewed interest, especially students of the Malta squadron, the largest, most active fleet of Christian galleys engaged in privateering in the sixteenth- and seventeenth-century Mediterranean.

Since the middle of the last century, authors such as Jean Mathiex have uncovered the high prices commanded by galley slaves in the Malta fleet. Michel Fontenay, Godfrey Wettinger, and more recently Anne Brogini have analyzed the phenomenon in detail; it applies as well to other Christian armadas.[23]

---

20 Marchena Giménez, "Vida y los hombres," 261–423.

21 Heras Santos, "Los galeotes de los Austrias"; Martínez Martínez, *Forzados*, 21–55.

22 Zysberg, *Galériens*.

23 Mathiex, "Trafic et prix de l'homme," 161–62; Fontenay, *Esclave galérien*; Wettinger, *Slavery*; Brogini, *Malte*, 259–62, 360–61.

Pierre Boyer and then Zysberg refer to it in their studies on French galleys, and Salvatore Bono in his work on the papal fleet. For squadrons belonging to the Hispanic Monarchy, there are mentions in Maurice Aymard's work and, more recently, in Eva Serra's on slaves in the Galleys of Catalonia and Bernard Vincent's on the Galleys of Naples.[24] Specialists in the field, though limited by the types of documents available (essentially, muster rolls and lists of slaves that contain few details), have continued to speculate about the slaves' ages, the length of their service, and their rate of survival at the oars.

Historians' interests in the field have gradually turned to new questions, including, in recent years, the mentality and religious beliefs of slaves and convicts in the galleys. The initial study by Bartolomé and Lucile Bennassar was not immediately followed up, but Gianclaudio Civale returned to the theme in his work on the Inquisition of the Sea, created for the Spanish navy around the time of the Battle of Lepanto (1571).[25] Eva Serra, for the Catalan galleys, and David Wheat for the little-known Spanish ones in the Caribbean, have focused on slaves from the Morisco minority, while Manuel Martínez has studied gypsies in the Galleys of Spain.[26]

This latest trend is linked to a renewed emphasis on the Mediterranean as a zone of contact between civilizations. Galleys, the emblematic vehicle for conflict between Christendom and Islam in the sixteenth and seventeenth centuries, are attracting renewed attention from practitioners of the new political and military history, and the great events in which they participated are being viewed through a more modern analytical lens. It may seem at times that there are only a few stories worth telling, but the ways of telling them are infinite, as we see from the resurgence of interest in the famed Battle of Lepanto. A few years ago, Manuel Rivero suggested that the Christian victory there revealed a broad European consensus—both Catholic and Protestant—on the idea of a crusade. Shortly afterward, Alessandro Barbero devoted a hefty volume to diplomatic negotiations and contacts between the Ottoman Empire and the Christian powers in the two years before the battle.[27] In a similar vein, Philip Williams has questioned the classic claim that, after the battle, the Mediterranean gradually lost importance in both Spanish and Ottoman strategy. His monograph demonstrates the persistence of the crusading ideal and the relevance of political and military clashes between the two empires in the late

24 Boyer, "Chiourme," 59; Zysberg, "Galères," 423; Bono, "Achat d'esclaves"; Serra i Puig, "Galeres catalanes"; Vincent, "Esclaves," 843.

25 Bennassar, *Chrétiens*, 433–36; Civale, *Guerrieri di Cristo*, 129–50.

26 Wheat, "Mediterranean Slavery"; Martínez Martínez, "Gitanos," 412–21.

27 Rivero Rodríguez, *Batalla de Lepanto*, 293–98; Barbero, *Battaglia*.

sixteenth and early seventeenth centuries.[28] In view of this long, rich historiographic tradition and its wide range of focuses and interests, it is legitimate to ask what contribution or analytical perspective can still be offered.

In June 1618, the notary Vicente de Hermosa sent a report to the Supreme Council of the Inquisition on the problems presented by the Islamic religion aboard the Galleys of Spain. Among the crews, hundreds of slaves and convicts of Morisco origin openly displayed their adherence to Islam and lived "with as free a conscience as if they lived in a land where it exists, under the very nose of the Inquisition and in mockery of it." At that time, a mere four years had passed since all Moriscos from Castile and Aragon had been expelled from Spain. That massive deportation had been justified by the supposed religious treachery, apostasy, and conspiracy of those descendants of the old Mudejar communities in the Iberian Peninsula, and it was claimed as a great victory of the Hispanic Monarchy against the infidel, undertaken to preserve its subjects' Christian souls.[29] But at the same time, in one corner of that all-Catholic monarchy, a notary was reporting that the galleys had become new Morisco villages, where Islam was preserved and practiced under the indifferent gaze of the king's officers.[30]

This report to the Inquisition on religious freedom among galley rowers brings up a number of issues. Even leaving aside the difficult conditions of the men's work, state of health, and life in general, we clearly still have much to learn about the relationships, social life, solidarity, and conflicts among members of those crews. In those long, narrow royal ships there were Turkish, North African, and Morisco slaves and captives, together with Christian convicts of many nations and creeds, seized in war or condemned by royal or Church tribunals. They shared their benches with freemen, who hired out their labor, while sailors and soldiers of different origins paced the decks beside them alongside renegades, officers, and occasional passengers of every origin and social rank, nobles, men of the cloth, and sometimes even princes and kings. In that crammed, undivided space, no one could be indifferent to his fellow travelers. Judde de Larivière observed that aboard a Venetian galley under those conditions, relationships among persons of different social strata could develop that were impossible, or not nearly so easy, in any other milieu.[31] In the Spanish squadrons, although the rowers included fewer freemen, personal connections also acquired a special character, with a closeness and

28 Williams, *Empire and Holy War*.

29 Benítez Sánchez-Blanco, *Tríptico*, 207–33.

30 AHN, Inquisición, libro 1.241, fols. 63–64.

31 Judde de Larivière, *Naviguer*, 47.

indifference to rank that were unthinkable anywhere else under the Hispanic Monarchy. It was a situation that appalled the Inquisition.

It is interesting, as well, that Vicente de Hermosa called the Spanish galley squadron a *pueblo*, meaning both "a village or town" and "a people or nation." By that, he undoubtedly meant the body of rowers, but he was also referring to a unique space that followed its own rules, relatively indifferent to maintaining norms of proper behavior or preserving Christian souls that were in constant contact with infidels. It will seem strange that such practices were permitted in ships that conveyed and defended the cultural and political values of the Christian prince who armed them, ships that represented the sword and shield of Catholicism in the Mediterranean. But the demand for rowers to propel the galleys, and the no-less-pressing need to keep the strongest and most skilled among them in decent health, favored a permissive and relaxed climate that mitigated, to some degree, the harshness of such a confined, exposed, and painful life. Still, the fact that those who commanded the galleys could allow all this without fear of Inquisitorial justice makes us realize that this *pueblo* was more complex than it first appeared.

Recently Louis Sicking, in a wide-ranging monograph on the admiralty in the Low Countries under Philip I and Charles V, revised Jan Glete's thesis on the fiscal-military state. Sicking believes that the appearance of permanent armadas responded not to a wish to control the sea but to the monarchs' determination to control the population that lived on the coasts. A good portion of the Hapsburgs' most precious resources were concentrated on those inhabitants, but they had to identify and overcome strong local and territorial interests of a political and economic nature that were protected by a range of administrative and juridical traditions. The growth of the admiralty from the late fifteenth century onward allowed the monarchy to develop a naval policy in its broadest sense, clearly based on a monopoly of violence in its ships and against its enemies at sea, but also—significantly—on dominance over coastal dwellers and their traditional institutions, through the exercise of royal jurisdiction.[32]

Along these same lines, Alain Berbouche has argued that Cardinal Richelieu's reform proposal for France, initiated in 1629, assumed that the monarchy's greatness would be based on a powerful war-fighting navy. But he never lost sight of a parallel objective, the development of institutions that established a primary, essential prerogative of the king—his jurisdictional supremacy in

32 Sicking, *Almirantazgo*, 29–34.

administering justice over all seafaring men, and over the territories where they were based and from which they drew their resources.[33]

The present study seeks to enter this debate by analyzing the various aspects of how governance and jurisdiction were exercised in the galley squadrons of the Hispanic Monarchy. We will defend the thesis that each squadron of galleys was like a little viceroyalty, an archipelago of tiny islands, perhaps the smallest and most densely populated jurisdiction in the Catholic king's realm, one that had arisen for a variety of motives. Galleys that captured other ships on the high seas, laid siege to North African ports, or joined galleys from other kingdoms in pursuit of common political ends were acting in the name of the king's sovereign power to conduct offense and defense against enemies of his country, a power delegated -pro rex-, in this case, to the leader of each squadron, its captain general. For a capture to be just or an alliance legitimate, the king's representative had to back up his actions with force—the force of rowers and cannon, to be sure, but also the force of legal jurisdiction.

These ships' very mobility presented another sort of challenge, to which they responded by affirming their jurisdictional authority. Galleys used up their stores quickly and completely and carried little cargo. If the objects of their pursuits were distant, coordination with other units poor, or the weather unfavorable (just a few of the adverse conditions they could face), they would have to put into port on varied coasts, in several kingdoms, and of course under different jurisdictions. This supplied many occasions for conflict (over the purchase of stores, the bad behavior of crews on shore leave, or any other factors that could lead local or royal authorities to take sides in a dispute arising from the presence of a galley in their port). The independent jurisdiction of galleys, which gave each of those small, exclusive territories its own legal standing and a high degree of autonomy, was an effective tool in keeping inconvenient incidents from prejudicing the operation and effectiveness of a ship or its squadron. Hermosa the notary was well aware of this fact, but in our day we have not yet fully analyzed how that state of affairs originated, developed, and acquired legitimacy; what constitutional framework supported it; and how the prevailing legal powers on land might resist it. The first part of our study will be devoted to these issues, paying particular attention to the legal doctrine that justified the galleys' special privileges. It will be useful to think of them as simply one more of the corporations or *universitates* of the Hispanic Monarchy.

As corporations and also as political spaces, galleys can be understood as flourishing frontier societies in miniature. This concept has informed the

33 Berbouche, *Marine et justice*, 17–22.

debate about the modern Mediterranean in recent years, based on a revised concept of frontier relations that adopts a decentralized, nonnationalist point of view. The sea is seen as porous, as anything other than monolithic or closed; emphasis is placed on interchange, cultural permeability, and the circulation of persons and ideas.[34] This change is helping to overcome the "Europeanizing" view of Mediterranean history, inherited from the nineteenth- and twentieth-century era of colonial domination, which saw territorial or institutional absorption as a natural result of the spread and establishment of superior models from the old continent. In this sense, the squadrons of Spanish galleys were not only a means of military, defensive, communicative, and territorial structuring affecting the Iberian Peninsula, North African ports, the islands, and Italy—areas of conflict but also meeting places between Mediterranean Christian and Muslim societies. They also undoubtedly constituted a privileged frontier space. Whether on the rowers' benches, in frequent skirmishes with other ships, or during their stays on land, men of the galleys were accustomed to interacting with others and often understanding them.

The external dimension of this interchange is equally profound, if perhaps less obvious. Meetings on the high seas did not always end with seizures of ships and cargoes or the capture and enslavement of defeated crews, and landings did not invariably result in fighting or in the flight or death of attackers or defenders. Even in the galleys, which had been designed for war—and at a time when defense of one's religion was a common cause of conflict—there was space for understanding. We must therefore revisit a number of clichés that are very much alive in readers' minds and that form part of traditional histories of Mediterranean naval warfare.

The negotiation of ransoms is perhaps the best example of how galleys participated in, and validated, one of the most profitable economic activities in the Mediterranean. In addition, their perennial need for supplies led their crews into a range of commercial transactions, whether legal or fraudulent. Every man aboard participated in them according to his means and regardless of his religious beliefs; in our second chapter, we will explore this little-known and largely unsuspected phenomenon. Each person involved might not have been playing by the same rules, but for this very reason we should analyze such activity in order to understand how that commerce, and the legislation that governed it, interacted with (or helped to reconfigure) the legal and institutional structures that regulated Mediterranean trade.

34 Bertrand and Planas, *Sociétés*, 1–20.

The present study is part of the project "Mediterranean Reconfigurations: Intercultural Trade, Commercial Litigation and Legal Pluralism" (ConfigMed; No. 295868) of the European Research Council, directed by Wolfgang Kaiser. In these five years of research, I have amassed many debts to colleagues and friends. I express my gratitude, first of all, to Lluís Guia Marín for his initial advice, to Juan Francisco Pardo Molero and Rafael Benítez Sánchez-Blanco for their help throughout the writing, and to all my colleagues in the Historia Moderna section of the Departament d'Història Moderna i Contemporania of the Universitat de València. I also wish to acknowledge the patience and support of all the members of the ConfigMed project, in particular Rémi Dewiere, Leila Maziane, Eloy Martín Corrales, and Wolfgang Kaiser. The list of friends with whom I have shared hours of toil "chained to the benches" in the archives is endless, but I cannot forget Alberto Marcos, Davide Maffi, Eduardo de Mesa, Cecilia Tarruell, José Miguel Escribano, Marco Legnani, and Daniel Hershenson, together with all the archival personnel and especially my friends from the Archivo General de Simancas. Further, this book would not exist without the unfailing support of my parents and my sister, to whom it is dedicated. I have always heard stories about the ships and shipyards of the port of Valencia, where both my father and my grandfather worked all their lives. Although my profession has led me to follow a different path, this is my contribution to the family business.

CHAPTER 1

Galleys on the Coast!

The Hispanic Monarchy began to transform its naval forces in the Mediterranean after the conquest of Granada in 1492.[1] The impulse came originally from Castile, which needed to reconfigure its Mediterranean policy after having absorbed the long coastline of the former Nasrid kingdom.[2] Its objective was twofold. On the one hand, it hoped to devote more stable resources to guarding the coasts and the Strait of Gibraltar; on the other, it sought to overcome the obstacles that, up to that time, had made it difficult to organize the royal armadas and achieve the Crown's immediate goals. Naval mobilization had been sporadic—there was no consistent royal policy for shipbuilding, and every summer there was a scramble to gather and launch a sufficient number of ships.[3] In practice, the Crown relied too heavily on renting and requisitioning, making naval campaigns uncertain and ineffective. At the end of the fifteenth century, Ferdinand and Isabella dreamed of extending their sway over North Africa. By conquering and occupying several port cities, they sought to control part of the commercial traffic that flowed northward through the Sahara to the coast.[4] It was not so much the conquests themselves as the later maintenance and defense of the captured ports that required stable communications with Spain, but that aim was hard to achieve with the current naval policy in Castile. Clearly, the emerging Hispanic Monarchy had to take decisive steps to create a permanent naval force, but aside from the obvious logistical and financial challenges involved there was another factor to consider: creating a permanent fleet meant changing prevailing policies, which might destabilize the delicate web of institutions in the places where royal jurisdiction was now to be imposed. A balance would have to be found between preexisting legal tradition and the necessary changes required by a new, more effective royal command of the sea.

1 Szmolka Clares, "Fuerzas navales," 138.
2 Mira Caballos, "Armada," 38.
3 Navarro Sorní, *Calixto III Borja*, 81–86.
4 Escribano Páez, "Actores."

1 The Jurisdiction of the Galleys

The Galleys of Spain were born of a confluence of defensive needs, dynastic aspirations, and commercial motives. It was hoped that they would discourage the corsairs who harried the Spanish Mediterranean coasts, to the benefit of economic activity on shore; at the same time, they were expected to open and maintain new markets and defend them by patrolling the trade routes. The level of royal intervention they represented, while it took a new form, was in fact a modernization of long-held goals. The galley fleets built on existing achievements while eliminating or transforming other elements that stood in the way of the rulers' plans. Our intention here is not to reconstruct this process from its origins in any exhaustive fashion; in any event, as Miguel Ángel Ladero Quesada reminds us, we know very little about how Castile exercised its military jurisdiction over the sea and the coasts during the Middle Ages.[5] But we must make a few general observations in order to create a framework for the new developments that we will be analyzing.

1.1 *Continuity and Change under the Catholic Monarchs*

The obvious first step was to define the jurisdictional space that the new, permanent naval squadron and its leaders would occupy. From the thirteenth century onward the Crown of Castile had been establishing jurisdiction over its coasts and navigable rivers by strengthening the office of *almirante mayor* (high admiral). This figure was responsible for the logistical organization and command of temporary fleets and also, through the admiralty tribunals, held broad jurisdiction over maritime traffic and any commercial conflicts that arose from it. The comprehensive authority of the post reflected an attempt to regulate the Crown's military and commercial jurisdiction in these areas, and its great challenge was to ensure that this theoretical framework led to practical results. In fact, the high admiralty failed to become fully established during the fourteenth and fifteenth centuries, largely because of shifting royal policies. At times, it was reduced to a position at court that held little power, and by the beginning of the fifteenth century it effectively belonged to one family, the Enríquezes.[6]

Although the issue is still debated by historians, the current view is that, but for a few exceptional cases, the *almirantes mayores* of Castile had only a limited impact on maritime commercial activity, so that local consulates still took

5 Ladero Quesada, "Almirantazgo," 71.

6 Calderón Ortega, *Almirantazgo*, 73–150, 218–22.

the lead in conflict resolution. There is somewhat more disagreement about the military influence of the office. But there is no doubt that Ferdinand and Isabella took that responsibility too away from the high admiral and conferred it on another position, also of long standing but readapted to the new interests of the monarchy—*capitán mayor del mar* (grand captain of the sea).[7]

The high admiral of the sea was the direct precursor of two other emblematic posts under the Hapsburgs, *capitán general del mar Mediterráneo* (captain general of the Mediterranean) and *capitán general de escuadra* (captain general of squadron). Restoration of the office was clearly meant to recover for the Crown a broad strategic jurisdiction that had been left in the hands of the nobility but was now essential for conducting the monarchs' new naval policy. There was also a legal consideration: although the post had fallen into disuse, it already formed part of the jurisdictional order, subsumed under legal tradition and maritime custom. It was not a new institution alien to that juridical milieu. In the past, it had included responsibilities similar to those of the admiralty and therefore could justify its actions without undermining the admirals; it thus grew into a parallel institution that slowly leached power away from its rival and transferred it to the Crown. Here, we propose to establish which elements of juridical tradition were adopted in creating the Galleys of Spain and the patents of the captain general, which elements were discarded, and which others represented a true innovation in the two areas that converged under its jurisdiction, the military and the commercial.

In the fifteenth century, the admiralty of Castile held jurisdiction over every city, town, village, seaport, river, and loading dock of the Crown. José Manuel Calderón has studied the title of *lugarteniente del almirante mayor* (lieutenant of the high admiral) granted to Don Íñigo Arteta and has shown that the office's ordinances and statutes had to be obeyed by every legal entity in Castile and by all the king's subjects irrespective of sex, status, rank, and condition. The authority of the post thus extended to the Crown as a whole, though it fell with special force on all those professionally involved with maritime affairs: captains, shipowners, skippers, mates, masters, sailors, seamen, fishermen, and all other persons who took to the sea.[8]

The many ship-related endeavors listed under Artieta's title show how heavily the post influenced all those people's activities, both internally (maintaining discipline over the men who served in the royal fleets) and externally

7 Calderón Ortega, *Almirantazgo*, 224.

8 Calderón Ortega, *Almirantazgo*, 228–29 n. 201.

(involving vessels and persons whom the admiral or his delegates might encounter while at sea or in port). From the time of the *Partidas*, the thirteenth-century law code of King Alphonse x the Wise, every authority on the seacoast or the bank of a navigable river had to recognize the admiral's (and his delegates') civil and criminal jurisdiction when they sailed as a fleet, in every matter that had to do with the sea—in all things exactly as if he were the king.[9] His power extended to legal cases related to corsair activity, the export of strategic products, or any type of commercial contract.[10]

It is hard to define precisely how responsibilities were transferred from the admiralty of Castile to the high admiralty of the sea. The first years of the fleet's existence, up to at least 1504 or 1505, were taken up with organizing defensive structures in Granada and establishing the jurisdiction of the High Admiralty of the kingdom. About ten years earlier, in 1495, Ferdinand and Isabella had signed the first *asientos* (contracts for administering the fleet) with Garci López de Arriarán and Juan de Lezcano, but the documents merely granted them the title of captains of the royal armada.[11] It is reasonable to assume that these patents still fell under the jurisdiction of the admiral, though Ladero Quesada affirms that almost simultaneously, in 1496–97 when Princess Joanna traveled to Flanders, the admiral had exerted his traditional logistical and military authority for the last time, an authority that had scarcely been used in previous years.[12] We can hazard, then, that when the first contracts were signed the admiral was no longer in charge of Mediterranean naval policy but had not yet been replaced by a fully formed new institution—that was still in the process of being defined. Antonio Jiménez Estrella suggests that although we do not have the original ordinances and instructions to the captain general of the kingdom of Granada, he must have supervised and controlled the fleet along its coast.[13] This notion would be consistent with the problems of indiscipline and fraud that, according to López de Coca, caused tension between the admiral of the kingdom and contractors of galleys in that early period.[14] It seems that the monarchy, which did not govern its galleys directly, still preferred to avoid granting broad authority to private contractors and left their oversight to its trusted men in Granada. This was entirely different from the traditional authority of the admiral, a surprising fact if we consider that his jurisdiction

9 Pérez Embid, *Almirantazgo*, 25–28.

10 Calderón Ortega, *Almirantazgo*, 218–22.

11 López de Coca Castañer, "Reino de Granada," 98.

12 Ladero Quesada, *Armada de Flandes*, 75.

13 Jiménez Estrella, *Poder*, 32–34.

14 López de Coca Castañer, "Reino de Granada," 99.

seemed to fade away in Castile just as the Catholic Monarchs were moving firmly toward a centralized bureaucracy, since earlier rulers had used the admiralty in particular as a tool to strengthen the central government.[15] In any case, and contrary to appearances, the functions of the admiralty were far from extinguished, although to identify them we must bear in mind the restructuring that Castile had undergone after its union with the Crown of Aragon.

In October 1501, Ferdinand the Catholic granted Gonzalo Fernández de Córdoba full power to make war on the Turks. In his instructions he recognized him as "our leader and captain general over the armies of land and sea with the broadest authority and power," informing him that as such he enjoyed free rein in military action and enjoyed all the prerogatives pertaining to the office. He could act swiftly against the enemy "as it might be in our own person." Finally, and since the kingdom of Sicily would be the base of operations, the king placed him above the other officials of those ports and warned of consequences if any of them contradicted the royal decree.[16]

This document granted very broad powers that were not limited to the governance of the armada. It confirms that at least from the beginning of the sixteenth century the monarchy had removed the management and command of the armadas from the admiralties of Castile and Aragon and conferred them on this new office. It held complete jurisdiction over the administration of justice in any squadron that might be formed, and also over all actions connected to purchasing supplies, mobilizing troops, seizing prizes, and making profits. The latter concessions recognized the voracious consumption of men, food, and money in the fleets and their constant need to requisition those resources along the coasts where they sailed (to mitigate the ever-present dangers of insubordination and desertion, which risked the destruction of the armada).[17] To avoid such dangers, the monarchy recognized the captain general right to

15 Pérez Embid, *Almirantazgo*, 26.

16 "[T]erra marique exercitum ... ducem et capitanum nostrum generalem ... cum amplissima facultate et potestate ... generalis capitaneus armorum, possistis facere et exercere omnes et quoscumque actus quos duces et capitanei nostri armorum generales ... et omnibus prerogativis superioritatibus et facultatibus ad dictum oficium pertinentibus et spectantibus. ... [V]os solus locumtenentes vester iuxta potestatem ... cum promptam et expeditam ... faciatis iuxta criminum et excessuum ralis ac armorum capitaneus noster ... personam nostram pareant. ... [P]er has easdem spectabili viceregi nostro magistro justiciario eiusque in officio locumtenenti, judicibus nostre Magne regie Curie, magistris racionalibus, magistro portulano, thesaurario et conservatori nostri regni patrimonio, advocatuque fiscali, capitaneis, juratis ceterisque aliis officialibus dictorumque officialim locumtenentibus presentibus et futuris sub ire et indignaciones nostre incursu penasque." Suárez Fernández, *Política internacional*, 6:279–82.

17 Fernández Duro, *Historia*, 2:409–15.

intervene in the markets of ports that supplied the galleys, and also in local and territorial jurisdictions whenever a civil or criminal case on land involved a member of the fleet.

These orders clearly continued a substantial portion, though not all, of the prerogatives that admirals had previously enjoyed. In Castile, the admirals maintained their authority over commercial traffic—even more directly at that time, through the admiralty's controversial tribunals.[18] Therefore, the new admirals did not control onshore economic activity as a whole, but only what was directly related to supplying the fleets.

The effects of this separation of competencies would not have seemed new along the coasts patrolled by the armadas. Although the existence of a permanent galley squadron was a change, the ships were few (no more than three or four at a time between 1495 and 1523, according to Mira Caballos),[19] and the men who contracted for them did not seem to enjoy much autonomy. The truly destabilizing factor was the presence of an admiral with power to interfere in normal commercial transactions, like that granted to Fernández de Córdoba in 1501. But his position, unlike the first Galleys of Spain, was not yet permanent.

By the end of the Catholic Monarchs' rule, most of the fleet was still occasional, as was the office that managed it. In 1502, the admiralty was conferred on Íñigo Manrique,[20] and on several occasions beginning in 1505 it passed to Pedro Navarro and to a series of captains general of the kingdom of Granada's coast.[21] After Isabella's death, command of the Galleys of Spain moved into a new phase. Contracts were renewed in 1504,[22] and from 1505 Ferdinand the Catholic involved several Catalan shipowners in managing the squadron, though historians disagree on the title they were given; they have been called both *capitanes* (captains)[23] and *capitanes generales* (captains general).[24] In the absence of their patents, we cannot know whether the position's jurisdiction had changed.

In any event, the presence of Catalan contractors in command of a Castilian squadron, and the naming of a Castilian like Fernández de Córdoba to an armada with broad jurisdiction over the Aragonese kingdom of Sicily, illuminate the most significant new institution taking shape during those years, the Capitanía General de la Armada (Captaincy general of the Fleet). Although the post was

---

18 Calderón Ortega, *Almirantazgo*, 232–34.
19 Mira Caballos, "Armada," 45.
20 Suárez Fernández, *Política internacional*, 6:283–84.
21 Fernández Duro, *Historia*, 1:65–103.
22 Szmolka Clares, "Fuerzas navales," 116.
23 Fernández Duro, *Historia*, 1:66.
24 López de Coca Castañer, "Reino de Granada," 99.

not yet permanently established nor its jurisdictional reach clearly delineated, it enjoyed certain general prerogatives that applied to both kingdoms. It was therefore becoming a common and general institution in all territories controlled by the Hispanic Monarchy in the Mediterranean, and its offices were held by the subjects whom the king considered most capable or respected at the time, irrespective of their origin. The intent was certainly to make them the driving force of a new naval policy, and above all instruments of the monarchs' jurisdictional power over naval warfare and its associated conflicts—this at a time when, by no coincidence, a similar process was taking place in many other aspects of the Hispanic Monarchy.

1.2 *Culmination of the Process: from Andrea Doria to Don John of Austria*

The necessary step toward completing this shift was obviously to institutionalize the office of captain general of the sea, to end its temporary status and the sense of a brief and finite commission that still clung to it. First, however, there would have to be more investment of resources, and new contractors capable of sustaining permanently a larger number of galleys would have to be drawn into the service of the monarchy.

The reign of the Hapsburg Charles V (Charles I of Spain) began with a degree of continuity. Between 1518 and 1520 the Valencian Hugo de Moncada was placed in charge of several royal projects with the title of admiral; his instructions have not survived, but they were probably mere renewals of earlier patents. He was unable to suppress the growing threat of Barbary pirates and the gains of the Barbarroja brothers. At the same time, his early plans to increase the number of galleys patrolling the coasts by raising a new squadron in the Crown of Aragon met with a lack of strong support, and there were doubts about whether to devote resources to the defense of the land or of the sea.[25]

In the end, the final events of Charles I's second sojourn in Spain capped the long series of changes that had begun at the end of the fifteenth century. The monarch, anticipating his (perhaps final) departure from the Iberian Peninsula in 1528, with his minister Gattinara began to institute a regency that would preserve the image and legal presence of the sovereign in his realms even when he was physically absent. One result was a profound reform of territorial governance in the Crown of Aragon that broadened the capacities and jurisdictions of the viceroyalties through a closer link to royal tribunals. The latter, from

---

25 Pardo Molero, "*Per terra*," 64–70.

that point onward, were configured as advisory councils to the viceroys whose members also served as *auditores* (judge advocates) to the king.[26]

As the king was departing in 1529, Hernando Enríquez, admiral of Castile, expressed his bitter regret that his hopes of ingratiating himself with the Crown were now finished. Over the preceding years, Charles had done away with the last remnants of the old admiralty—its tribunals.[27] By then, the Crown of Castile had recovered all its authority to oversee trade on its coasts, with significant consequences. Until shortly before, admiralty tribunals had often caused conflicts by establishing controls over the export from Castilian harbors of all items considered strategic, particularly grain and wine, the most prized products consumed in the galleys.

Reform of the model of government on land, and the reestablishment of old prerogatives for controlling shipping out of coastal ports, are relevant for understanding a third phenomenon that probably also took place at this time—though we lack full documentation for the evolution of patents for admirals of the fleet from the early sixteenth century. Between 1527 and 1530, the Hispanic Monarchy finally achieved its goal of increasing the number of galleys in its service and strengthening its operations in the Mediterranean.[28] Contracts signed in turn with Álvaro de Bazán, Rodrigo de Portuondo, and Andrea Doria allowed larger fleets to be organized, redefining Charles I's foreign policy.[29] Although this change was crucial in itself, it was accompanied by an internal one of equal importance (independent of the resources invested at any given moment, the possible future number of galleys, or the vicious circle represented by alternating direct and indirect management of naval forces). We find its seed in the contracts granted to Andrea Doria in 1528 and 1530, which accorded him two basic prerogatives. The first was the right to purchase huge supplies of wheat (for feeding the crews) from any region of the kingdom where galleys were anchored. This gave Doria, among other things, a commercial advantage that helped him attract new and more powerful contractors and keep them loyal to him over time. It was made easier by the fact that the monarchy was no longer burdened with other jurisdictions, like that of the admiral, that might have stood in the way of such concessions. But the real change in the rules of the game was the combination of this prerogative, which merely corrected and extended a common, well-known privilege, with a second one, to be explained below.

---

26 Rivero Rodríguez, *Edad de oro*, 77–78.

27 Calderón Ortega, *Almirantazgo*, 145–47.

28 Pardo Molero, "*Per terra*," 72.

29 Thompson, "Galeras," 97.

We cannot be certain if such a thing had happened before, but the special political and reformatory events of those years suggest that its appearance was not coincidental. The first contract with Andrea Doria made scant mention of the jurisdiction that the monarchy would grant him in order to increase his authority; that power was essential if he were to engage in exporting wheat without meeting resistance. There was a single allusion, taking up little more than a line, that nonetheless marked an innovation of great significance. The contract declared that the king, because of his respect for and confidence in Doria, ordered the "granting of his patent of captain and lieutenant general [over the galleys and any other armed vessel] like the one that the illustrious Don Hugo de Moncada holds from His Majesty."[30]

With these words, a contractor capable of maintaining a large number of armed galleys over a long period—of offering a *de facto* squadron in permanent service—was given authority to govern not only those ships but all the monarchy's galleys in the Mediterranean with the title of captain general of the fleet. At this point, the office ceased to be in some sense temporary (the composition of most fleets having been temporary up to that time, except for a handful of stable squadrons). The captaincy general of the sea became a permanent position, exercising its rule over a collection of permanent squadrons that might grow over time—and did, because contractors like the Dorias continued throughout the next century to renew their agreements with the Catholic kings.

Many things changed with the advent of a new model of coastal defense, consisting of a number of permanent squadrons of galleys under a general whose authority was broad and continuous. To begin with, men could now aspire to a set of posts, the *capitanías generales* of each squadron, that carried broad privileges in daily life, delegated by the monarch and his lieutenant general of the sea. Because these posts increased in prestige and offered opportunites for earning honors through service to the monarchy, they attracted members of the great noble families and created a deep bench of leaders or "heads."

As a second result, the jurisdictional structure of the permanent galleys changed as well. Internally, the judicial power wielded directly by galley captains declined; now, the captains general of each squadron, and above them the captain general of the sea, were the figures to whom appeals would be directed. If authority became less direct at the galley level, it was also more continuous and predictable. In theory, the king's jurisdiction over galley crews was strengthened, and potential changes did not end there. Externally, the king's

30 "[D]espachar la patente de su capitán y lugarteniente general conforme al que tiene de su Majestad el ilustre don Hugo de Moncada." Fernández Duro, *Historia* 2:366. In fact Hugo de Moncada had died a few months earlier.

galleys, in constant movement from one coast to another, came to be under the jurisdiction derived from the privileges of the admiral of the fleet; in theory also, the full authority of that position (unlike that of the former admiralty) was really exercised, especially and in practice while the royal armada was at sea, since that fleet was no longer temporary but permanent.

There might have been no problem for ports and docks visited by the king's galleys if the ships had still been as few as before along the coasts of Granada, Valencia, and Catalonia. But by the early 1570s, Philip II had increased the total of his galleys to 168,[31] and the squadrons' growth called for a redefinition of the situation of galleys in port. Throughout the century, ports along the coast were visited with increasing frequency by royal galleys that brought not only hungry and thirsty crews but also their own legal privileges, creating the potential for conflict. Once again, it may be no coincidence that while Charles I was reforming the internal governance of the monarchy by consolidating the system of viceroyalties, management of the galleys was also evolving. New structures of governance and jurisdiction established the system of squadrons and came to regulate a different kind of territory, a different *pueblo*, a different Hispanic *universitas*.

The jurisdiction of the king's admiral and lieutenant of the sea (the name of the post varied throughout the sixteenth century) grew to its broadest scope by 1568. In that year, its name was fixed as *capitán general del mar Mediterráneo* (captain general of the sea), a title used fairly consistently until about 1700. Don John of Austria was put in command of the war against the Ottoman Empire as the superior of all captains general and every other rank in the fleet; further, in the king's name (*pro rex*), he commanded every jurisdiction—civil and criminal, high and low (the technical term was *mero et mixto imperio*, delegation of absolute power)—possessed by the monarch. His position authorized him to decide and execute in all legal matters, including those of such weight, nature, and importance as to normally require intervention by the sovereign, with every power and liberty that "the Emperor [Charles's] captains general of the sea have had and held heretofore." The patent therefore carried the force that derived from the legal and juridical traditions of ancient medieval institutions and the Roman law that had inspired them.

Although the post united certain special powers that had to be respected by all of "our subjects, greater and lesser, of any degree, dignity, title or preeminence," in every territory of the Hispanic Monarchy in the Mediterranean,[32]

31 Thompson, "Galeras," 98.

32 AGS, Estado, libro 38, fols. 1r–3v.

and in spite of the lofty language of the decree, the existing situation was not significantly changed. The monarchy now effectively controlled a preexisting jurisdiction acknowledged by maritime custom, adapted to new political needs and conditions.

1.3 *The System in Its Maturity: from the Conquest of Portugal to the Thirty Years' War*

Although the parameters of the office reached their maximum extent under Don John of Austria, we cannot claim that they were perfectly delineated after 1568. Even in the most active years of Mediterranean naval policy, the post was not entirely stable, because the monarchy did not always confer it automatically on a captain general of a squadron; it might go to a military man with special prestige and experience at sea or to a member of the royal family. Philip II, from the 1560s to the end of his reign, did grant it great continuity, designating first Álvaro de Bazán and later Giovanni ("Gian") Andrea Doria, great-nephew of Andrea. But the post could actually disappear if the man who held it was deployed elsewhere or left the service, as happened in 1601.

The 1580s marked the beginning of changes that were significant for understanding how the the jurisdiction of this post developed. Álvaro de Bazán used the Journey to Portugal in 1580 and above all the conquest of Terceira Island in the Azores in 1583 as laboratories for consolidating the office of *auditor general* (judge advocate general) of the fleet, with profound implications for the administration of justice in the squadrons. Once the captaincy general of the sea was stabilized, it had to be endowed with an institutional structure that could support the disciplining of crews and defend its prerogatives against external interference in a permanent and practical way. We will have more to say below about the development and impact of those changes. We will now analyze whether, as management of the captaincy general responsibilities was developed and perfected, it was interrupted when the post disappeared at the beginning of the seventeenth century, and if that circumstance propelled new changes.

The armada organized for the conquest of Algiers in the summer of 1601 provided the spark that eventually led to the suppression of the admiralty of the sea. Around the time of King Philip II's death and Philip III's succession to the throne, Gian Andrea Doria was about to retire from the service, and his planned successor, his son Carlo Doria, was inexperienced. Captains general of the other squadrons saw a perfect opportunity to strip the Genoese family of its command of the sea. Competition among them turned the expedition against Algiers into a disastrous failure, after which Gian Andrea Doria decided, suddenly and unilaterally, to retire.[33] The resulting scandal at court stripped him of his title of captain general of the sea almost on the spot,[34] with an important consequence—the post, rather than be conferred on an captain general of a squadron, remained vacant for more than a decade.

In the following years, a new trend developed that helps us to understand a process little noticed until now, the creation of the new post of *capitán general de escuadra* (captain general of a squadron), parallel to that of admiral of the sea. The early seventeenth century is a propitious time for studying the phenomenon because, while Philip II in his later years had promoted the creation of land-based militias throughout his realm,[35] his son Philip III began by establishing maritime militias, that is, new squadrons of galleys. By no coincidence, between 1598 and 1604 the Galleys of Spain were divided to allow for two new squadrons, the Galleys of Flanders and the Galleys of Portugal, while the king tried to persuade Catalonia, Valencia, and Sardinia to arm at least a small number of galleys apiece.[36]

The pacts that the king made with each territory provide insight into how the royal armadas were coordinated in the absence of an captain general of the sea; into how the monarchy balanced its aspirations with the objectives of local legal institutions by handing out privileges, prerogatives for naming officers, and sources of funding for each new squadron; and into what degree of autonomy the new units enjoyed. Since this new activity occurred more than a century into the Crown's naval policy, we gain perspective into the results over that entire period and now observe the final step in a process of more-or-less deliberate change. Here, we cannot make a full comparative analysis of the jurisdictional aspect of the patents of each new squadron, but we can study one of the most representative cases of the age.

In 1599 Philip III tried to extract a promise from the Cortes of Catalonia to arm a squadron of four galleys. The negotiations were difficult, but an agreement was eventually reached that illustrates the juridical framework for each squadron in its territory of origin. While the various estates sought favorable economic concessions for maintaining the galleys (an issue we will discuss in the next chapter), sections of the approved text show clearly how the principality of Catalonia sought to gain effective control over the ships while minimizing the influence of any future captain general of the sea. Although

---

33 Lomas, "Juan Andrea Doria"; and see Bunes Ibarra, "Felipe III."

34 ADP, scaffale 85, busta 23: Loano, Gian Andrea Doria, 11 March 1602.

35 Ruiz Ibáñez, *Milicias*, 29; Mora Casado, "Milicias," 55–58.

36 Olesa Muñido, *Organización*, 510–11; Muñoz Altabert, *Corts*, 180–87; Guía Marín, *Sardenya*, 76–77.

it recognized that when that office existed the Catalan squadron would have to obey its orders, it was agreed that that could only occur when the captain general of the sea was actually present on the Catalan coast. At all other times (probably the majority), jurisdiction would rest with the captain general of the squadron, to whom the principality would grant the powers and controls with which we are already familiar—full authority in administering both civil and criminal justice. Further, although the king retained the right to name the Catalan captain general, he agreed to follow the recommendation of the principality's deputies. And finally, the strategic post of *auditor* would remain in the hands of those deputies and Catalan *oidores* (civil judges), so that the *auditor* would pronounce sentence according to the constitution of the principality and could assume prosecutorial functions when necessary.[37]

This type of agreement could be altered, however. In 1616 the Duke of Lerma negotiated with the monarchy to arm a squadron to protect the coast of the kingdom of Valencia; he was accorded the same privileges as above but, since he was a private contractor, the office of *auditor* would be overseen not by the civil judges of the kingdom of Valencia but directly by the Council of War.[38] In Naples, on the other hand, the post of *auditor* of the squadron was supervised by the *auditor* general of the kingdom's military administration, which answered to the viceroy.[39] Local arrangements varied, then, as a function of the monarchy's capacity to reach more-or-less advantageous agreements with each territory or individual; but as a common principle, the privileges of each squadron had to be respected by every viceroy, captain general, noble, prelate, judge, and minister of every kingdom and territory of the monarchy.[40] In theory at least, all the squadrons enjoyed a greater or lesser degree of judicial autonomy not only in their territory of origin but also on all the coasts of the Catholic monarch and his allies. The prevailing jurisdiction endowed each squadron with a unique, privileged frontier character, even without the collaboration of the captain general of the sea.

In spite of all this legislation, the squadrons experienced a slow and progressive decline, detectable from the late sixteenth century and resulting from increasing difficulties with financing and the growing participation of large sailing ships in Mediterranean naval warfare. In contrast, Philip III during the second half of his reign made notable efforts to revitalize his galleys, first by issuing ordinances and attracting new contractors and later by reintroducing

---

37 AGS, Estado, 459. Consulta del Consejo de Estado, Madrid, 23 January 1616.
38 AGS, Estado, 1945, n.d.
39 AGS, Estado, 1425, fol. 114.
40 AGS, Estado, libro 38, fols. 3v–5r.

the position of captain general of the sea. The situation did not improve after the king appointed Emmanuel Filibert of Savoy captain general, whether from economic difficulties or from the new commander's lack of skill. The Duke of Osuna operated his naval forces with surprising freedom in Naples in those years,[41] considering that at the time there was an captain general of the sea in the Mediterranean with the same broad powers that Don John of Austria had enjoyed.[42] Toward the end of Philip III's reign, the post seems to have become a merely honorific one, but that is hard to judge since we know little about its role during the Thirty Years' War.

These issues aside, we have determined that the office underwent no significant changes in its jurisdiction after the Battle of Lepanto (1571) and that parallel growth in the prerogatives of all captains general of squadrons gave them similar and sufficient powers and autonomy. We still need to establish whether this authority actually protected both the galleys and their crew members or if, as had happened before with the admiralties, it existed more in theory than in practice. For this, we must study the relationships that developed between officers of the galleys and local authorities in the ports they visited, and between the squadrons' crewmen and residents of those towns. Only then can we assess the impact of changes in traditional jurisdiction, whether the squadrons achieved the true freedom of movement they sought, and to what extent the ports accepted and respected their presence. Perhaps then we can consider and analyze the galleys as a corporation, a *universitas* that expressed the polycentric nature of the Hispanic Monarchy.

2 Galleys and Ports: Profiles of a Complex Relationship

In 1656 a virulent plague assailed the city of Naples. Rumor had it that it had begun in the port when a group of soldiers from Sardinia had disembarked, and had spread from there; at that point, the stories became less precise. Everything pointed to a ship called *El Sol*, but it was also whispered that "others speak of a certain captain of a trireme who had come from Sardinia"[43] (i.e., that it had been brought by the captain of a galley). The detail is of interest because the soldiers came from a place where the plague was known to be present,[44] and yet the ship had been allowed to unload. More significant, even

41 Redondo, "Lucha," 395–416.
42 Lomas, "Galeras de España," 147–58.
43 Renzi, *Napoli*, 370.
44 Manconi, *Castigo de Dios*, 36–88.

during the epidemic's worst months in the city the port was not quarantined and the movements of soldiers and royal ships continued.[45]

This admittedly extreme example illustrates a problem that must have existed in many coastal cities: except in cases of storms, contrary winds, high seas, or a direct order from the sovereign, almost nothing could prevent a squadron of galleys from entering or leaving a port. There must have been times when intimidation by an armed crew or local authorities' wish to avoid trouble might act in the galleys' favor, but what prevailed was the exercise of a jurisdiction that could be either respected or questioned but that always protected the galleys from external interference while tolerating their abuses. By studying the conflicts that often attended the galleys' presence in port, we can analyze the practice of a jurisdiction that we now know of only in theory. We will begin with the external aspect of juridical practice, that is, how it related to other jurisdictions.

2.1 *The Galleys: a Vehicle for Concord*

We should first make clear that conflict was only one feature of the relations between galleys and the ports where they docked, and that it coexisted with commoner and more symbiotic activities. The best known is probably trade. The arrival of galleys, especially when a whole fleet was being armed, created commercial opportunities that stimulated local industries and required manpower; that increased the income of many families.[46] In the next chapter we will attend to these important issues, and now say only that these were not the only reciprocal interests between the two *universitates*.

The most frequent contacts between galleys and ports took place when ships were loading and unloading soldiers, equipment, or arms, making short stopovers, or seeking shelter (more or less urgently) from bad weather at sea. But under the Hispanic Monarchy there was another type of ritual or symbolic visit: high-ranking royal officers and ecclesiastics were often in transit between the Iberian Peninsula and Italy. The travels of viceroys and ambassadors were the most conspicuous, and produced some of the most dramatic contacts between residents of a coastal port and crew members of a galley squadron.

Between December 1622 and May 1623, after the coronation of Philip IV, a large number of the new king's trusted deputies sailed for Italy while others who were leaving their posts there returned to Castile by sea. These movements produced welcoming ceremonies—at the ports of arrival and ports of

45 Fusco, "Istituzioni," 100.

46 Saavedra Vázquez, "Formación de armadas," 55–76.

call along the way—that were recorded in contemporary accounts. As the galleys bearing the Count of Castro and his family approached the port of Genoa, they were greeted by a salvo of artillery, and two senators received the visitors after the ship dropped anchor. The Genoese representatives offered the count the friendship of the Republic of Saint George, inviting him to come ashore, where a welcoming committee of local nobles, surrounded by excited residents, was waiting to escort him to the Senate. There, the count returned their courtesies, making a public show of the Hispanic Monarchy's affection for the people of Genoa.[47]

The Duke of Pastrana, Spain's new ambassador to Pope Gregory XV, arrived by galley in Civitavecchia to similar acclaim. The port's cannons were fired and the people rejoiced, since they usually received gifts, alms, and other welcome gestures, like the freeing of prisoners, from the pontiff on such occasions. The Orsini family, Dukes of Bracciano, were normally in charge of receiving important visitors to the port but, unable to be present on this occasion, they compensated Pastrana handsomely—his galley was escorted farther south to the castle of Palo, where hunts and other entertainments were often prepared for distinguished visitors. There, the new ambassador was feasted while awaiting the Pope's delegation, which escorted him along a road lined with enthusiastic crowds to his first audience with Gregory.[48]

These visits served to renew ties of friendship and reciprocity between the Hispanic Monarchy and its chief allies in the Mediterranean. Their components varied according to local custom, but the opening ceremony was usually the same. A squadron of foreign galleys was welcomed warmly as the symbolic vehicle for a good relationship and lasting alliance, with local officials making a display of every step of the ritual, seconded by residents of the port. Naturally, these celebrations meant more in those ports where the man disembarking was not a foreign ally but a minister charged with exercising power in the port itself and the rest of its territory.

The Duke of Alba arrived at the port of Naples in the Christmas season of 1622 to take possession of his viceroyalty. He did so "accompanied by many galleys adorned with various standards and banners, and the whole city was excited by the boom of cannonades from the castles." A city official boarded the duke's galley, welcoming him and inviting him to disembark along a richly decorated gangway.[49] During a ritual procession to the palace, the duke met all the city's leaders, making a show of the continuity of royal power, while behind

47 ASV, Segretaria di Stato, Avvisi, 9, fols. 177r–181v.

48 ASV, Segretaria di Stato, Avvisi, 9, fols. 135r–139v; Visceglia, *Città rituale*, 270–79.

49 ASV, Segretaria di Stato, Avvisi, 9, fols. 1r–6r.

him, his soldiers followed the tradition of stealing the gangway's luxurious fabrics.[50]

That same year saw the death of Emmanuel Filibert of Savoy, captain general of the Mediterranean Sea and viceroy of Sicily since 1619. His own inaugural journey to his kingdom had been more typical of a sailor fearful of the sea (and therefore of God)—he visited the principal sanctuaries along his route before arriving with his galleys at Palermo. As his ship dropped anchor, it was saluted by the port's artillery, after which the city's representative came aboard and invited the viceroy to disembark. With this ceremony completed but before stepping on land, Emmanuel made a gesture from the stern of his galley seeking the approval of his predecessor, the Duke of Lemos, who awaited him on the pier. After the two exchanged a few courteous words, Cardinal Giannettino Doria, the city's archbishop, presented the newcomer with a gold-plated chair that symbolized his rule over the kingdom. Only then did the new viceroy disembark, amidst applause and the firing of arquebuses throughout the city; he rode through garlanded streets to the royal palace. The next day, after visiting the church of Monreale and the principal men of the town, he took ship to Messina, where an almost identical ceremony awaited him.[51]

In both cases the reception of a new viceroy began with a ceremony that followed preordained rules. First, there was a jubilant welcome for the galleys, as if their arrival presaged a happy, prosperous future for the people. This display doubtless served to honor the figurative arrival of the monarch, incarnated in his new lieutenant, through a dramatic and grandiloquent spectacle that served as propaganda and, above all, as a vehicle for social cohesion and adherence to the monarchy and its legitimate power.[52] The galley was thus transformed into a ritualized space, but one distinct from the other powers that converged on the event. When groups of city fathers were received on board, they resembled the delegations that, on land, would await visitors at the borders of their own jurisdictions; it was understood that although the ships rode at anchor within the port, and ships and port city belonged to the same king, the galleys constituted a different territory, whose limits and privileges must be respected like those of any other frontier. Only when the viceroy stepped onto the pier did he actually enter the city, to be received by other officials who had been awaiting him beyond the "border."

In these scenes of public festivity, the galleys—especially when they were the principal actors—were asserting their legal autonomy vis-à-vis that of the

50 Hernando Sánchez, *Reino de Nápoles*, 111–12.

51 ASV, Segretaria di Stato, Avvisi, 8, fols. 463v–464r.

52 García Bernal, *Fasto público*, 233–51; Ferrer Valls, "Fiestas públicas," 43–51.

authorities gathered to receive them. Such ceremonies were organized whenever a fleet set out on campaign, but even more so when it returned victorious. The triumphal entry of a fleet shared with the journeys of viceroys and ambassadors many theatrical features designed to promote the monarchy's political and ideological program among the people. Maria Antonietta Visceglia recalls how, to receive the victorious admiral Marcantonio Colonna in Rome after the Battle of Lepanto, two models for conceiving and expressing his victory were competing: the allegory of Christ's entry into Jerusalem, which stressed its spiritual nature, and the classic trope of the Roman imperial triumph, which emphasized its political one.[53] This tension between *christianitas* and *romanitas* existed within the Hispanic Monarchy as well and could be displayed dramatically through its galleys.

In October 1618 the Duke of Osuna, viceroy of Naples, sought to express his devotion to the Virgin and the protection she extended to his fleet by ordering that before it sailed, every vessel anchored in the port of Naples incorporate a Marian allegory into its banner and fly it next to the royal standard. The raising of the banners caused a sensation in the port "that a great crowd ran to see," setting off a wave of euphoria in remembrance of Lepanto almost fifty years before.[54] The act transformed an omen for a safe journey into a memory deeply rooted in the collective imaginary. While promoting the notion of a shared spiritual crusade just before a new campaign, it also strengthened the people's belief in the monarchy's political objectives and, in this specific case, in the viceroy's service, dedication, and good governance.

At these events the local people marveled at the galleys. News that wounded but gallant officers were leaving the ship, the sight of captured slaves, and tales of the amazing speed with which the rowers had completed the journey circulated widely.[55] Therefore, "to give some additional entertainment to the populace," an order might be issued to print "a broadsheet with a key to the captains and the insignia of the galleys," so that people could forget their own cares and enjoy those stories.[56] These were the right moments to strike up the drums in the public squares and recruit other men to honorable service at sea.

The galleys could also threaten public order at such times, however. The great raising of banners that Osuna ordered in Naples in 1618 ended with the violent expulsion of the crowds gathered on the piers, after a baker attending

53 Visceglia, *Città rituale*, 220–24.
54 ASV, Segretaria di Stato, Avvisi, 8, fols. 265r–266v.
55 ASV, Segretaria di Stato, Avvisi, 9, fols. 198r–202v.
56 ASV, Soldati, 2, fol. 93.

the spectacle was stabbed in the melee.[57] A few years earlier, in 1611, the kingdom's galleys had come into the same port escorting a large captured ship, and "so great was the mass of people who came to see them that some were trampled underfoot."[58] In 1623 a great artillery salvo in Málaga had caused gunpowder stored in a Spanish galley to explode, resulting in many deaths.[59] Although the arrival of galleys in a port carried great symbolic weight, their presence was always problematic, even if the worst thing the local authorities faced was the people's excitement. Excitement, in any case, was better than fear.

2.2 *"That Is Spain's Flagship, and This Is the Pope's Fortress"*

On every Christian shore in the Mediterranean, the greeting was the same. When galleys approached a port, they showed their good intentions by firing their cannons three times, or four if the standard of the local ruler's squadron was visible within the port. An answering shot from the port meant that they were welcome. Through this symbolic but essential exchange both jurisdictions, visitors and hosts, expressed their mutual respect and paved the way for a neighborly relationship that would be, ideally, as cordial as it was brief. For many coastal towns, a visit by galleys was a temporary problem that they dealt with as best they could, through a ceremony that was less rich and symbolic than some others but designed to keep the peace. After the required exchange of salutes, and just as in more important landings, the governor of the port would send a boat to assess the visitors' intentions. These forays, aside from issuing the expected polite invitation to disembark, were a chance to examine the quality of the ships' people, the number of soldiers on board, and how much hunger showed in the faces and bodies of the rowers. Whenever possible, a landing could be avoided by promising enough water and provisions to satisfy the officers.[60] But if the visitor was a friend, or if there were heavy seas and threatening winds, other solutions had to be found.

Marco Antonio Zani, a former captain at Lepanto and commander of the Pope's navy,[61] described such a situation in a letter to Duke Giacomo Buoncompagni written from Civitavecchia in December 1577. The previous day nine Spanish galleys, loaded with soldiers bound for Flanders, had appeared outside the port. Bad weather, and news of a strong Turkish squadron to the north, had persuaded them to lay over there, and their general was seeking both

57 ASV, Segretaria di Stato, Avvisi, 8, fols. 265r–266v.
58 ASV, Segretaria di Stato, Avvisi, 4, fols. 271r–274r.
59 ASV, Segretaria di Stato, Avvisi, 9, fols. 191r–195v.
60 ASV, Segretaria di Stato, Particolari, 13, fol. 140r.
61 Guglielmotti, *Storia della Marina*, 7:4.

provisions and the support of the three galleys that Gregory XIII maintained at the time. To hold off any trouble, Zani received the general with "caresses and the usual welcomes," while smilingly denying him both supplies and the loan of any galleys to help the expedition.[62] Many years later one of his successors, Giovanni Moroni, would write that when polite words were not enough they would be accompanied by "the usual attentions, plus reinforcing the troops of guards by day and by night, as I have done on other similar occasions."[63]

Resisting a hungry crew, though it did not happen often, could prove a poor strategy. The republic of Genoa once asked Gian Andrea Doria to judge such a case from his position as the Catholic king's captain general of the sea. In July 1603 three French galleys anchored in the port of San Remo, seeking shelter. Their negotiations with local authorities to obtain refreshment must not have gone well, because their commander let a number of soldiers disembark and raid local gardens while the ships' artillery, though apparently without ammunition, fired on the town. Terrified soldiers from the little fort that guarded the harbor fired back at the galleys, killing nine people.[64]

There is unfortunately no mention of this incident in Prince Doria's later correspondence, but clearly the secret to success at such times was a little permissiveness. Many coastal towns knew that galley crews usually wanted just two basic necessities, water to drink and firewood to keep them warm, and that if these were not offered readily they would be seized outright. Because that fact was well known in Civitavecchia, its residents did not try to prevent Gian Andrea Doria's three galleys from collecting wood in January 1569—after all, the ships were helping them by defending the coast. But the wood had to be reserved for the ships' own consumption and could not be sold commercially.[65] These concessions could be abused, however. In June 1620 the monastery of San Jerónimo near Seville complained that a plot of land it owned next to the River Guadalquivir was regularly invaded by crewmen from the Galleys of Spain, who cut down its trees "not only for the galleys but to sell [the wood] in the city." Philip II had signed a judgment in the friars' favor in 1588, but it had done them little good in the face of the squadron's jurisdiction, which protected its men's actions.[66]

Commanders of the galleys knew that their jurisdiction favored them, and they sometimes managed to have their hosts assume the costs of their stays in

62 ASV, Segretaria di Stato, Particolari, 3, fol. 100.
63 ASV, Segretaria di Stato, Particolari, 13, fols. 55–56.
64 ADP, scaffale 86, busta 27: Gian Andrea Doria, Pegi, 11 July 1603.
65 ASV, Segretaria di Stato, Particolari, 3, fol. 8.
66 AGS, GyM, Consulta del Consejo de Guerra, 9 July 1620.

port. One illustration is a case from beyond the Mediterranean. In early 1599 the galleys armed by Federico Spínola to serve in Flanders stopped over in Santander; the stay was supposed to be short, but the expedition was delayed there by winter weather. At first the situation was manageable; there were leftover supplies in Santander from an earlier campaign that provided clothing for some of the men and tents on deck to protect them from the cold. But food began to run short.[67] Most of the soldiers were billeted in nearby towns while a skeleton crew manned the ships. Eventually a local doctor had to be found, and soldiers began to be arrested for "the little debts they have run up after not receiving their pay."[68] Although the soldiers were genuinely in need, some were arrested not for failing to pay for food but for debts from other activities such as gambling. When the sum to pay them finally arrived, their officers had to admit that "it was impossible for the soldiers to be disciplined enough to spend their pay on food, because some would gamble it away, others would spend it on clothing, and others would take the money and desert." The officers, realizing that once the salaries were frittered away the troop might disintegrate, decided not to distribute the funds at all; instead, they kept them to buy food for the crewmen still on board.[69] That meant that local residents had to keep providing for the soldiers billeted on them, while those impoverished men kept causing trouble in the towns. The officers protected them, petitioning the king to remind the Santander authorities not to interfere with the galleys' jurisdiction by arresting their soldiers.[70]

If a port was visited by a foreign squadron this problem did not disappear, but it might be handled with different strategies. Port authorities had to consider their sovereign's alliances, and their behavior should always honor their ruler, but there were ways of avoiding trouble. In 1638 Giuseppe Mattei received a request from eight Neapolitan galleys to enter the inner harbor at Civitavecchia and take shelter from a contrary wind. Because Mattei knew that the 500 soldiers on board could cause conflicts, "I told him politely that it was not a good time to receive him in port, and treated with courtesy all the officers who came on land."[71] Flattering the officers maintained good relations with Spain while avoiding a massive disembarkation of soldiers, with all its risks.

Still, it was often hard to avoid receiving galleys whether the polite forms were observed or not. Two years earlier, in May 1636, the Papal port had

---

67 AGS, GyM, 539: Tomás de Aguirre, Santander, 27 January 1599.
68 AGS, GyM, 539: Fernando de la Riva, Santander, 28 January 1599.
69 AGS, GyM, 541, fols. 71–72.
70 AGS, GyM, 539: Fernando de la Riva, Santander, 28 January 1599.
71 ASV, Segretaria di Stato, Particolari, 13, fol. 106.

awakened to a squadron of galleys anchored just offshore. No signal was offered for several hours, until finally at noon the ships began to move toward the inner harbor—still without firing the usual salute. Faced with this action, the castellan first fired an empty cannon, then sent a shot wide, and finally launched a ball that grazed the lead galley's mast. Only then did that ship send out a boat to request free passage for the Galleys of Spain. The castellan replied that while the galleys might belong to the king of Spain, the fort belonged to the Pope, and he would not admit them without the proper courtesies and signs of respect. The galleys finally gave the salute, and though the official preferred not to receive them, he had to consider the diplomatic consequences of a denial; therefore, he opened the harbor and accepted a short but difficult visit in which both sides had to overcome their mutual distrust.[72] The squadron commander, for his part, restrained his soldiers and "made his people act with great modesty." Meanwhile, the admiral of the papal galleys, while "not failing in courtesy toward him," reinforced the garrison in the arsenal and surrounding territory "to make our people aware that we have served our lord correctly," that is, to let residents know that the visitors would not disturb the peace.[73] He achieved his aim on this occasion, but many others were not so fortunate.

The port of Cartagena was a provisioning site for the armadas of the Hispanic Monarchy and therefore saw constant traffic of galleys and soldiers;[74] it had to live daily with the sort of problem that the castellan of Civitavecchia had faced with the Galleys of Spain. That squadron visited Cartagena regularly and seems to have grown more careless over time. In the early summer of 1602 Carlo Doria, contractor for the Galleys of Genoa then en route to the Strait, found the entrance to Cartagena's inner harbor closed off. When he asked the reason, the local authorities replied that a few days earlier the Galleys of Spain had arrived, faced the entrance to the port, and refused to salute the castles—they wanted to enter without observing any of the proper forms. After the local governor denied them entry, the ships had taken revenge by burning every local boat they could find, so the city had refused to receive any galleys at all until the king answered their complaint.[75] Clearly, these cities had relatively little recourse if galleys decided to abuse their privileges.

Quarrels like this one, arising from each side's assertion of its dominance, were frequent and of more than anecdotal importance. Both parties were insisting on their position within the political or jurisdictional order of that

72 ASV, Segretaria di Stato, Particolari, 13, fol. 61.
73 ASV, Segretaria di Stato, Particolari, 13, fol. 67.
74 Lomas Cortés, "Armada de Felipe III."
75 ADP, scafalle 82, busta 27: Domenico Sevo, Cartagena, 6 July 1602.

special web of relationships; each was trying to gain space at the expense of the other, or at least to not lose the status it had already claimed. Conflicts about expressing the proper courtesies to galleys and ports, or about respecting and honoring each prince's flag, dramatized the weight of every sovereign in an alliance, the limits of friendship, and the role that each ruler sought to play in Mediterranean politics. On a humbler level these disputes—occasional ones like the layovers in Civitavecchia, or more permanent ones in the galleys' home ports—expressed rights that the parties thought they had earned or aspired to earn. They demonstrated how continual insistence on the galleys' jurisdiction affected institutional networks on land.

2.3 *Soldiers, Sailors, and Townspeople*

There were never any guarantees that both sides would respect minimal norms of courtesy and maintain a cordial tone. When officers allowed shore leave for soldiers and sailors, those men often disturbed the peace, and officials in the ports knew that their own laws would usually not be obeyed.

One constant cause of disorder among galley crews in the Mediterranean, often punished by the authorities, was gambling. In 1571 a report to Pope Pius V contained advice on improving discipline in the armada of the Holy League, with the vice of gambling figuring among the greatest concerns: "By day and by night they do nothing but gamble, young men and old, and it is as if they joined the fleet only for the folly of gambling."[76] Gianclaudio Civale has noted that the habit grew out of the long periods of idleness aboard the galleys, when card games were widespread and so popular that it could be dangerous to forbid them. Therefore, although officers tried to maintain discipline by not allowing too much freedom, they were careful not to impose new limits on games of chance.[77] If officers were not too strict about gambling on board ship, it is understandable that they did not try hard to control it among soldiers and sailors who went ashore, especially since the activity was a useful escape valve.

Sometimes, however, gambling did not relieve tension but had the contrary effect. In 1599 Philip III spent several weeks in Barcelona for the meeting of the Cortes. Gian Andrea Doria's galleys had conveyed him there from Valencia, where he had just married Marguerite of Austria.[78] While Philip planned to travel on to Madrid, the galleys had remained in port to guard the coast while the king was in residence. It was one more occasion for galleys to take part in public festivities, in this case for the sovereign's welcome presence in the city

76 ASV, Miscelanea Armadi, 2:116, fols. 139–41.
77 Civale, *Guerrieri di Cristo*, 111.
78 Lomas Cortés, "Renovar el servicio."

after a long absence; but some soldiers took celebration too far. The fleet had landed on May 17, and six days later the king ordered in person that, to avoid "the disputes that began today between the soldiers and the locals ... there may be no gaming tables on land, because that is the road to many sorrows." In just those few days, two residents of Barcelona had been killed, and all men with shore leave were sent back to their ships, not to return to land until they received new orders.[79]

The 1571 report had tried to shed more light on the problem. If gambling proved uncontrollable, it was largely because at every rank on board, including that of captains general, "they have done nothing but gamble for hundreds and thousands of gold *scudi* ... they have lost bets of here six, there twelve, and even twenty-four thousand, to the ruin of their estates."[80] Gian Andrea Doria and his sons were all famously dedicated cardplayers who did not set the best example for their crews, although excuses could always be made. In spite of all the criticism of gambling in military treatises,[81] officers generally treated the practice benignly. A game of cards was a confrontation or struggle between gentlemen that could impart values important to a soldier: thirst for victory, competitiveness, the development of strategies for survival. Like defeat in battle, it taught gentlemen how to fight with honor and control their emotions at all times. Both wins and losses helped to channel the frustrations and tensions of life on board, defusing them in more-or-less controlled fashion while setting an example to the rest of the crew. Despite all appearances, gambling had psychological and educational benefits for the men, plus other ones useful to the officers charged with managing the galleys. As Pedro de Toledo, captain general of the Galleys of Spain, wrote to the king in 1610, "Gambling ... is the means of finding willing men [*buenas bollas*, i.e., *buenaboyas*] on land," so the practice had to be allowed a certain freedom.[82]

This last assertion is a curious one. *Buenaboyas* were volunteers who worked for a salary and formed a very small proportion of a galley's rowers.[83] While officers were always on the lookout for men to fill the benches, volunteers were not a significant force, at least not in the Galleys of Spain. Pedro de Toledo's report makes clear that gambling was actually more useful on board ship, since sometimes a convict who had served out his sentence could be forced to keep rowing to pay off a debt. These two types of cases might add up to a good

---

79 ADP, scaffale 82, busta 18: Alonso Muriel, Barcelona, 23 May 1599.

80 ASV, Miscelania Armadi, 2:116, fols. 139–41.

81 Eguiluz, *Discurso*, 215–22.

82 AGS, GyM, 742: Pedro de Toledo, Madrid, 21 May 1610.

83 Lomas Cortés, "Galériens."

number, but we cannot judge their extent. We can assume, however, that officers in the galleys both encouraged gambling and generally kept it under control. They could turn to their advantage certain negative effects that, although condemned by the Church, were justifiable in the special *universitas* of a galley as a way of cultivating and supporting its crew.

Perhaps in the galleys gambling could help to serve the king of Spain, but ports, like other towns visited by troops,[84] found that gaming tables might act as traps for careless residents; in spite of the towns' best efforts, there would be fights and murders. In late December 1603, while ships were docked at the fortified port of Oran, "a quarrel arose between a sailor from the galleys and a butcher from Oran, resulting in the butcher's death." The sailor tried to escape but was caught before he reached his ship, setting the scene for a confrontation. The captain general of the galleys demanded the prisoner's return, but the governor refused to release him and closed the gates to the fort so that the remaining crewmen could not reach their embarkation point at Mazalquivir. As soon the Council of War learned of the problem, however, resistance came to an end. Its letter to the king explained that the governor was "obliged to return … the imprisoned sailor who had killed the butcher, and Your Majesty should reprove [him] for having detained seven galleys for twenty-four hours with a clear danger of losing them, confining inside the gates of Oran all those who sailed in them."[85]

Because soldiers had relative immunity on land and local authorities could not always resist them, indignant residents sometimes took justice into their own hands. In early August 1577 several galleys filled with Spanish infantry dropped anchor in Civitavecchia on their way to Genoa. Captain Zani, as usual, had tried to ensure "that no news got about," but there was such a crowd at the port that confusion ensued. In the midst of it all a Spaniard decided to urinate against the corner of a house, and angry neighbors began to stone him, injuring him in the head. Other Spaniards, hearing his cries, ran to help their comrade while more residents joined the fray, and the violent melee ended with four more Spaniards wounded; others fled from the city, and still more sheltered in a nearby church and a lady's house. The Pope's soldiers closed the gate between the town and the port to hem the men in and avoid further bloodshed, but that only provoked the visitors to draw their swords and try to hack the gate to pieces. An unlucky dyer on the other side was pierced by a blade and died. The Spaniards did not fare much better—when at last the tumult subsided

84 Ruiz Ibáñez, "Juegos de azar," 301–9.
85 AGS, GyM, 624, fol. 111. See Lomas Cortés, "Esclave captif."

and Zani asked the commander of the galleys to order his men back on board, several of them arrived gravely wounded, and one soon expired.

Although Zani immediately ordered the galleys to sail away, he also seized the occasion to complain about how little zeal the commissioners of the port, in charge of administering justice, showed in pursuing such outrages: "If there were justice here such things would not be done, for whenever galleys come here there is always some homicide, and all because the local people are too insolent. The rumors begin with them, and if punishment were meted out the first time there would be peace the next time, and they would not try to do what they did. ... If local people kill someone from a galley or ship, that is to say foreigners, they settle everything by paying five *giulii*[86] to the commissioner." To make matters worse, while everyone was distracted by the skirmishes with the Spaniards, two of the Pope's captains had fought a duel on the other side of the city.[87]

Perhaps Zani had forgotten to report that the galleys' own people, beginning with those under his command, were partly responsible for the anger of Civitavecchia's residents and the indolence of its commissioner. We find one example in early November 1623. A soldier from the papal galleys newly arrived in port was ordered by a captain on the pier to lead him to the vicarage. His companions objected and started a fight with the captain's underlings that ended in arquebus fire; two men drinking in a nearby tavern were struck by bullets and killed.[88] In an atmosphere in which violence broke out so often (in separate incidents, but too-frequent ones by many accounts), it is unsurprising that residents of ports where galleys anchored regularly were, just like the crews, both victims and perpetrators of conflict. Even so, quarrels with angry civilians paled beside the ones that arose between galley crewmen and soldiers who guarded the ports.

One example sheds light on this last type of conflict, even though Spanish squadrons were not involved. In 1600 the Pope's galleys stopped over at the Spanish fortified port of Porto Ercole. Once they had dropped anchor, their lieutenant ordered some sailors to escort a few slaves to collect water on shore,

---

86 "[S]e qua ci fosse giustitia non si farebbero simile cose, che ogni voltga vengono galere qua sempre interviene qualche homiccidio, et tutto per causa di questi della terra che sono troppo insolenti, che da loro cominciano li rumori che si fossero castigati una volta l'altra volta starebbero in pace, et non cercarebbano di fare quel que fanno ... che se questi della terra ammazzano uno o di galera o di barca, o sia foresteri, con cinque giulij che diano al detto commisario accomodano ogni cosa." A giulio was a coin worth one-tenth of a Roman escudo.

87 ASV, Segretaria di Stato, Particolari, 3, fol. 403.

88 ASV, Segretaria di Stato, Avvisi, 9, fols. 302r–306r.

but after landing they were confronted by a group of Spanish soldiers, and in the resulting quarrel a sailor was killed. The lieutenant, who had witnessed the scene from his galley, ordered the trumpet blast that meant "all hands board ship," but the governor of the fortress, unwilling to let matters rest there, commanded his artillery first to sink the boat carrying the sailors and slaves back to their galley and then to fire on the galleys themselves. The boat managed to stay afloat and the lieutenant, to put an end to the firing, offered to parley. But he claimed that the sailors who had caused the fracas had not reached their boat but one had died on land, so that punishment should befall only those who had wounded many crewmen by bombarding the visitors from the port. The Spanish governor, who disagreed, waited till nightfall to fire on the galleys once more, forcing them to weigh anchor and sail away with all speed.[89]

These cases suggest a few general conclusions beyond their chronology, the squadron involved, and the place where the incident occurred. It is obvious that whether the relationship established was friendly or hostile, the authorities of ports where galleys anchored usually accepted the ships' jurisdictional autonomy. That acceptance was somewhat diluted on land, which became the battleground for imposing one system of justice over the other when a crime involved persons from both sides of the frontier. But if on land there was some margin in favor of local justice, there was no such power over the galleys. Perhaps the ships' cannons were dissuasive enough that local officials did not dare to pursue delinquents all the way to the deck, but it seems that no one really questioned that the royal standard that flew over the Spanish squadrons (or the French, Tuscan, Papal, or Maltese ones) conferred on those ships the status of a territory apart.

As with all rules, there were exceptions. We saw above how in the autumn of 1606 soldiers of the captain general of the kingdom of Portugal actually came on board to try to free two prisoners from a galley anchored in Lisbon. But the incident was rare, threatened to cause tremendous bloodshed, and was quickly resolved in the galleys' favor.[90] All these cases, even the last, show how far the monarchy was willing to go to render its squadrons immune from external interference, even if they sometimes exceeded their authority.

This was the situation in ports of the Hispanic Monarchy that received the king's galleys, but it obtained at other Mediterranean ports as well. In towns that obeyed other rulers, the squadrons' legal autonomy was likewise respected, despite occasional flares of resistance. Whether motivated by treaties of

---

89 ASV, Segretaria di Stato, Spagna, 53, fols. 244–45.

90 Lomas Cortés, "Justicia y gobierno."

surrender, offensive or defensive alliances, mutual interests, or simple maintenance of cordial relations with neighboring powers, the relationships of port officials with foreign galleys followed, in times of peace, almost identical practices—the same salutes on arrival, the same courtesies on land, and very similar reactions to conflicts that arose.

Virtually everyone understood the limits of those relationships, and it is clear why sailors and soldiers from the galleys sometimes behaved badly on land and why local populations might respond with violence. It would be a mistake to think that systems of justice in ports visited by galleys accepted the situation willingly, no matter what gestures might be made toward good relations. Justice related to the galleys did not spring up fully formed; it was shaped gradually through a series of ordinances, legal prudence, and the experience derived from conflict resolution. It appears that the creation of permanent squadrons, led by captains general who possessed much of the military authority of the ancient admiralties, changed the balance of power in institutions along or near the coast. But to understand the process fully we must explain how the galleys were endowed with the resources and structures they needed to put into practice the autonomy that they held in theory, both at sea and on land. We need to know how the galleys articulated their defense and whether the structures that allowed it remained the same or had evolved since the temporary fleets of the fifteenth century.

3 Between Naval Tradition and Military Innovation

A separate jurisdictional space for the galleys was constructed, as we have learned, to protect them from possible interference by land-based justice. We have also explained how their legal prerogatives were not linked to the existence of a particular squadron (that is, they did not belong to the galleys) and that these prerogatives could vary in scope, even reaching full autonomy, depending on the moment and especially on the identity of the person who enjoyed them.

One could object that after 1531, when the galley ordinances established by Álvaro de Bazán were approved, and especially after 1607, when the new broader, revised ordinances for the Galleys of Spain were introduced, the situation changed. Galley regulations then provided more detail about how powers were conferred in practice on the captains general, strengthening their ability to deal with their ships' geographic dispersal, the temporary absence of an captain general, and problems arising from the presence of disembarked crewmen on land. Application of the ordinances allowed a power that had been mainly hypothetical to become actual, at a time when naval infrastructure was growing in size and complexity and the posts of captain general of the sea and captain general of a squadron were undergoing fundamental change. But this supposition is difficult to demonstrate.

3.1 *Galley Ordinances and Corsair Customs*

The chief aim of the 1531 ordinances was to systematize the governance of the ships and, above all, of the men who sailed in them. The initial clauses sought to fix the salaries of the freemen on board (officers, soldiers, and buenaboyas), the food rations designated for each group, and the percentage due to each crew member of any captured prize. So that contractors would be sure of securing the galleys' basic provisions, especially grain and wine, they were guaranteed "fair prices,"[91] meaning concessions that gave them an advantage in the markets, a factor that attracted important men of business to the king's service. We will explore this issue further in the next chapter, but here we will establish how these ordinances introduced a new factor that protected galley crews on land.

There was certainly an improvement in the ability to intervene in the markets, an important aspect of the development of the galleys' economic and commercial jurisdiction. But the form of governance introduced in 1531 and expanded in 1607 (there are references to intermediate ordinances that remain undocumented)[92] was in fact virtually unchanged from the uses and customs that had regulated the arming of corsair galleys for centuries. There is clear influence here of the legal tradition of Mediterranean commercial navigation. According to the *Llibre del Consolat del Mar* (Book of the consulship of the sea) of Barcelona, a list of naval customs, a man who signed on to a corsair galley armed by a private individual had a right to four things. First, the contractor had to inform him of the quantity and quality of the galley's provisions, so that every potential crew member could evaluate the risks of the assignment before accepting it. Further, the admiral chosen by the contractors to lead the expedition had to pledge that everyone on board would receive his daily ration of food, his salary, and the percentage of any profits due to him.[93] For strategic reasons, of course, it was better if royal galleys did not reveal their exact logistical conditions, but it is clear that the basic rights of crewmen under the Hispanic Monarchy were exactly those enjoyed for centuries by men in galleys that sailed with letters of marque. This fact suggests that the squadrons were

91 Marchena Giménez, "Vida y los hombres," 434–40.

92 Marchena Giménez, "Vida y los hombres," 41.

93 Moliné i Brassés, *Costums marítimes*, 185–88.

formed not only for political (particularly defensive or offensive) reasons but also for economic ones, expressed through a series of regulations much like the rules for corsair activity. It supports the notion that those regulations were essential to the galleys' survival, even when their actions were represented as the results of political, religious, or civilizational conflict.[94]

The 1531 ordinances did introduce a few new factors, however, meant especially to regulate the governance of the unfree persons aboard—slaves and especially convicts—who were much more numerous than in a galley with letters of marque. Those men received no pay and had no contract for supplies, but they were guaranteed sufficient amounts of food.[95] They were also bound, like the freemen, by a set of rules that again showed continuity with traditional legal practice and lend support to our concept of the squadron as a corporation or *universitas*.

In exchange for the rights and provisions described above, every crew member of a galley armed for commercial purposes had to acknowledge its admiral's full power to employ all means of coercion necessary for good governance of the vessel. The admiral had sworn an oath to the ship's contractors, and then every man at every rank swore loyalty and homage to the admiral, in life and in death. Having received this verbal assent to his jurisdiction, the admiral could impose harsh physical punishments on any sailor or soldier who refused his orders or caused damage to the ship's cargo. A violator could be "flogged round the ship" or, in more serious cases, have his ears cropped.

The heaviest punishments were reserved for officers, especially *cómitres*. By the sixteenth century some duties of that rank had passed to skippers and captains, leaving cómitres (something like second mates) as simply the officers in charge of overseeing and maintaining the rowers. But in the fifteenth century, a cómitre had been more like a captain,[96] the galley's first officer and the one charged with administering justice on the spot. For him to violate his oath of loyalty and homage to his admiral was the worst possible offence, punishable by impalement, with a single limitation—his authority over the crew ended the moment they set foot on land ruled by another jurisdiction. This exception is important because, as we know, in the galleys of the sixteenth and seventeenth centuries the ships' jurisdiction followed each crew member even onto land.

The squadrons of the Catholic monarch, in their ordinances, followed the same ritual oath-taking that applied to corsair ships, with a few variations.

94 Williams, *Empire and Holy War*.
95 Marchena Giménez, "Vida y los hombres," 438.
96 Calderón Ortega, *Almirantazgo*, 227.

The *oficiales de sueldo* (financial officers)—the *veedor* (inspector), *pagador* (paymaster), and *contador* (purser), all charged with the squadron's financial and logistical administration—swore to the captain general that they would perform their duties faithfully. In turn, they received the captains' oaths to command their ships well. The rest of the crew accepted the authority of their captain general at the muster (known as the *alarde* or *muestra*) that preceded any new expedition, when new men were entered into the lists and inactive ones crossed off.[97] In this way, the captain general of the squadron received the fealty of everyone aboard his galleys, all acknowledging his position at the pinnacle of that unique legal and juridical universe, just as the inhabitants of a territory did at the start of a new sovereign's reign.

In contrast, the ordinances of royal squadrons did not contain the list of crimes and punishments included in Barcelona's naval regulations, which were recognized by private admirals' jurisdiction. This was probably because titles like that of admiral of Castile already assumed them, giving that office the capacity to "pass justice on all those who … go absent without leave or escape, or steal something or fight so as to cause injury or death,"[98] rules that the captains general' jurisdiction later inherited. Although the 1531 and 1607 ordinances stated that the squadron's captain general should carry out all their prescriptions with strict justice and employ all his powers in commanding the vessels,[99] they did not specify how that justice should be administered, or where, or under what assumptions. Those faculties, therefore, were privileges belonging to, and defined by, the title that the captain general obtained from the monarch; subsequently, the crew swore to obey them. The ordinances protected the galleys inasmuch as they belonged to the king, as did all the ships' people, and above all they protected the commercial privileges that ensured the continuation of the whole enterprise. But we must also conclude that the protections extended to sailors, soldiers, and slaves on land were not connected to the galley ordinances, but must be sought elsewhere.

3.2 *Convergence with the Tradition of Military Privileges*

The *Partidas* of Alphonse x the Wise stated that those sailing in a royal fleet constituted a "great host" (*hueste mayor*).[100] According to Covarrubias's dictionary *Tesoro de la lengua castellana* (1611), *hueste* at the time meant "an army sent into the field against the enemy";[101] therefore, crewmen in a fleet were

97 Marchena Giménez, "Vida y los hombres," 438.
98 Calderón Ortega, *Almirantazgo*, 217–18.
99 Marchena Giménez, "Vida y los hombres," 434–40.
100 Calderón Ortega, *Almirantazgo*, 223 n. 181.
101 Covarrubias, *Tesoro*, 482, s.v. *hueste*.

legally considered members of an army on campaign, and as such they enjoyed a whole series of long-standing privileges well established in Roman law. Since these formed part of the norms that regulated discipline in the legions, we find them in clauses on military affairs (*De re militari*) in law codes such as Justinian's *Digesta*. There, we see how soldiers in wartime had certain advantages in making a will, for example, while their commanders could administer severe punishments, ranging from flogging to execution, depending on a man's rank and the nature of the crime; that jurisdiction extended to offenses such as disorderly conduct, insubordination, and above all desertion. The combination of those two principles produced norms in Roman law that strongly recall cases we have already seen. One example will suffice here. According to the *Digesta*, if a soldier committed a crime of a military nature the punishment should conform to military justice; therefore, if a soldier who fled after committing a relatively minor offense was caught by another authority, he should be turned over immediately to his superior with a report on the incident.[102] But at the start of the early modern age this measure did not apply in every situation but was confined to the jurisdiction of the high admiral, which as we know extended only to the sea and the lands along the coasts.

In thirteenth-century Castile, military penal legislation began to be built on legal principles of Roman origin, and that still held true when the Hispanic Monarchy needed to modernize its military structures in the early sixteenth century.[103] We can observe this process in the judicial arena by comparing Ferdinand and Isabella's "Great Ordinance" of 1503 with the Ordinance of Genoa of 1536. In both it is easy to identify crimes and their punishments with those described in the *Digesta*, and René Quatrefages has observed that we can also trace a loss of autonomy by infantry officers parallel to that suffered by cómitres in the galleys.

In cases that straddled military and civil society, however, military jurisdiction was still not wholly independent of the civil variety. The Great Ordinance of 1503 decreed that in Castile, cases involving both soldiers and civilian residents should be heard only by the *corregidor* (local crown magistrate), even in places where an *alcalde de las guardas* (a military judge, who dealt with disputes between soldiers) was present. They also specified that if no corregidor was in residence, the military judge must hear the case together with local magistrates. While the *Digesta*, recognizing that a soldier might commit both military and civil crimes, called for punishment according to the nature of the

102 Rodríguez de Fonseca, *Digesto*, 120–21.
103 Martínez Ruiz, "Legislación y fuero militar," 2:12.

offense,[104] that does not appear to be the spirit of the 1503 ordinances. Though some military matters fell under the corregidores' jurisdiction,[105] the fact that military judges had to collaborate with local courts suggested to Quatrefages that punishments meted out to soldiers in these situations owed more to civil than to military justice.[106]

In 1536 Charles v laid down the directives for organizing his troops in Italy, creating the system of infantry regiments (*tercios*); at the same time, he made a significant alteration to the internal administration of justice in those units. The change, which does not appear in earlier ordinances, established the *auditor* as the figure delegated by the general of a regiment to administer justice within it.[107] Unfortunately the 1536 Ordinances were less explicit than those of 1503 in defining how conflicts involving both military and civil justice should be handled; they noted only that the *auditor* would find and pass sentence in cases "between parties." Therefore, it is hard to determine the limits of that jurist's powers. Further, since new permanent troops of soldiers were being established outside of Castile and Aragon, it is not clear whether they fell under traditional Peninsular laws or whether innovations were introduced, as was happening during those years in the strengthened system of naval squadrons. We wonder, then, why judicial limits were so vaguely defined in the 1536 Ordinances when they could easily have incorporated earlier Castilian legislation.

We must bear in mind that *auditor* did not replace the *alcaldes*, who continued to serve in units of the Guards of Castile.[108] Their areas of responsibility made sense within the traditional organization of that kingdom, but they could not readily be transferred to a different geographical and legal space such as Italy. There was always a duality between the internal and external logic of Spanish military administration[109] and its handling of justice. The office of *auditor* belonged more to the external realm, after units were created that might serve under a variety of foreign jurisdictions. Historians have shown that a crucial factor was the definitive adoption of Roman law in a process that culminated in 1587 with the ordinances that Alessandro Farnese ("Farnesio") issued in Flanders.[110] These specified the precise functions of the judicial officers of

104 Rodríguez de Fonseca, *Digesto*, 119–20.
105 Lunenfeld, *Corregidores*, 13–21.
106 Quatrefages, *Revolución*, 185–86, 199–200, 384.
107 Quatrefages, *Revolución*, 323.
108 Martínez Ruiz, *Soldados del rey*, 2:15.
109 Quatrefages, *Revolución*, 225–70.
110 Portugués, *Colección*, 38–45.

the regiments, especially those of the *auditor*, and are considered the foundation of the administration of military justice under the Hapsburgs.[111] But little has been written about the process of evolution itself, that is, how the *auditor* position evolved from its introduction without a clearly defined scope in 1536 to a sharper delineation of its authority in 1587.

One might argue that since our purpose is to define legal jurisdiction for the galleys this excursus has been unnecessary, but that is not the case. In the sixteenth and seventeenth centuries soldiers who sailed in the galleys did not belong to specific naval units but were assigned at random to whichever ones were operating at the time. Therefore, two legal systems coexisted aboard ship, the naval one based on maritime custom, and the military one that soldiers brought on board with them and retained when they disembarked at a Mediterranean port. It is no coincidence that *auditores*, either general (*auditores generales*) or attached to squadrons (*auditores de escuadra*), began to appear on galleys after 1536. It is essential to understand their origin, the nature of their functions, and at what point their duties became fixed if we are to grasp the squadrons' legal universe, which not only protected the crews but also, as we shall see in the next chapter, justified their participation in maritime traffic and influenced the evolution of legal practice in the Mediterranean.

3.3 *Roman Law and Experience: the Introduction of Auditores into the Galleys*

Juan Francisco Pardo has recently remarked that in the sixteenth and seventeenth centuries Spanish jurists habitually commented on and reelaborated Roman legal texts as they sought to understand and explain the institutions of their own time. They used a dialectical method, collecting sentences and opinions by authoritative voices of the past in order to formulate theses that justified the scope of a given office or institution. *Auditores* were merely *letrados* (lawyers), assigned by royal courts to help captains general perform the legal duties attached to their office and delegated by the king,[112] but once present they might play a role similar to the one they already performed in other royal institutions.

The name of the office provides an initial clue. For Covarrubias *auditor* meant "a judge who hears cases," and the term had been introduced because it was "used in Rome."[113] Jean-Marc Pelorson claims that it originated with the

111 Moreno Casado, "Ordenanzas," 431–39; Martínez Ruiz, *Soldados*, 2:16–17; Millán Garrido, *Justicia*, 21–22.

112 Pelorson, Letrados *juristas*, 68.

113 Covarrubias, *Tesoro*, 103, s.v. *auditor*.

auditor of the Apostolic Tribunal of the Roman Rota,[114] but that idea might actually derive from the example Covarrubias used in his definition. The word might also simply be a Latinization (*auditor* = lit. "hearer") of Spanish *oidor*, the chief judge in the monarchy's royal councils, *audiencias* (courts of appeals), and chancelleries. Perhaps this person was understood to be the chief judge of the captain general's appeals court, in parallel to the long-standing relationship between a viceroy and his royal appeals court.

Once the office had been created, it had to assume certain powers that, while still unclear, had an obvious goal: to provide military justice with a set of principles that would grant it greater autonomy and (as with other decisions relating to galleys) prove decisive in the viability and outcome of a campaign. Its actions probably determined the limits of prerogatives that were being strengthened at this time, as we already know. Through these and with the help of tradition, experience, and exemplary laws from the past—in edict after edict and campaign after campaign—*auditores* would gradually establish both general and specific principles that, while absent from the ordinances of 1536, must obviously have evolved beyond the ones articulated in 1503.

This hypothesis gains credibility in the light of evidence from the galleys. In 1596 Cristóbal Mosquera, a member of the Council of Castile and former *auditor* general of Philip II's fleet and army, published his *Comentario en breve compendio de disciplina militar* (A brief commentary on military discipline). There, he described the Battle of Terceira in the Azores under the command of Álvaro de Bazán, which had completed Spain's conquest of Portugal in 1583. As Mosquera acknowledged after narrating the campaign, the captain general of the fleet had charged him with defining the principles of military discipline that had obtained in the battle; in other words, with justifying the legal norms on which penal law had been based and distributive justice applied on that occasion.[115] Mosquera gave his reasons in the first pages of his work, pointing to the important context that we have been exploring: "For only a short time now ... a large armada of sailing ships [and] a squadron of galleys [has embarked] on seas never accustomed to supporting them," a situation that produced new challenges to the justice system.[116]

Cristóbal de Mosquera tells us how captain generals had exercised their jurisdiction over their crews up to that point. Because the ordinances did not name specific offenses and their punishments, before each expedition captain generals would publish an edict, shown to every man in the fleet, that set out

114 Pardo Molero, "Usos de Roma," 390–91.

115 Mosquera de Figueroa, *Comentario*, fol. 9.

116 Mosquera de Figueroa, *Comentario*, fol. 4r.

the rules of discipline that would apply. For the 1583 campaign Bazán listed the punishments to be imposed if a crewman deserted, turned renegade, blasphemed or insulted, was violent in word or deed, profaned a church, took revenge for a past affront, initiated an action without his officer's permission, took a mistress, sold his clothing or weapons, gambled without having funds, switched companies without leave, or even created confusion by shouting during battle. All these were frequent behaviors by crew members to which the ordinances did not refer.[117]

The most interesting revelation of Mosquera's work was that each captain general issued his own orders for the battle he faced, with the advice of his *auditor*. Orders were based on offenses drawn from normal military law, "taken from [previous] military [examples] and legal prudence so that both soldiers and seamen may be ruled and governed by them." There was therefore no obligatory model; rather, each commander relied on his own experience and tried to proceed with caution and in good order, "being moved by examples from the ancients, imitating at times the Romans and at times the Greeks and adopting the best of the Macedonians besides, through frequent reading of good books." Mosquera hoped to make Álvaro de Bazán's actions in 1583 a model for the future, while describing the origin and functions of the *auditor* or—which comes to the same thing—laying the legal foundations for a post that was still in the process of being defined.[118] Since Mosquera was a *auditor general* himself and wrote in his own hand, his work supports our hypothesis that he was setting dimensions for a new office, born of the 1536 ordinances. Although its publication was delayed, it coincides in time with Farnese's initiative, so the 1580s appear to be the decisive decade for the delineation of the *auditor* position.

It is easy to trace Roman law in both Farnese's 1587 text and Mosquera's chronicle of 1596. Farnese's ordinances defined the duties of the *auditor*, and other scholars have already written about its roots in the Roman legal tradition.[119] Mosquera's definition, however, though incorporated into a narrative, was the truly influential one for the squadrons. Above all it describes more accurately the origin and early justification of the post, in a way that helps us to determine the nature of the captains general' authority and their influence on the corporate structure of galley squadrons.

Late medieval jurists, and sixteenth-century ones during the reorganization of *audiencias* and viceroyalties, commonly identified the *audiencias* (which had replaced local magistrates' courts) with ancient Roman institutions and

117 Mosquera de Figueroa, *Comentario*, fols. 18v–19v.

118 Mosquera de Figueroa, *Comentario*, fol. 10.

119 Moreno Casado, "Ordenanzas," 431–39; Martínez Ruiz, *Soldados*, 2:16–17.

their extensive prerogatives. According to Juan Francisco Pardo, viceroys were interpreted as the modern equivalent of proconsuls and *audiencias* as modern senates.[120] Mosquera took up this interpretation in his own argument, adapting it to the contemporary posts of captain general and *auditor* of the sea. He attributed the origin of the judge in wartime to a decision by Hector of Troy, thereby linking it to the most remote of the *arcana imperii* of Rome, but above all he tried to identify *auditores* with praetors, the Roman magistrates who administered justice under the consuls. After that, it was easy to define the duties he considered proper to the post—adjudicating and meting out swift punishment in all civil and criminal cases, imposing sentences from the lightest to the most severe according to the gravity of the offense, and moving cases forward regardless of the delays typical of normal tribunals, "deciding them as active affairs of the field, making no official documentation or delay in them." This notion created a perfect equivalence between the captain general's jurisdiction and that of the "Emperor or commander of the army, which was supreme in the field and was granted to him in war," the *auditor* being the person who "provides justice in his [the Emperor's] name … in [the exercise of] his praetorship."[121]

The theatrical aspects of this position must have impressed both residents of the ports and soldiers and sailors in the galleys. In 1606 in Lisbon, when there was an attempt to free two prisoners from a galley at anchor, a witness reported that its captain, Diego Brochero, arrived at the port escorted by twelve arquebusiers.[122] Mosquera states that the *auditor* during his years of service always had "a guard of arquebusiers close to his person, just as, when praetors appeared in public, they were usually accompanied by six attendants [*lictores*]; unlike the great consuls, who had twelve, … because Praetors had only half the dignity of Consuls."[123] Such scenes may not have reminded many people of Roman times, but they did display the power of these men even to those of limited understanding and certainly conveyed a clear message to local authorities.

The expansion of *auditores*' powers appeared unstoppable. By Gian Andrea Doria's account, in 1592 and perhaps under the decisive influence of Farnese's ordinances, every one of the Catholic king's squadrons of galleys in the Mediterranean had its own *auditor*—except for the Galleys of Sicily, which were apparently petitioning to have one too.[124] Above all, Cristóbal Mosquera's

120 Pardo Molero, "Usos de Roma," 392–95.

121 Mosquera de Figueroa, *Comentario*, fols. 110v–111v.

122 AGS, GyM, 662, 3.

123 Mosquera de Figueroa, *Comentario*, fols. 111v–112r.

124 AGS, Estado, 1931, 8.

Compendio became the great reference for issues of jurisdiction and *auditor* relating to galleys. In 1620, the deputies and judges of the principality of Catalonia needed to know whether someone substituting for the *auditor* of its galleys enjoyed his same authority. Mosquera was the author most cited in explaining how that military judge enjoyed full exercise of all civil and criminal jurisdiction, not only in the galleys but also (and here he agreed with many ancient and modern writers) in "any place on land, despite the rule ... stating that judges' jurisdiction does not extend beyond his [*sic*] own territory ... [because] the jurisdiction of the *auditor general* over military men and subjects is not limited to that territory ... [for] it is not limited like that of an ordinary judge within the bounds of his territory ... rather his commission is more extensive, not having a designated territory ... rather he has competence wherever the crime is committed and and all guilty persons arrested appear before him."[125] Roman law had now been incorporated in its totality. The traditional jurisdiction of the admiralty, which had extended only to coastal areas, was superseded, and so was the Castilian tradition that placed limits on military judges and forced them to accept the authority of regular magistrates in certain cases.

3.4 *The Galleys' Jurisdictional Supremacy*

In 1621 Gabriel de Santans, a soldier serving in the Galleys of Spain, entered a tavern with his friends in the town of Tocina in western Andalusia. His conduct must have been disorderly, because soon he was exchanging "very hostile words" with the owner's servant, whom he wounded. A local magistrate ordered Santans confined in chains, but he did not remain in custody for long. When the Council of War heard of the incident, it ordered that the soldier be released at once to his captain general together with a written report of the case.[126] We learn from this incident that at least toward the end of Philip III's reign, the Hispanic Monarchy had established the two basic jurisdictional principles for defending the privileges of men from the squadrons—that *auditores* held

125 "[Por] cualquier parte de la tierra, no obstante la disposición ... por la cual está dispuesto que la jurisdición de los jueces no se extiende mas allá del territorio en el que está ... [porque] la jurisdición del auditor general de los militares, entre sus militares y súbditos, no se circunscribe al territorio ... [pues] no está limitada como la del juez ordinario dentro de los términos de su territorio ... por extenderse más su comissión, la cual no tiene señalado territorio, antes en qualquier parte que se comete el delicto es competente, y se le remiten todos los culpados que se huviere recogido." AHCB, Al.legacions jurídiques, 4:12, doc. 6. See Capdeferro i Pla, *Ciència*, 107–20.

126 AGS, GyM, 871: Petición de Parte, Madrid, 9 August 1621.

sway in any place where a soldier committed a crime, and that their authority also covered cases in which civilians were involved.

In the military Ordinances of 1632, which updated earlier ones of 1611, an article specified that no magistrate, on either Crown or noble land, could charge a soldier with any crime except robbery or treason.[127] The naval ordinances of 1633, however, stated that in cases of problems or quarrels between landsmen and sailors on shore the *auditor general* should not carry his orders to excess and should seek to avoid "competing in jurisdiction with ordinary magistrates."[128] Even as the jurisdiction of the *auditor* became better defined, authorities on land would still try to defend their own prerogatives.

There were certain limits that the galleys' jurisdiction was never able to overcome. By the rules of Barcelona's Consulate of the Sea, an admiral with letters of marque could never punish a crime on land, because that would interfere with civil justice;[129] by the same token, squadrons were barred from doing so. In February 1601 Marino Caracciolo, Prince of Avellino and a commander of Neapolitan galleys, strung up a scribe in the port of Savona for an unrecorded offense. His action infuriated both the port's *podestà* and Gian Andrea Doria, who, to keep the scandal from spreading throughout the republic of Genoa, condemned the act in the strongest terms, reminding the prince that the Catholic king's galleys could not punish anyone in a land with a different system of justice.[130] But since many other limits were less well defined, magistrates drew on the same tools that had already served the monarchy (i.e., the principles of Roman law).

In 1684 the city of Barcelona engaged the jurist Jerónimo Ferrer to try to limit the privileges that the military ordinances granted to billeted soldiers. He argued that sometimes soldiers were accused of nonmilitary crimes, ones typical of civilians rather than soldiers, and that before the new military ordinances came into effect a soldier who committed a common offense had been subject to civil justice. He concluded that the military ordinances could not always "transfer the Soldier from the Ordinary system to its own," since "under the ordinary [system] he would still enjoy military privilege" but only in matters pertaining to soldiering, for "in Catalonia the constitutions and municipal laws, having been made by His Majesty and the Cortes, belong to common law and do not recognize any higher one."[131] Clearly, the line between military and

127 BNE, Ms. 9422.
128 BNE, Ms. 8224.
129 Moliné i Brassés, *Costums marítimes*, 185–88.
130 ADP, scaffale 85, busta 20: Gian Andrea Doria, Loano, 6 and 8 February 1601.
131 AHCB, Al.legacions jurídiques, 4:12, doc. 13.

common law was variable rather than firmly drawn, and the monarchy took advantage of the fact, making its squadrons the vehicle for a political practice that, according to Jean-Frédéric Schaub, used jurisdictional conflict as a way of governing.[132]

Something similar happened in the navy. In principle, *auditores* had to do only with soldiers who shipped in the galleys, but if we recall Mosquera's account, Álvaro de Bazán's instructions before the 1583 campaign covered both soldiers and sailors in his fleet.[133] We wonder, then, about the coexistence in the galleys of two sets of ordinances, naval and military, that governed the crew. It may be that the superposition of both jurisdictions in the person of the captain general defused occasions for conflict; in any case, we have no reference to such cases. But we still must ask if sailors, and by extension any crewmen who went ashore, benefited from the privileges originally designed for soldiers or whether their privileges descended from the ancient prerogatives of the high admiral.

In November 1600 the Count of Santa Gadea, captain general of the Galleys of Spain, wrote a report to the king that sought a solution to the shortage of sailors in his squadron. He believed that better enforcement of existing ordinances was not sufficient and that the ordinances should be expanded. He suggested that sailors' privileges be made equal to those of soldiers, beginning by removing any crimes they might commit from civil jurisdiction and transferring them to the *auditor*, with the Council of War as the court of appeal. To achieve the maximum number of enlistments, he proposed extending that advantage to a radius of six leagues from fleet's anchorage. The count had other changes to suggest as well. Sailors should have the right to bear arms by day and by night in every kingdom under the monarchy, they should be exempt from arrest for debt, and their weapons and other property related to the sea should not be confiscated. They should even have a pew reserved for them in the main chapel of every church, in which they would be seated according to the merits earned during their service, and this list of privileges proposed many more exemptions from taxes and other economic benefits. In short, the Count of Santa Gadea hoped to improve recruitment by making sailors into a privileged collective.[134] This report tells us that, at least in the early seventeenth century, *auditores* oversaw each category of crewmen in the galleys according to its ordinances but that one current of opinion favored treating sailors and soldiers in similar fashion. When eventually the ordinances of 1633 stated that

132 Schaub, *Portugal*.
133 Mosquera de Figueroa, *Comentario*, fol. 18r.
134 AGS, GyM 567, 173.

the *auditor general's* jurisdiction extended to both soldiers and sailors, we do not know if Santa Gadea's wishes had actually come to pass or if the reference was to a single system that contained two sets of regulations.[135]

Theory aside, we can pay attention to practice by returning to a case already cited. When in 1603 a sailor from the Galleys of Spain killed a butcher in Oran, giving rise to the conflict we described, a special justice commission was convoked at court. It dictated that, though the governor of the fortress had the authority to punish the galleys' people when they came on land, the captain general of the squadron had been physically present at the scene and in that special circumstance had a higher jurisdiction in the case; therefore, the sailor should be set free.[136] In the end it did not matter that seamen of the galleys—sailors, convicts, salaried rowers, and slaves—were not protected by the law that protected soldiers; the high admiral's ancient prerogatives still extended to everyone in his fleet and to lands edged by the sea, and, if the captain general was aboard his fleet, nothing could stand against him.

This prerogative was so common that writers of treatises usually defended it. Juan Baños de Acevedo wrote in his *Política Militar de Príncipes* (Military policy for princes) that this type of "gift perhaps [can be] granted by setting aside the law, when changing it seeks only the public good";[137] in other words, service in war should come before other considerations, and certain issues should be glossed over that would be unpardonable in other circumstances. For the authorities in Mediterranean ports, the problem was not only the presence of the galleys' people in their towns but also how daily reminders of the galleys' privileged jurisdiction affected local residents.

We can best illustrate this state of affairs with a case from the papal galleys. In late July 1610 Giovanni di Luca, a resident of Livorno who had recently enlisted as a soldier in the Pope's galleys, ran through the streets of the port trying to board the ship on which he served while a column of smoke rose up behind him. It seems that while the squadron was tied up there, he had gone home and, by his account, had found his wife in bed with another man. In the resulting quarrel, his wife had died of a stab wound and her lover had wounded Giovanni himself. Livorno's governor, informed of the incident, came to the port and asked the galleys' commander to hand over the soldier, who had managed to board before he could be caught. But the commander refused on the grounds of respect for papal jurisdiction, and sent his *auditor* out to negotiate—Sixtus V had copied the Spanish model of governance for his squadron. It seems that

135 BNE, Ms. 8224.
136 AGS, GyM, 624, 111.
137 Baños de Velasco y Acevedo, *Política militar*, 247.

on other such occasions the conflict had been resolved by discreetly surrendering men who sought refuge in the galleys, but here the situation was different because Giovanni had already enlisted. While the *auditor* argued that the case should come under the galleys' jurisdiction, the governor countered that the Livornese was known for abusing his wife, that the accusation of adultery was a lie, and that Giovanni and some of his new shipmates had set fire to the house to cause a distraction and cover his escape.

The dialogue produced few results. The *auditor's* reasoning shocked the governor "because it introduced the idea that in Livorno, such a principal and proud fortress, there would be less concern for wrongdoing, since delinquents were assured of saving themselves in the galleys of other princes"; the people of Livorno should not believe that they could escape punishment for their crimes simply by enlisting or enrolling in the galleys of a different prince. The governor refrained from firing on the galleys out of respect for the friendship between the Grand Duke of Tuscany and Pope Paul V, but he could be pushed only so far; he ordered the *auditor* arrested, though he later proposed an exchange of prisoners.[138]

The conflict then rose to a higher level. The grand duke ordered the governor of Livorno not to release the *auditor* until the commander handed over the guilty man, and he wrote to the papal nuncio in Tuscany, the bishop of Torcello, asking him to mediate. But the nuncio, after consulting the Pope's nephew Cardinal Borghese and receiving new instructions, issued a warning to the grand duke. The latter's galleys, the Saint Stephen squadron, spent more time in Spanish ports like Naples and Messina than on the Tuscan coast, and if the duke insisted on changing the rules of the game in the present quarrel, the Pope would have the Spanish viceroys start to arrest soldiers who served under the banners of the Medici. The nuncio reminded the duke that when similar problems had arisen before, the proper procedure had been to respect the galleys' system of justice in the first instance and then appeal for the criminal's release to the sovereign who had armed the vessels. Those petitions tended to be granted, thus avoiding difficulties and respecting the rights of both sides while avoiding public scandal.[139]

Unfortunately, we do not know the result of this particular incident; the last news we have is that the grand duke held firm, and the papal galleys left Livorno without their *auditor* but with Giovanni di Luca on board.[140] Whatever the outcome, the case provides some insight.

---

138 ASV, Segretaria di Stato, Firenze, 15A, fols. 141–47.

139 ASV, Segretaria di Stato, Firenze, 15A, fols. 148–50.

140 ASV, Segretaria di Stato, Firenze, 15A, fols. 151–52.

The arguments the nuncio used to secure the *auditor's* release show how, when a foreign squadron of galleys was in port, both sides had an interest in respecting its jurisdiction over its own men when they disembarked. All princes owned galleys, and if one day a prince suffered from the presence of foreign galleys on his coast, on another day his own ships might be causing problems for a different state and ruler. All sides benefited if no one interfered with the others' autonomy and freedom of movement. This common consensus maintained the system of permanent Christian squadrons in good working order.

As a result of this tacit agreement, however, other potentially difficult situations could arise. The Spanish ordinances held that if a man enlisted in the galleys after committing a crime, by request of a civil magistrate his enlistment could be canceled and he could be handed over to local authorities. But there was no provision for a premeditated crime such as Giovanni di Luca's may have been.[141] The situation was more complicated if at least two squadrons under different princes were in port at the same time, because then crewmen fleeing from punishment could just enlist in the foreign squadron. In fact, Gian Andrea Doria complained in October 1588 that the recently created papal galleys had become a habitual and shameless refuge for delinquents sought by, or expelled from, other squadrons, so that a layover at Civitavecchia had become a danger for the fleets. Although he did not deny that Spanish ports such as Naples had similar problems, the practice seemed especially typical of the Papal States. Doria asked the Count of Olivares, ambassador to the Holy See, to seek redress from Sixtus v,[142] but at the same time the captain general of the sea admitted that not much cooperation could be expected from Spain. While for writers of treatises these betrayals were mortal sins, and for captains general they were the worst of crimes, what hurt one day could be of help the next. Although a soldier who tended to flee was not very trustworthy, the galleys were used to this type of behavior and, like all other European armies, they did not scruple to accept such men in times of need.[143]

In these cases the deference offered to the squadrons' jurisdiction strengthened their status as a border. As they sailed into an inner harbor, they brought with them and onto the coast a Mediterranean frontier to which any resident or crewman might resort to his benefit; he might eventually cross it, as bandits did when they escaped punishment by crossing the line between two kingdoms. Giovanni di Luca, like any other resident of Livorno, obviously

141 BNE, Ms. 8224.

142 AEESS, legajo 9, fol. 280.

143 González Cruz, "Deserciones."

understood that the presence of a foreign galley in port was not only a potential problem but also an opportunity. He knew that, by taking refuge on a galley after murdering his wife, he could create a jurisdictional conflict that would help him in the end, especially since he had enlisted as a soldier in the papal squadron beforehand.

Finally, what was an obstacle to magistrates in port cities became an advantage, even a necessity, for the squadrons. Their officers, with the sword of Damocles hanging over their heads, were in constant fear that desertions or sickness might make their ships inoperative. They had to defend their people to the end, in all circumstances, both to maintain morale and to make the harsh life on board ship attractive to landsmen. Civilians, attentive to how conflicts developed, envied the freedom of soldiers and sailors to set up their gaming boards and live their dissipated lives virtually free from punishment. In a society in which an individual's position depended on what privileges he enjoyed or lacked, life in the galleys was not always an accident to be endured; for some it was a temptation that rested on the special legal protections offered by service on land and at sea.

In the words of Juan Baños de Velasco, a kingdom without ports was like a chimney without fire—but so was a kingdom without warships.[144] Therefore, as Bernardino Barroso explained, it was essential to attract to the virtuous service of arms men who, though not sons of *hidalgos* or descended from ancient honorable families, wished by their actions "to raise up their progeny and successors in quality and dignity," just like "Tullus Hostilius, born to poor parents and raised poor on humble soil, [who] by his virtue and parts became emperor of Rome."[145] The profession of war was a privilege that the galleys defended jealously; like infantry regiments, they used it as a tool for recruitment, proclaiming the merits of military life while using wiles and stratagems to enlist the credulous.[146] The soldiers who disembarked on Terceira in 1583 were shocked that some Portuguese nobles had formed infantry units with their black slaves "against all the laws that forbid it ... giving them license to become men of war and fight, through which they could gain freedom and privileges."[147] In 1605, when the magistrates of Seville stripped the king of his right to seize soldiers from the Galleys of Spain for crimes of resistance, their captain general complained bitterly that "to avoid the inconveniences that follow from

144 Baños de Velasco y Acevedo, *Política militar*, 386.
145 Barroso, *Teoría*, 114. See Puddu, *Soldado*, 72–89.
146 Rodríguez Hernández, *Tambores*, 105–9.
147 Mosquera de Figueroa, *Comentario*, fol. 80v.

this ... for this reason no one wants to serve in the galleys unless they are useless sorts," and he asked that the privilege be restored.[148]

Behind this appeal lay a more serious problem. A few years earlier, after "very great disturbances between its [Seville's] officers and soldiers from the galleys ... which led to the arming of both sides," a soldier named Gaspar de Cuenca was violently seized by the *asistente* (the local equivalent of a corregidor) after having, probably accidentally, fired the arquebus he carried. To make matters worse, a few hours later "they sentenced him to be hanged without hearing any defense," so as to "pacify the city, since the galleys were in the river and the two jurisdictions were facing off." It seems that the official meant to execute Gaspar before his friends could react, but that proved impossible; the city was already in turmoil, having seen "the soldiers from the galleys [who] came marching in to the beat of a drum, prepared to free their comrade from prison." Under pressure from a corporal of the squadron, the asistente promised to investigate the soldier's offense and then surrender him, but that was only a sham. Before dawn, "quietly" and expecting a fresh attack from the soldiers, "for [the official] was so fearful of the soldiers and halberdiers who blocked the streets that he lost his reason," he hanged the prisoner, who "was found there in the morning at the prison door on a scaffold built in the middle of the street."[149] With this precedent, it was clear that granting jurisdiction over soldiers to local justice in Seville would be especially dangerous.

Galley crews, like other "military societies," were viewed with mistrust. But as Sabine Loriga has observed, it would be wrong to assume that a man who enlisted suspended his relationship with the outside world, that the new discipline would wipe away his self-concept and the baggage from his past, or that civil society would invariably take him for an aggressor. At a time when societies were divided into corporations and communities, institutions like galley squadrons did not separate or subordinate their members but legitimated and protected them in their relations with civil society, validating their behaviors and personal strategies. Therefore, we must remember the positive motivations, not always coercive or based on need, that generated loyalty to that way of life, to a corporation (the galleys) whose clichés and stereotypes have been constructed over centuries by literature and political and military history. We have to conceive of service in the galleys from the viewpoint of its members, understanding its people's internal dependencies and reciprocities, as well as

---

148 AGS, GyM, 605, 213.

149 León, *Grandeza*, 503–7.

how the base of that social body influenced its head (i.e., its officers, and also civil institutions).[150]

Although the bureaucratic and logistical development that increased the number of permanent galley squadrons reshaped the conflictive nature of those fleets in the Christian Mediterranean, civil society accepted their presence in its midst. It did so, in part, for the benefits that their protection brought, and in part perhaps believing in a collective obligation to support them, even if it meant tolerating gambling, recruitment, disorderly crews, and abusive or fraudulent commerce. Mistrust arose not because the frontier between ships and society was firm, but because it was porous—contact between crews and landsmen was too intimate. Galley squadrons became not only a site for dissension but also a tool for transmitting the monarchy's ideas and political culture, through their prominent role in public ceremonies even at times of conflict. Service in the galleys also functioned as an element of social protection, helping members to gain in dignity and improve their standing in the social order, even though the galleys' internal world was marked by profound inequality and discrimination, as we will see throughout the following pages.[151]

In the last instance, the prerogatives enjoyed by these corporations resulted from a long process of change, adaptation, and bureaucratic and jurisdictional modernization promoted by the monarchy, which first restored oversight and then incorporated earlier, even ancient, rights and privileges. These gave rise to a form of governance whose rules straddled medieval maritime custom and Roman-inspired military law. Those two principles defined the galleys as a unique territory in which the crews' oath of loyalty to their captain general made him the sovereign of that kingdom and, through Roman legal doctrine applied for the occasion by its *auditores*, the imperator of that naval militia. This conjuncton of ancient sources with medieval tradition constructed a political theory that gave permanence to the autonomy and privileges of the galleys and their people, but it also launched them inevitably into a more complex, centuries-old debate about the relationship between central power and local governments. When the galleys affirmed their jurisdiction, which was like that of any other institution and based on the same doctrinal principles, and magistrates of civil law responded, they were repeating patterns that Brian Tierney once explored in explaining the keys to constitutional thought in medieval and early modern Europe—debates about the

150 Loriga, *Soldats*, 9–23.

151 Loriga, *Soldats*, 45–46, 91–94.

legitimacy and the extent of authority, the idea of a mixed constitution, and the right to resist.[152] We shall take up these matters later on. First, having illustrated some of the problems that arose from applying the galleys' civil and criminal jurisdiction to Christian coastal lands in the Mediterranean, we will go more deeply into how those legal principles were expressed at sea and in trade.

152 Tierney, *Religion*, 103–5.

CHAPTER 2

Captures, Commerce, and Corruption

In October 1615 the *Generalitat* of Catalonia sent a protest to the Council of War. Prince Emmanuel Filibert of Savoy, recently appointed captain general of the sea and charged with revitalizing the Mediterranean galley squadrons, had required it to pay one-tenth the value of all prizes seized by the Galleys of Catalonia as required by the ancient rights of the admiralty, which his office had inherited.[1] The dispute, which had arisen a year earlier, awakened a long-standing fear of the Catalan deputies: that the ample jurisdiction granted to the prince could interfere with their control of the galleys they armed and the profits they earned from them.

The Galleys of Catalonia, like all the Catholic king's other squadrons, enjoyed enormous privileges. By an agreement made in 1599, the Generalitat had to impose a series of fiscal charges to cover, first, the 80,000 libras assessed for arming the four galleys, and later the squadron's annual operating costs. To do so, it pledged to commit the *bolla* (a kind of customs duty) of the city of Barcelona and to levy tariffs on the sale of playing cards, the export of fruits and vegetables, grain, wine, oil, fish, and certain textiles, and the import of silk from Valencia, wool from Castile, and leather.[2] In exchange, the king granted the Catalans the right to export, free of any type of tax, 500 *salmas* (a measure of tonnage) of Sicilian wheat a year and up to 48,000 Castilian ducats annually. They were also allowed to purchase all those "munitions, provisions, and other things necessary for those galleys, free of all tariffs, paying the fair price for them," and were exempt from any other duty, including the one owed to the admiralty, on the profits they earned from seizing ships.[3]

Clearly these privileges, common to the jurisdiction of all galley squadrons, granted Generalitat deputies exceptionally favorable access to every market under the Hispanic Monarchy. Their intent was to ensure the survival of the expensive squadron, but of course they also offered many chances for its managers to enrich themselves. In fact the Marquis of Almazán, viceroy of Catalonia during the dispute with the Prince of Savoy, had complained repeatedly about the situation. Though the squadron had been sailing for only a few years, the deputies showed scant interest in keeping it operational; they armed only

1 AGS, GyM, Consulta del Consejo de Guerra, Burgos, 9 October 1615.

2 Gilabert Tomàs, "Defensa."

3 AGS, Estado: Consulta del Consejo de Estado, 23 January 1615.

two galleys a year and devoted them to prize-seeking, so as to profit from their built-in commercial advantage.[4] Under the circumstances, it was natural for the Prince of Savoy to seek some of those gains, and for the Generalitat to feel that its share of the profits from the galleys was under threat.

1 Prizes, Embargoes, and the Audiencia de las Galeras

This problem was well known and affected galleys beyond Catalonia. The Hispanic Monarchy routinely exempted owners of corsair ships from paying taxes on the prizes they seized.[5] The measure, designed to encourage defense of the coasts, also brought continual conflicts because many persons motivated only by "greed for prizes" committed excesses.[6] This problem could never be resolved, but it has served, first, to define the relations between the monarchy and the merchants who conducted its maritime trade,[7] and second, to explain one of the squadrons' commonest responses to the high death rate among rowers and the need to preserve themselves at all costs. Just as in privately armed ships, Philip Williams explains how the nature of each squadron was based on the logic of prize-seeking, on the success or failure of a type of warfare in which one either attacked or was pursued. If a galley were to maintain itself, its resources—above all, slaves—had to come from seizing enemy ships.[8]

By analyzing this theory we can explore the second jurisdictional dimension that captains general of the galleys inherited from the old admiralties: their power over trade, maritime trade in this case. We can then assess the effect of ship captures on the finances of the galleys, specifically those of the Galleys of Spain. More broadly, we shall consider the role of capture in Mediterranean commerce and whether its judicial practice affected conflict resolution in cases of prize-seeking, smuggling, and embargoes.

1.1 *Ship Capture and Its Benefits to Crews*

Each galley squadron had a different profile, and all varied in the specific economic gains they made from corsair activity. Letters to court by officers of the Galleys of Spain speak of their chronic need for rowers and their occasional

4 AGS, GyM, 796: Marquis of Almazán to Philip III, 6 December 1614.
5 AGS, Estado, 1945: Consulta del Consejo de Estado, 23 October 1615.
6 AGS, GyM, 800: Consulta del Consejo de Estado, 26 March 1615.
7 Ruiz Ibáñez, "Juegos de azar"; Ruiz Ibáñez and Montojo Montojo, *Entre el lucro y la defensa*.
8 Williams, *Empire and Holy War*, 51, 114.

captures of large numbers of new slaves at sea. These facts suggest that the squadron depended heavily on prize-seeking to maintain itself, especially since its leaders were always lamenting their lack of financing. The royal galleys had to protect the Peninsula's long Mediterranean coast, the supply routes for North African outposts, trade across the Strait of Gibraltar, and the galleons that sailed to and from the Indies; on every watch, they came into contact with all sorts of ships, making it easy to seize precious resources, especially human ones. Luckily, their account books reveal this economic activity in fairly complete form for several years in the early seventeenth century, allowing us to gauge the impact of corsair activity, an important aspect of their commercial privileges, on their finances and manpower. This time spans a period of low-level warfare[9] that also saw the definitive stabilization of the office of *auditor* in 1605.

Some scholars have remarked on the Hispanic Monarchy's difficulties in defending certain strategic routes. Beatriz Alonso, for instance, noted the problem in the Oran-Cartagena passage, which became a veritable hunting-ground for North African galliots during the crucial summer months.[10] Less has been written about the Spanish advantage on very short routes, like that between Tétouan and Algiers, where North African merchants sailed in the same season. In June 1616, Gabriel de Chaves, captain of a galley that seized many prizes during those years, captured a 200-ton ship on that route manned by about a hundred Turks and Moriscos.[11] Three years later, the Galleys of Denia, a satellite of the Spanish squadron, heard that the Algiers flagship, loaded with merchandise, had sailed alone out of Tétouan. They decided at once to give chase, spurred by the rumor that it carried goods "of great value"—between gold, silver, jewels, pearls, purple dye, and many Jewish, Turkish, and North African captives who might be ransomed, the first estimate hinted at a fabulous fortune of several hundred thousand ducats.[12]

These examples, and others we could cite, suggest that the Galleys of Spain could have realized enormous gains from their corsair activity. One hundred captured slaves could have solved the shortage of rowers at a stroke, and the treasure from the flagship, distributed to the crews, might have solved the economic problems of all their soldiers and sailors. But in the event, 70 of the 110 people seized in 1616 were Moriscos who were set free, while the galley's cargo was swindled away in the twinkling of an eye (a lawsuit was brought for fraud),

9 Jamieson, *Lords of the Sea*, 78–79. See Williams, "Strategy."
10 Alonso Acero, *Orán-Mazalquivir*, 460–66.
11 AGS, Estado, 813: Consulta del Consejo de Guerra, 8 June 1616.
12 AGS, GyM, 846: Consulta del Consejo de Guerra, 20 December 1619.

so that we do not know its actual value or whether the crew gained anything from the prize.[13]

Despite some grandiloquent pronouncements, the usual fortunes of the Galleys of Spain in the early seventeenth century were much more modest, as their account books reveal. Although not every ledger registers sales of prizes or the resulting income, we do find traces in the accounting from 1605 to 1611 and 1614 to 1619. For the first period, we see a ship sold in 1605 for a little over 1,150 ducats, paid at public auction by a town councillor of El Puerto de Santa María. Curiously, there was no further sale before December 1608.[14] We do know that another prize from the period, a ship that Pedro de Toledo captured in 1607, was auctioned for 97 ducats but sold only in 1610; therefore, it appears on the books for the period 1609–11, during which time no other such sale is recorded. The accounts are somewhat out of phase with the sales of captured ships, which tended to accumulate—in 1614–16 there is record of a few small payments for two Turkish ships seized in Málaga, probably sold between 1612 and June 1614, a period for which we have no data.[15]

Two ships were sold in the second half of 1614, a small one taken at Gibraltar in June and auctioned for 152 ducats, and a Moorish settee captured by Captain Chaves in July along the Barcelona coast and knocked down for 187 ducats. In 1615, total income was similar but came chiefly from other settees that Chaves had seized the year before. In January, Jacome Rebella of Barcelona, a merchant captain, bought a Turkish settee captured the previous December for 120 ducats, while Francisco de Acosta of the same city acquired a Turkish ship—one of the ones seized in 1614—for 1,386 ducats. At an unknown date Domenico Barrile, a resident of Cartagena, became the owner of an Algerian ship called *Nuestra Señora del Rosario* and all its cargo for 4,279 ducats, and we find the sale of the Tétouan galliot that Chaves took in 1616 for 250 ducats.[16]

Finally, among sales of prizes for the period 1617–19, a Turkish caravel taken at Tétouan in February 1617 was sold to a resident of El Puerto de Santa María for 145 ducats. In this case, the cargo too is recorded—the more than 400 arrobas of oil it carried brought 600 ducats, 100 jars of olives brought 40 ducats, and 34 quintales of figs brought 50 ducats. We also know that Chaves, while conveying the Duke of Feria to Italy, captured two settees, one in Peñíscola and one in Oropesa, and sold them immediately at auction, with all their rigging,

13 AGS, GyM, 858: Melchor de Borja to the Marquis of Santa Cruz, 28 August 1620.
14 AGS, CMC, 3ª Época, 1436.
15 AGS, GyM, 795: Accountant Miguel de Luyando to the king, El Puerto de Santa María, 6 April 1614.
16 AGS, CMC, 3ª Época, 2940–41.

sails, and artillery, to Gabriel Sanza of Peñíscola for 410 ducats.[17] In all, in the fourteen years of campaigning that include 1605–11 and 1614–19, the books of the royal accounting office (Contaduría Mayor de Cuentas) list sales of prizes to a value of about 8,717 ducats, to which we should add two more sales from 1611 that are not described in full detail and not included in the total.

Of course these accounts may contain errors. A letter of June 1618 relates that a galley en route to Seville seized a brigantine with twenty-three North Africans and two Christians aboard, but there is no record of its sale, probably because it was not bought until 1620.[18] We know that in May 1616 another North African ship, pursued by the Marquis of Santa Cruz off Fuengirola, went to the bottom, so of course it was never sold. Other ships may have sunk as well, but there are no great discrepancies when we compare records of sales with the squadron's correspondence. It is curious that auctions of ships' cargoes are mentioned only twice, but perhaps most ships simply contained little of value—many of the captured vessels were small, and almost half of them brought less than 200 ducats at auction, while two others brought less than 300 ducats.

In light of all this, it seems that for the Galleys of Spain no great gains derived from corsair activity along the coasts, since captured prizes were relatively few; instead, there were occasional windfalls that had little effect on the squadron's total income. Certain monies did accrue to officers, however, if they were able to collect them. The accounts record that Captain Gabriel de Chaves received a stipend of 100 ducats for his active role in prize-taking, though as often happened, that amount was paid out only in small occasional sums. The ledger for 1602–3 mentions that a commission had been charged with appealing to court for payments owed to galley captains and their sailors for prizes taken in 1591–92.[19] In November 1616, the paymaster Fernández de Villegas, returning to his post after an absence, found that only 260 ducats from sales of prizes had been recorded.[20] Captains general sometimes made improper use of those funds. In 1599, the Marquis of Santa Cruz spent some on new dresses for his sister Doña María, just named lady-in-waiting to the queen.[21] Many stipends from the monarchy to crew members had to come from sales of prizes, and it was essential that payment be made regularly; it was problematic, therefore, if that failed to be done.[22]

17 AGS, CMC, 3ª Época, 3324.
18 AGS, GyM, 834: Marquis of Santa Cruz to Philip III, 24 June 1618.
19 AGS, CMC, 3ª Época, 397.
20 AGS, CMC, 3ª Época, 3324.
21 AGS, GyM, 553, fol. 231.
22 AGS, GyM, 571, fol. 162.

Even captains general had trouble collecting their share of prizes. Emmanuel Filibert of Savoy did not collect what was owed him as captain general of the sea (3,200 ducats for the period 1612–16) until 1618. The Marquis of Villafranca, who had ceased to be captain general of the squadron years before, was still drawing small sums in 1618 on the value of the prize taken in 1611.[23] Unsurprisingly, both men demanded their back pay in a bitter lawsuit that lasted for years.[24] The profits from sales of prizes were so small and so late that in most cases the galleys' paymaster would satisfy those delayed debts with amounts that the Genoese Vincenzo Squarciafico, based at court, drew on his agents in Seville.[25]

1.2 *Acquisition of Slaves*

One might object here that our analysis ignores the immediate benefit gained from seizing ships (a larger number of rowers) and the income derived from the sale of human beings, which was a factor in other Mediterranean squadrons.[26] But even here the account books tell another story, though the data they offer are few. During our fourteen-year period there is only one brief reference to a deposit from a collective sale of slaves captured by the Galleys of Spain. On May 30, 1617, a bill of 4,900 ducats was presented in Seville for an "order of payment to the Commissioner General [of the Crusade] for 158 slaves and three Moorish ship captains whom the Galleys of Spain took in prizes captured between the year 1610 and February 1617."[27]

The amount is correct. By the 1607 ordinances, slaves captured by the squadron could be sold only to the king, at the price of 30 ducats a head and 100 ducats for North African captains, giving us a total close to that of the bill.[28] But we must ask if this was really a sale of surplus "stock" to the king. It might represent instead an accumulated payment for all the slaves taken during those seven years and now serving in the galleys, to be distributed among the crews, after discounting the jewels (the captain general's portion, usually the best valued slave), according to each man's allotted share of prize money. Unfortunately, because the books are in disorder and the paymaster's distribution policy is unclear, we cannot tell if the sum was actually shared out. We must look elsewhere to learn whether a seizure of large numbers of slaves by the squadron could lead to this type of sale en masse.

23 AGS, CMC, 3ª Época, 3324.
24 AGS, GyM, 795: Martín de Quijano to Philip III, 24 May 1614.
25 AGS, CMC, 3ª Época, 3324.
26 Brogini, *Malte*, 358–64.
27 AGS, CMC, 3ª Época, 3324.
28 Marchena Giménez, "Vida y los hombres," 456.

We first find that the Galleys of Spain made a purchase from the Galleys of Catalonia in February 1615. For the sum of 2,700 ducats, they bought 87 slaves captured by the Catalan squadron, again at the official price of 30 ducats per head, seeming to confirm the shortage of slaves just at the time mentioned in the letter of May 1617.[29] We can relate this purchase to the normal practice in those years, by which the Council of War gave the squadron large occasional sums for buying slaves; that also suggests that the squadron was usually a buyer, not a seller. During our period, there is a single reference to a deposit for that purpose, of 14,000 ducats in 1608, but accounts from 1608 and 1609 register no large purchase of slaves. Therefore it appears that, except for certain special opportunities like the one in 1615 (there was another in 1610 that we will discuss below), those monies were spent in other way.[30] Perhaps, instead, individual slaves were bought at intervals over time, so that although there was a large budget for slaves, the need for them was not really so pressing.

There are a few entries for slaves bought from private owners. Between 1605 and 1608 only two sales were recorded, three slaves in 1607 and two in 1608, from residents of El Puerto de Santa María, Cartagena, and Cádiz, for a total of 361 ducats.[31] Larger purchases were made during the next three years. In 1609, in seven transactions, twenty slaves changed hands at a cost of 1,945 ducats. The next year only two were bought, though for a high price of 309 ducats, and none was bought in 1611.[32] We can conclude that around the time of the large bank deposit of 1608, only twenty-seven slaves bought from private owners entered the galleys, for a total price of 2,615 ducats (i.e., about 96 ducats per head).

This limited number of sales acquires meaning if we compare it with the sales of "useless" slaves in the period 1605–8. Throughout 1605, the galleys sold eight slaves who could no longer row, one in January, one in February, two in August, and four in December. Curiously, they were bought by members of the squadron itself. The wife of the purser Juan Alfonso de Molina bought one; another purser, Durango, bought two; the secretary Bartolomé Rincón, one; Bartolomé de Alzate, probably related to a third purser, Carlos de Alzate, also bought one; and the Count of Niebla, former captain general of the squadron, two. Their total cost was 290 ducats, and if we add another 80 ducats from a ransom, the average price of an individual was 53 ducats (i.e., almost double the rate the king paid, even though these slaves were "useless").

---

29 AGS, CMC, 3ª Época, 2940–41.
30 AGS, CMC, 3ª Época, 1436.
31 AGS, CMC, 3ª Época, 1436.
32 AGS, CMC, 3ª Época, 1570.

The year 1606 saw similar stories. That year, four slaves were sold—to the captain of a galley, the purser Molina's wife again, Dr. Jerónimo de los Cobos (the galleys' physician), and the private citizen Juan Ocampo—for an average of 42 ducats. In 1607, only one slave was sold, for 30 ducats, to a resident of El Puerto de Santa María, though we could add two female slaves confiscated from an indebted supplier, at 148 ducats for both, and a ransomed man for 60 ducats. No sale took place in 1608.[33] During the next three years, 1609 saw the sale of Hamete from Tétouan for 20 ducats, Alí from Larache (who had lost a leg to a cannonball) for 54 ducats, and another ransomed man for 72 ducats. No transactions occurred in 1610, and in 1611 the only one involved a ransom. Those four sales came to 206 ducats, so over the three years the total number of individuals bought or ransomed was nineteen, for almost 1,000 ducats in all.[34]

Therefore at this period the sum spent on buying slaves was more than double that earned from selling them, based on twenty-seven bought and nineteen sold. It is reasonable to suppose that, as the ordinances allowed, the income from sales was reinvested in new purchases as opportunities arose, and that the uneven market prices (since a useless slave cost less than a healthy one) were compensated for by the Council of War's special fund. It seems clear that galley officers were particular beneficiaries of the few slaves sold by the squadron. Because of high prices, they would prefer not to fill their benches with rowers from public slave markets except on rare occasions.

Another source of purchases came not from individual sales but from the captain general's privilege of buying shipwrecked men, inherited from earlier times of the admiralties. It was rare to obtain slaves in this way, and there is no case in the account books before 1609. The first one registered involved a single North African from a Moorish brigantine that ran aground at Cádiz; he was bought for 90 ducats.[35] The detail is significant because, in 1600, the Count of Santa Gadea had bought five slaves shipwrecked off Tarifa for more than the official rate set by the king for galley prizes, opening a debate about whether their price should be fixed at 30 ducats; apparently, that had not occurred.[36] In December 1609 there was a larger shipwreck in Ayamonte involving thirty-four men. After some talk of taking them to Portugal,[37] in the end thirty of them ended in the galleys according to the accounts from 1610. In 1611, another eighteen slaves were taken from a shipwreck in Cabo de Gata, but there is no record

33 AGS, CMC, 3ª Época, 1436.
34 AGS, CMC, 3ª Época, 1570.
35 AGS, CMC, 3ª Época, 1570.
36 AGS, GyM, 566, fol. 173.
37 AGS, GyM, 727: Duke of Medina Sidonia to Philip III, Sanlúcar, 30 December 1609.

of their sale prices, only of the cost of transporting them.[38] In all, shipwrecks provided forty-nine slaves in only those three years, bought with the special fund set up in 1608. Rights to shipwrecked men were obviously a significant element to be added to those captured through fighting on the high seas.

We cannot understand the makeup of the galleys' slave population in these years without considering the largest and most significant source of slaves in the first two decades of the seventeenth century—the Morisco rebellion that broke out in the kingdom of Valencia in October 1609, which proved of enormous benefit to the Galleys of Spain. Letters written at the end of that year show that the Marquis of Villafranca had managed to channel into the squadron a good portion of the Moriscos who had been enslaved after their defeat. The approximate number was two hundred men,[39] and an account-book entry for 1610 confirms that the total might even have been slightly larger. On April 30, 1610, the Galleys' paymaster noted an outlay of 2,274 ducats for 224 Morisco slaves from Valencia, an average price of 10 ducats per person.[40] This was the lowest amount paid for any purchase in the years under study, and shows how the galleys probably benefited from the saturated slave market in Valencia after the uprising. At the same time, it explains why there were so few purchases of new slaves in the years following.

It is much harder to calculate the number of new Moriscos who joined the galleys through captures of North African ships in the following years, because those who could prove their noninvolvement in corsair activity could be deported again. For example Andrés Hernández, a Morisco from Baeza and a slave on the galley *San Martín*, had been taken aboard her with four other slaves in August 1613. The squadron had paid a private citizen 20 ducats for him, but less than a year later he could show documentary proof that after being sent to North Africa, he had decided to turn Christian; he had sailed for France with a skipper, who cheated him and cast him ashore at Marbella, where he had been caught and sold into slavery. On reviewing his case the Count of Salazar, the commissioner of the expulsion, ordered him freed and he was sent back to North Africa in April 1616.[41]

Even while Moriscos were increasing the ranks of slaves, the dearth of captures soon returned the squadron to its usual state of scarcity. Doubtless one reason was not its lack of skill but competition with the Armada of the Ocean Sea, which was sailing in the same waters at the time.[42] Just as in June 1615,

38 AGS, CMC, 3ª Época, 1570.

39 Lomas Cortés, *Puerto de Dénia*, 219.

40 AGS, CMC, 3ª Época, 1570.

41 AGS, CMC, 3ª Época, 2940–41.

42 AGS, GyM, 813: Consulta del Consejo de Guerra, 8 June 1616.

when rowers had had to be bought from the Galleys of Catalonia (their surplus had perhaps inspired the Prince of Savoy's demand for part of their profits in that year), in June 1618 a similar deal was made—the purchase of thirty slaves from the galleons of the armada which, since just the beginning of that season, had already seized four ships.[43]

In short, not only did the Galleys of Spain find it difficult to fill their rowers' benches with their own captures; neither could they buy many slaves from civilians on shore nor make up their numbers with shipwrecked men, although the latter formed an important component. Clearly, the chief source of slaves for the galleys was other royal squadrons, from which men could be bought at a fixed, lower-than-market rate that depended on current supply and demand. Our data suggest that the payment order for the 158 slaves captured from 1610 to 1617 referred not to the sale of surplus men (the Galleys of Spain had no surplus in those years) but rather to the exact number of slaves seized from captured ships who ended up on the rowers' benches. On the theory that a squadron's operations and prestige were measured by its success in prize-taking, it seems that the Hispanic Monarchy's oldest and best-known squadron had a series of bad years where slave capture was concerned. It remains an open question whether, as a result, the number of rowers fell to a dangerously low limit.

We have no account of deceased slaves for the full period, and lists of rowers must be treated with caution because (possible cases of fraud aside) they rarely offer a periodic, total count of the squadron's men. But one useful document is a report prepared by the Dorias in 1638 that calculates the cost of maintaining four galleys for the kingdom of Sardinia, which reveals that under normal conditions the average death rate was eight slaves per galley per year.[44] If we accept this figure, assume that the Galleys of Spain had the same number of slave rowers as contracted galleys, and recall that this squadron consisted of nine vessels in those years, we can conclude that it needed about seventy-two new slaves per year. In the decade 1609–18, for which records are fairly complete, 573 slaves came aboard (though the number would be slightly higher if it included purchases from private citizens between 1612 and 1618). Therefore, throughout the decade, the squadron seems to have been able to replace, in one way or another, about fifty-seven of the seventy-two new men required each year. These incomplete data suggest that the squadron was more or less able to maintain its crews, though the general tendency was negative, a fact

43 AGS, GyM, 834: Emmanuel Filibert of Savoy to Martín de Aróztegui, Madrid, 19 June 1618.

44 ADP, scaffale 70, busta 24: "Calcolo della spesa necessaria per mantenimento d'una galera ordinaria della squadra del signor principe Doria."

explained in part by its falling back on reinforced galleys.[45] The main problem was the small number of captures, though we must note that slaves formed only a small part of the rowers in this squadron—most of the men were convicts.[46] To fill out the picture of the income produced by the galleys' actions at sea, we must consider not only the struggle against the Turks but also commercial warfare with Christian enemies of the monarchy.

1.3 *The Audiencia de las Galeras and Embargoes*

In December 1598, the recently crowned Philip III proved his intent to continue the war in Flanders by decreeing the seizure of every Dutch ship then trading along his coasts or able to be captured at sea.[47] Only a few days later, the king announced the first results: six vessels taken in Guipúzcoa, two in Galicia, twenty-four between Oporto and Lisbon, nine in the Algarve, five in Ayamonte, fifty-seven between Sanlúcar, El Puerto de Santa María, and Cádiz, three in Seville, six in Cartagena, and two in Alicante. Other important jurisdictions such as Málaga had not yet reported their numbers.[48] Though there is no record of the Galleys of Spain having made any specific capture, their officers played an important role. Half of all the seizures passed through the hands of Alonso de Velasco, the squadron's inspector general, who had been charged with applying the edict on the coast between Sanlúcar and Cádiz; he was helped by its *auditor*, who inventoried the ships and their cargoes and arrested their crews.[49]

The galleys benefited from these embargoes just as they did from captures—by appropriating the rowers and selling the ships. We do not know the end result, but early in the process, by December 16, the galleys had gained seven *maestres* (merchant captains), six *contramaestres* (boatswains), and seventy-three seamen.[50] These numbers must have increased as captured men arrived from faraway ports, though we know that many remained in prison and never boarded a ship. Our information about ship auctions is also incomplete, but in March 1599 the six vessels seized in Cartagena were still waiting to be sold for the squadron's benefit (and the captured sailors were still awaiting the arrival of the galleys where they would serve). According to the purveyor Miguel de Oviedo, their assessed value was 9,200 ducats, a significant sum. In just a few

45 Williams, "Past and Present."
46 Heras Santos, *Justicia penal*, 312.
47 Gelabert González, "Entre 'embargo general'."
48 AGS, GyM, 561, 26–30.
49 AGS, GyM, 561, 76.
50 AGS, GyM, 539, 187.

months from 1598 to 1599, and in just one port, the squadron had apparently earned from these seizures more income than from the sale of prizes taken in all of 1605–11 and 1614–19, though we must treat this information with caution. Miguel de Oviedo also reported that the ships had been knocked down for less than their asking price when no buyers appeared, and in the end some of them even had to be sold on credit.[51]

It is easy to see how this situation arose. The auction price of ships might have fallen because such a large number had been embargoed. But above all, once the embargoes had been decreed, many merchant captains appealed the *auditor's* decisions, making him justify whether "it is a legitimate prize or not, and where they come from" before an auction could be held. Because the process was not always simple or conclusive, purchases must have become even more uncertain—and this was not the only problem caused by the edict.[52]

The *auditor* Mosquera de Figueroa wrote that cases involving galleys should be brief and efficient, avoiding "the scrupulous rigor of ordinary judges," because the forms, rituals, and "substantial ... superstitions of common law" created delay and "loss of time" that worked against the needs of an army on campaign. Therefore when a *auditor* prepared his cases, he should not give "occasion for seeking out lawyers"; he should avoid at all times "the loud chattering of prosecutors, the damaging ruminations and irrelevancies that some lawyers, with a narrow reading of the law, use to persuade and, if they can, to change the judge's mind." Nor was he obliged to "listen to litigants when they wished to speak to him privately; [they should speak] publicly in his court, so that cases can be better understood and decided swiftly." The *auditor* was not bound by "the practice of civil, canonical, or municipal law, which are characterized by the written exposition of the case, a response by the opposing side, assignment of times and deadlines, the appearance of witnesses, and documents, without which ordinary justice is nothing."[53]

---

51 AGS, GyM, 541, 163.

52 AGS, GyM, 548, 88.

53 "[L]a vocinglera parlería de los procuradores, las dañosas cavilaciones y impertinencias con que pretenden persuadir algunos abogados, con un cierto rigor de derecho, para derribar si pueden la voluntad del juez ... [sin obligación de] oir a los litigantes en particular cuando le quieren hablar en secreto, sino públicamente en su tribunal, para entenderse mejor las causas y acertar en ellas brevemente ... [No está ligado a] la práctica del derecho civil, canónico y municipal, que consiste y se diferencia por la presentación del escrito, contestación del pleito, asignación de términos y plazos, producción de testigos y escritos sin los cuales el juicio ordinario no es ninguno." Mosquera de Figueroa, *Comentario*, fols. 112v–114v.

The elements needed for sound and swift military justice were not limited to the squadrons, but followed the type of summary judgment outlined in the judicial system of Castile, as María Paz Alonso Romero explained years ago.[54] That system allowed for a prompt decision on the fate of a corsair ship and was occasionally applied to merchant ships and other types of Mediterranean commerce. On the nearby coasts of Muslim lands, a "plain and sincere" eyewitness statement could carry more weight than a written document when two parties sought a quick resolution and preferred not to go to court.[55] On the other hand, when *auditores* used the same procedure, they could become persons "of absolute power and a strong hand,"[56] making their decisions a threat not only to crews and ordinary magistrates but also to skippers and armers of ships.

In September 1600, a group of galleys brought the *auditor* Juan Ossorio to Huelva. On disembarking, he ordered an armed troop of soldiers to enter the town and arrest two residents, Diego Juan and David Barbero, and a French merchant, "Pablo Guillermo," on charges of avoiding the embargo by trading for the Flemings with their own ships, thus eluding seizure. Ossorio then confiscated their merchandise, valued at more than 5,000 ducats, together with an unknown sum of money, "causing a great uproar." The local magistrate soon objected that those acts impinged on his jurisdiction, that the three well-known residents had been unjustly charged, and that the *auditor* had exceeded his authority in applying the embargo to men who were good subjects and faithful Catholics. Besides, since the galleys' people were not involved in the case, he demanded a full report and the immediate return of all seized persons, vessels, cargoes, money, and legal briefs. The magistrate wrote to the Council of War, which replied that it first needed to study the case, requiring copies of all briefs and their assessment by an expert.[57] With any decision thus delayed, there would be no immediate auction of the ships, but nor would either side in the case receive prompt satisfaction.

This type of conflict with the regular justice system, which arose from jurisdiction over offenses against the laws of maritime commerce, was as common as those involving crimes that seamen committed on land. It almost always followed the same pattern: a *auditor* ordered an embargo and passed sentence within a few days; a local official, usually a corregidor, objected and appealed

54 Alonso Romero, *Proceso penal*, 287 ff.

55 Greif, "Contract Enforcement."

56 AGS, GyM, 846: Consejo de Guerra, 1619.

57 AGS, GyM, 572, 361.

the case; and everything was delayed while the Council of War weighed in on the jurisdictional dispute. Occasionally, however, the roles were reversed.

In January 1605, several merchants of Cádiz brought suit against Adam Veart before the corregidor of El Puerto de Santa María. That skipper, a native of Havre-de-Grâce, had anchored in Cádiz for a few days while he bought salt to take to the fishing grounds off Newfoundland, but the men of Cádiz insisted that he was really a pirate. Three years before, while they were trading in North Africa under license, Veart had boarded their ship and stolen their cargo, and they now demanded his arrest and the seizure of his vessel. The corregidor confiscated his sails and weaponry to keep him from resisting or escaping while the charge was investigated. But as soon as the inspector of the galleys learned of the situation, he embargoed the ship, arrested its crew, inventoried its cargo, and forwarded the case to the *auditor*, who called on the corregidor to relinquish it. The judge advocate insisted that since it involved a crime of piracy at sea, it fell under the jurisdiction of the captain general.

The case seemed complicated at first. Because Veart had changed ships and crews since the incident of three years before, he claimed that the present embargo and arrest were illegal. He was only a quarter-owner of the company, so the *auditor* was trampling on the rights of the other owners. But these arguments proved useless. No one expected a quick decision, because of the jurisdictional dispute involved, and the Council of War had not yet been consulted on whether the *auditor* could take the case away from the corregidor of El Puerto and whether an embargo could be declared at all. But in short order the arrested seamen were already rowing in the galleys and the Duke of Medina Sidonia had requisitioned the vessel for guard duty in the Strait of Gibraltar.[58]

Sometimes jurisdictional disputes arose even between different military units, inevitably with the ships' armers on the losing side. In December 1604, a merchant vessel from Emden, a German port near the border with Holland, loaded with wood from Galicia to transport to Seville, was seized off Lisbon by a ship from Dunkirk bearing letters of marque from Archduke Albert of Austria and his archduchess, Philip II's daughter. The corsairs had boarded her believing that she belonged to an enemy ("from a bad country"), but after identifying the cargo and its origin, they realized their mistake. Reluctant to lose any possible profit, however, they towed her to a bay near Cascaes and demanded 500 escudos in exchange for her captain's release. But the governor of

58 AGS, GyM, 683, 219.

the local castle, informed of their presence, alerted the ships of the Armada of the Ocean Sea, just then anchored in Belem. While the corsairs and their prize were soon in the hands of the squadron, the captain of the German ship was still very far from seeing justice done.

On the one hand, the armada's *auditor* claimed the case because his ships had captured the corsairs. On the other, the *auditor general* of the kingdom of Portugal asserted his own right to it, because soldiers from regiments under his jurisdiction had served on the armada, boarded the corsair and its prize, and arrested the crew. As an additional complication, the *auditor* of the Galleys of Portugal also claimed a role—the armada's people, unable to tow the two ships themselves, had asked his galleys for help in bringing them into port, and therefore his own squadron had taken part in the capture and he, too, had a right to hear the case.

Each side began to prepare its briefs while calling on the other to withdraw. The first to leave the field was the *auditor general* of Portugal, but his colleagues continued the fight to defend their own interests. The galleys wished to declare the Dunkirk ship a legitimate prize and auction it off, but the armada sought to seize it by embargo for its own squadron; it would receive no economic benefit, "because His Majesty does not consider as prizes ships that are embargoed for his service and manned by people from his armadas." In March 1605 the Council of War called on both *auditores* to show proper deference to each other. But what interests us most is that after four months of litigation both ships were still stranded in port—the *auditor* of the galleys was still not entirely convinced that the German vessel was not an enemy one—at great financial cost to their armers and crews.[59]

Faced with all the usual delays that resulted from appeals against the *auditores*' decisions, some chose simply to accept their jurisdiction. In June 1601 some of the armada's ships, together with the Galleys of Spain, captured five Flemish vessels as they tried to cross the Strait. Because the Count of Santa Gadea commanded both squadrons at the time, he put the *auditor* of the Galleys in charge of the case. Each ship was to be charged separately, and statements would be taken from officers and crewmen, through several interpreters, over a period of days.

All the testimony pointed in the same direction. Four of the vessels were Dutch, though armed by different people, and had been returning to Amsterdam after trading in several Italian ports; near Málaga, they had decided to form a convoy to defend their cargoes against the dangers of the Strait. The

59 AGS, GyM, 651, 29–32.

fifth ship was not Dutch but had taken the precaution of joining the others, and so had been caught along with the rest. With this information in hand, the *auditor* arranged several "plenary trials," a type characteristic of Castilian summary justice. In each trial the crews' statements were verified and each captain was asked "if he wished to defend himself in the case and claim his right to justice, for which he would be assigned a lawyer, a representative, and a stipend." But all the skippers declared that they had no defense to present, that their shipmates' statements were true, and that they would accept their sentence. All they asked in return was freedom to go home with their men. As a result, after a two-weeks trial on 14 July, the *auditor* confiscated the four Dutch ships and their cargoes "as a legitimate prize" and ordered the crews set free. He decreed that the fifth ship could continue its voyage, and offered its captain safe-conduct in exchange for a fine of 200 maravedis for having traveled in such bad company.[60]

Mosquera de Figueroa explained that although *auditores* were exempt from all the ceremonies of common law, they should conform to those of natural law and the law of nations. In doing so, they had to respect the three principles that effected, informed, and decided any trial and without which their jurisdiction could not operate nor their "court" be legitimate: confessions, necessary proofs, and legitimate defense.[61] It appears that the trials of the Dutch ships involved the practical application of Mosquera's legal doctrine, since it was based on witness statements and respected the skippers' right to a legitimate defense. It is not so clear that other proofs were considered, but in this case the captains agreed to the process, and the *auditor* may have found the offense to be flagrant.

The captains did have the right to an attorney and a representative, but demanding them carried its own risks. The month of July 1601 happened to be an intensely busy one for the *auditor* of the galleys. Aside from the case of the Dutch ships, he faced the complaints of a group of Irish merchants and merchant captains whose vessels and cargoes had already spent some time embargoed in Cádiz and El Puerto de Santa María. In that case the crew, having spent two weeks on the rowing benches while the *auditor* considered their crimes, had claimed their rights and sent a delegation to the court in Valladolid asking for help. While awaiting a reply, they had spent all their money on food. When their case was finally heard and they were set free, they found their ships too damaged to put to sea, and for both repairs and sustenance they would need

60 AGS, GyM, 582, 81.

61 Mosquera de Figueroa, *Comentario*, fol. 114r.

the funds that they were now, unsuccessfully, demanding from the Galleys of Spain.[62]

There were times when a ship's crew and its cargo suffered different fates. On September 7, 1598, a few weeks before the general embargo was declared, a Dutch vessel was seized because it came from rebel territory. In this case, its captain and the French merchant who had chartered it demanded their rights, so the galleys' appeals court (the Audiencia de las Galeras, as the scribe Leonardo Garguillo called it) heard the case. It was an example of the second sort of procedure that could take place before that body. A lawyer and interpreters were sought, and the licenciate Pedro de Armenta was named as defender and representative of the ship's absent armers, its captain Juan Garbaransen, and the French merchant Rocher Bolin. It was decided that for the opposing side a supervisor of the galleys, Juan López, would represent the royal property of the Catholic king. After five weeks of arguments the *auditor* found against the ship's captain and its armers, declaring it forfeit along with its artillery, powder, weapons, rigging, sails, and supplies. But while sentencing the captain and crew to row in chains, he freed Rocher Bolin, together with all the cloth and other merchandise in the hold, based on clauses in the recent Peace of Vervins.[63]

There is no mention in this trial of intervention by the French ambassador to help free Bolin and his cargo, but diplomatic pressure was often exerted in such cases. The usual complaint was that captains general of Spanish squadrons were not only pursuing Muslim ships but also seeking prizes from other nations, in an attempt to "take [from them] for supplying their galleys." This was the charge leveled against the Spanish ambassador in London, Pedro de Zúñiga, in 1607, after the Galleys of Portugal were said to have "seized large sums of money from different English [ships] for payment" of the squadron. Its captains general, the Count of Elda, had to prepare a report containing statements by several Englishmen that denied such seizures and showed, with an example from 1605, that he was obeying the terms of the Treaty of London. In September of that year, his galleys had captured an English ship loaded with cod that was sailing off Cape St. Vincent "without a passport and without the permits required by the treaties and capitualtions." The *auditor* had initially held that the seizure was legitimate, but a royal order had forced him to reverse himself, even though the ship and its cargo had been "properly condemned."[64]

62 AGS, GyM, 581, 76.
63 AGS, GyM, 561, 218.
64 AGS, GyM, 684, 116, and 120.

Such gestures were not unusual. In August 1618 John Digby, England's envoy extraordinary to the court of Philip III, requested that twelve Englishmen condemned to row in the Galleys of Portugal be freed. The Council of War reviewed their case and, though some of them had been sentenced for piracy, decided to release them; it recalled that James I of England had freed about one hundred "priests and laymen who were condemned, some to life in prison, for their Catholic religion" as a favor to the Spanish ambassador in London, the Count of Gondomar.[65] We observe here how galley squadrons could serve not only as instruments of warfare but also as tokens of peace and amity between princes; treaties usually included clauses that guaranteed freedom of trade between their respective countries and the mutual freeing of men sentenced to serve in their ships.

For example in February and March 1599, in accordance with the twentieth provision of the Peace of Vervins,[66] all French prisoners were removed from the squadrons—though men of that nation soon returned to them, as we see in a document from 1613. In May of that year the French consul in El Puerto de Santa María called on the Prince of Savoy to respect a decree by Philip III freeing all French prisoners, in particular those who were in the galleys awaiting the outcome of their trials. The captain general of the sea replied, however, that the only Frenchmen serving in the squadrons had been definitively condemned. He attached a list of their names, crimes, and sentences, giving us an insight into the severity of sentencing by the Audiencia de las Galeras in those years, at least as it pertained to the French.

In 1613 the ten Galleys of Spain held fifty-two Frenchmen among them. Only four of those had been sentenced for crimes related to piracy, and only two had been tried before a *auditor*. The rest had arrived from up to fifteen tribunals from all over Castile. The majority came from Madrid, Granada, and Valencia, and their commonest crime was robbery. Aside from thieves, there were rapists, murderers, adulterers, impersonators of soldiers, profaners, and blasphemers, though only two were serving life sentences. Sixteen were sentenced to six years, fifteen to four years, and eleven to ten years; therefore very few had served since the beginning of the century. The longest-serving prisoner in the squadron, Ramon Butar of Toulouse, had been rowing since the *Audiencia* of Valencia had imposed his life sentence in 1602. Most of the men (forty-two) had arrived in the galleys between 1609 and 1612. We can conclude that during

65 AGS, Estado, 2515: Consulta del Consejo de Estado, 18 August 1618.

66 Haan, "Dernière paix."

this period an average of ten Frenchmen a year were sentenced to the galleys, only two of them for crimes of piracy, in 1611.[67]

There are several ways to interpret the absence of seamen from the 1613 lists. Some sentences condemned the ship and its cargo but freed the crew, especially if the men acknowledged their responsibility, as the four Dutch crews did in July 1601. There was also the effect of diplomatic pressure. In 1607 the French ambassador intervened with the Council of War to free three corsairs from Havre-de-Grâce from the galleys: Jean de Lone, Dionis de Nigule, and Thomas Venart, the last of whom could be the Adam Veart accused of having robbed merchants from Cádiz off North Africa in 1605, or perhaps his brother. It seems they had served a year and a half of their ten-year sentences, and although their crimes were serious, the council judged that by showing them mercy "on other occasions the same thing [may] be done in France for subjects of Your Majesty."[68] It is unsurprising, then, that when two ships (from Holland and Danzig) were intercepted near Algiers in July 1609 without "the right dispatches" (making them susceptible to capture), it was decided to grant them "liberty without taking anything from them, so as not to create lawsuits over issues of interest, and to remove opportunities for ambassadors to present complaints, even if they are unjustified."[69]

It is hard to determine how far these practices extended. As with all aspects of the administration of justice in the galleys, the summary and expeditious nature of the *auditores*' decisions defies systematic analysis. Few of their trial records have survived, because only a few of those cases appealed to the Council of War are known. We can only guess at many others, since embargoes did not count as prizes and therefore appear only rarely in the account books. In only two ledgers have we found a specific section on embargoes, for the periods 1614–16 and 1617–19. From them, we learn that on August 17, 1616, the galleys embargoed a French ship in Cartagena, though they received no immediate benefit pending appeal of the case to the Council of War. Up to that point, the seizure had produced only expenses (for bringing Fray Juan Bressae to the port in December to hear the prisoners' confessions, for guarding the vessel, and for preparing reports of the case to send to the council). The accounts also reveal that in November 1617 the council finished reviewing another appealed embargo, of a ship taken in Barcelona from Domingo Felipe, who was already serving

67 AGS, Estado, 2643: Consulta del Consejo de Estado, 14 May 1613.

68 AGS, GyM, 669, 337.

69 "[L]ivertad sin thomales ninguna cossa, por no llevar pleitos en materias de intereses, y quitar las ocasiones que desto toman los embajadores para formar quexas, aunque no sean justificadas." AGS, GyM, 726: Luis Fajardo to Philip III, 1 August 1609.

a ten-year sentence as a rower. In that case, the squadron was able to auction off the ship for almost 4,200 ducats. At about the same time, another embargoed ship was awaiting the result of its case in Seville. The ship embargoed in Cartagena in 1616 finally saw its cargo sold (the exact date is unknown), bringing a little more than 60 ducats from the auction of 26 quintales of wheat.[70]

Though there is little information about income, we can also consider spending. Between 1614 and 1616 the squadron paid somewhat more than 3,000 ducats for prizes and another 1,400 ducats for embargoed ships.[71] With the exception of special decrees like Philip III's in 1598, respect for treaties, diplomatic negotiations, and lengthy appeals to the Council of War largely limited any economic benefit to the galleys from the application of laws of commerce; at least for 1614–16, those embargoes brought in less money than prizes did, although corruption could also have played a part.

Throughout these years, there was constant criticism of the *auditores*, especially for abuses they committed. In November 1598, for instance, the *auditor* of the Galleys of Spain was sued for threatening men with the rowers' benches if they disagreed with his imposition of the general embargo.[72] In fact, the Council of War set up a committee to investigate his actions during the process, and although proof of his offense was hard to establish, both he and his scribe were arrested and accused of appropriating part of the profits from the embargoes.[73] The network of depositaries and guarantors was so extensive that it is difficult to follow the trail of the stolen funds, which eventually emerged only in small quantities.[74]

During these months, a lawyer from El Puerto de Santa María perpetrated another fraud, helped by his former title as *auditor* of an infantry regiment. Passing himself off in Lisbon as the *auditor* for the Galleys of Spain, he unlawfully seized several German vessels and condemned them for almost 2,000 ducats. His deceit discovered when the seizure was appealed to the Council of War, he was imprisoned on a bond of 10,000 ducats, the estimated value of everything he had stolen.[75]

In 1607 the squadron's *auditor*—the real one this time—was again denounced for fraudulent dealings with the embargoes. It seems that in 1602 he had impounded a ship from Calais for smuggling and exacted a fine of 8,000

70 AGS, CMC, 3ª Época, 3324.
71 AGS, CMC, 3ª Época, 1454.
72 AGS, GyM, 561, 63.
73 AGS, GyM, 564, 254.
74 AGS, GyM, 565, 278.
75 AGS, GyM, 677, 787.

ducats, but soon afterward the viceroy of Portugal accused him of exceeding his authority and taking on several cases relating to the embargo against the Dutch that rightly belonged to the *auditor* general of the kingdom. Investigation revealed that he had defrauded the royal treasury of more than 20,000 ducats.[76] Clearly, the embargo business could prove very lucrative not only for the squadron but also for its *auditores*, though official accounts may not reveal the fact (among other reasons, because they too were fraudulent). It is clear from all this that as squadrons and their tribunals achieved permanent consolidation, they conditioned and changed maritime trade in the zones that fell under their influence.

In a recent work on corsair warfare and the right to prize-taking, Rita Loredana Foti explains how different monarchies, in trying to dominate the seas, constructed a legal doctrine in which the principles of the law of war (*ius belli*) were combined with other motives arising from commercial law (*ius mercatorium*)—such as the need to safeguard Christian interests at sea—and the law of prizes (*ius predae*; the latter fell under the jurisdiction of the old admiralties which, since the thirteenth century, had regulated captures at sea and the legal cases resulting from them).[77] This doctrine, by employing the discourse of the crusade, justified the corsair aspect of the war against Islam[78] but was also applied to commercial competition with Christian enemies. We recall that Hugo Grotius published his *Mare liberum* in 1609 in response to new pressure by the Hispanic Monarchy against Dutch maritime trade.[79] It is reasonable to consider whether Grotius's work arose from such circumstances (the consolidation of squadrons and of their jurisdiction over trade through *auditores*' courts, which were acquiring their definitive outlines in those years). Further, we can multiply the actions of the Galleys of Spain by those of ten or twelve other active squadrons. An undoubted result was a more efficient form of naval warfare, together with speedy resolution of lawsuits related to smuggling. All this could produce, or encourage, new reflections on the limits to control of the seas and to freedom of navigation. We must also ask whether captains general of the squadrons were conscious of these doctrines when they challenged a Christian merchant ship or attacked a Muslim vessel (whether legal discourse made them implacable defenders of the crusade or if, on the contrary, space still remained for contact and collaboration). We must determine to what degree

---

76 AGS, GyM, 677, 787.

77 Foti, *Giudici e corsari*, 17–44.

78 Fontenay, "Place de la course."

79 García Arias, "Estudio preliminar."

squadrons like the Galleys of Spain, in their incessant search for resources, could benefit from their proximity to North Africa, beyond the sale of prizes and the contraband activities that they, too, in theory, ought to pursue.

2 Cross-Cultural Trade and Control of Smuggling

In early July 1618 three galleons from the Armada of the Ocean Sea spotted a flotilla of eight vessels that were flying no flag. King Philip III had ordered the armada, together with the Galleys of Spain, to block the Strait of Gibraltar against a Dutch fleet; therefore the Spaniards, unable to determine the ships' origin, sent a caravel to approach them peacefully and ask who they were. The strangers made no answer "any more than as if they were mute," but scarcely had the caravel drawn away than they "raised a red banner of war with the arms of Venice and ... without saying more ... fired all their artillery."[80] The episode helps to explain how the initiation of combat could be justified and when a seizure was considered legitimate. According to the *auditor* Mosquera de Figueroa, before any fighting began there should be an attempt at peace to avoid "the spilling of blood." That should be accomplished through ambassadors bearing an offer of peaceful relations, similar to the behavior of a squadron when it solicited entry into a port—in a show of good will, it would accept a visit by local authorities. In encounters at sea the squadrons should play that role, demanding acknowledgment of the Catholic king's precedence. They then had the right to board the opposing ship and, if warranted, to seize it and arrest its crew.

An attack on the sacrosanct person of the ambassador—which the Venetian ships had been careful to avoid in 1618—was a justification for capture; as Mosquera explained, that had happened on Terceira Island when the Marquis of Santa Cruz's emissaries had been fired upon, giving them ample motive to launch the invasion.[81] While many documents reveal such captures, others describe encounters between squadrons and suspected corsair ships in which the latter allowed the galleys to approach, board, and conduct an inspection, after which they were free to sail on. Only if they resisted by fleeing or firing on the galleys could they be pursued, boarded violently, and captured. Whenever the galleys were the stronger force, it was prudent to cooperate with them, especially in the face of a possible embargo. That was why the captains of the four

80 ASV, Segretaria di Stato, Spagna, 60E, fols. 218–20.

81 Mosquera de Figueroa, *Comentario*, fols. 34r–35r.

Dutch vessels brought before the *auditor* in July 1601 had pleaded to be freed on the grounds that none of them had resisted boarding.[82] Dutch and German ships in July 1609 had escaped punishment by "entering the armada asking for Simón Dançer"; that is, they approached voluntarily as a sign of peace. Reports on that particular incident help us to analyze how well captains general understood the legal doctrine that protected their actions in war, and through them we can also study the collaboration that lay behind those conflicts.

2.1 *Between Religious War and Collaboration: the Action of Tunis, 1609*

Many actions involving galleys, even if taken against the infidel, had a purpose beyond the predatory; sometimes, they reflected concrete political aims of the monarchy. One example was the expedition in July 1609 that destroyed twenty-one ships belonging to the English corsair Howards ("Uguarts" in Spanish documents) and to Kara Uthman Dey ("Cara Çumanday") in the Bay of Tunis. According to the official report, the profit derived from the attack was only 50 reales, because the occasion "was about service to Your Majesty, and the one thing [sacking the ships] could not be achieved without impeding the other."[83] In fact in 1601 Gian Andrea Doria, writing to the viceroy of Sicily, had expressed concern that some at court believed "that prize-taking is prejudicial to the galleys" and wanted the activity forbidden; though the prohibition never happened, there was clearly a debate about its possible benefits.[84] The most interesting aspect of the Action of 1609, however, was that, after the attack, the Spanish fleet was kept in the bay for three days by bad weather, requiring some minimal communication with the Muslim authorities—especially after the Dey had sent a letter demanding an explanation for the aggression. Luis Fajardo's reply, and the final response he received, have survived among the reports on the Action that were sent to the Council of War, and they clarify why Fajardo admiral of the Armada of the Ocean Sea argued that the law was on his side and the Dey denounced the injustice he had suffered.

By the account of the fleet's admiral, the attack had been organized "to punish the pirates who in this Mediterranean sea, against the laws of Our Lord God, of justice, and of nature, are robbing ... and worrying ... and disturbing the Christian republics and destroying their subjects' trade." As Francisco de Vitoria explained, the only just cause for war was a grave offense that threatened the survival of the republic.[85] The same principle had obtained in Alphonse X's

82 AGS, GyM, 582, 81.
83 AGS, GyM, 726: letter by Luis Fajardo, 4 August 1609.
84 ADP, scaffale 85, busta 22: Gian Andrea Doria to the Duke of Maqueda, 2 November 1601.
85 Peñera, "Estudio introductorio," 127–33.

Partidas—that the only reasonable motive for war was protection of subjects and their property and revenge for an enemy attack;[86] jurists of the Hispanic Monarchy naturally invoked this legal principle to justify the role of the galleys. The Catalan Cortes, in creating the Galleys of Catalonia in 1599, had argued that Turks, Moors, and other enemies—all corsairs and pirates—were interfering with trade through their attacks and robberies, enslaving Christians and separating them from the Catholic faith, and forcing subjects of the monarchy to spend great sums on ransoming them, funds that the infidels later used to increase their fleets and redouble their attacks.[87] This disturbance of the peace, damage to the patrimony and honor of the Catholic king's subjects, and looming danger to the republic had given Fajardo the right to set those ships afire, especially because "as has been seen after that recent action … they have not sought advantage from anyone"; that is, the action was not intended for economic gain. It was therefore an act not of piracy but of legitimate defense, backed by justice and God's natural law. As Vitoria had explained (following Thomas Aquinas), in such cases a defensive war could not be won without an offensive one, which could be waged legitimately as one of the eternal laws, norms, and rules that governed the actions of men.[88]

Fajardo's invocation of the divinity also carried a strong charge, since from the Christian standpoint the fact that the authors of the offense were enemies of the Catholic faith reinforced the legality of the response. The Alfonsine code had already noted that since Antiquity there had been three reasons for waging war, one being "for the People to increase their Faith and to destroy those who may wish to confound it." In the sixteenth century this principle established the legal discourse of opposition to the Ottoman Empire and North African Islam. Gregorio López de Tovar, in his edition of the *Partidas* published in 1576, devoted a long gloss to this point, full of references to earlier authorities.[89]

Another notable argument in Fajardo's missive was that the Spanish were responding not only to the damage to Christian republics but also to the fact that the enemy "is robbing even its own peoples, something that cannot be allowed even among barbarians." A continual point of debate among Spanish jurists and intellectuals in the sixteenth century was the idea of barbarism and the extent to which the Hispanic Monarchy could conquer and educate idolaters and bring them to the faith. Ginés de Sepúlveda and Bartolomé de Las

86 López de Tovar, *Siete Partidas*, 551–52.
87 AGS, Estado, 459: Consulta del Consejo de Estado, 23 January 1616.
88 Peñera, "Estudio introductorio," 105.
89 López de Tovar, *Siete Partidas*, 552–61.

Casas had sparred over the issue in the congregation of Valladolid in 1550.[90] Domingo de Soto, though generally sympathetic to Las Casas's position, argued in his own treatise on justice and law that one could take up arms against a tyrannical government and even overthrow it when it persecuted the Christian religion or its faithful.[91] The presence of Christian captives in Muslim lands and Christian rowers enslaved in Muslim galliots legitimized the capture of ships that represented unjust Muslim rule on the seas—and, in this case, the burning of vessels that had been armed and equipped to oppress Christians.

Fajardo's reasoning went even further: "It is a wonder that the lord kings of Tunis, having such ancient obligations to the Crown of Spain and knowing its great power in the past to conquer this kingdom and many others, should wish to give occasion [for war] by protecting these robbers, a damned and excommunicated people." The comment was meant to evoke the vassalage that Charles V had imposed on Tunis's rulers, making the attack a just punishment for rebellious subjects; Fajardo urged them "to seek a remedy by clear signs ... and with it preserve the good concord and recognition that prevailed in the past." This affirmation of the power of the monarchy and its right even to seize the enemy's land recalls Diego de Covarrubias's words in book 6 of his *Regulae Peccatum* (1571): that it was not merely licit but obligatory for Christians to fight against infidels, since they held and usurped lands that had once belonged to Rome and the Christians.[92] This reasoning justified the Catholic monarchs' attempts to expel Muslims from North Africa and Turkey and provided legal backing not only for assaults and occupations of those Muslim lands but also, by extension, for the attempt to banish them entirely from the Roman mare nostrum. As Miguel Ángel Bunes has noted, one of the basic defenses of the monarchy's expansion into North Africa was the notion of reviving the classical world,[93] and Fajardo seems to have known that very well.

The admiral's final argument was that the Dey of Tunis had sheltered the English pirates. This was not a religious issue like the others but a breaking "of peace treaties between Christian princes and republics"[94] such as sometimes interfered with embargoes, as we saw above. The treaty signed by England and Spain in 1604 established free trade between the two powers,[95] so the English corsairs in the Bay of Tunis were violating it by preparing to attack Spanish

90 Soto, *Controversias.*
91 Soto, *Controverias*, libro V, cuestión III, 153.
92 Covarrubias y Leiva, *Regulae*, Lib. VI Part 9 & 10, 157–207.
93 Bunes Ibarra, "Marco."
94 AGS, GyM, 726: Luis Fajardo to the Dey of Tunis, 1 August 1609.
95 Abreu Bertonado, *Colección*, 243–94.

merchant ships, and their guilt extended to the Tunisians. But "Cara Çumanday" was not of the same mind. He replied that he did not understand the double standard and was not breaking the laws of justice and nature "by having ships that course on the sea or maintaining a free port or admitting ships of another nation," because "Christians do the same in Florence and Malta and other places in Christendom, where they arm themselves ... for these actions, from which our nation could be harmed." He was unaware of any violation except that committed by France, which, after signing a treaty of friendship with the Grand Turk, was allowing its corsairs to continue seizing and selling North African merchant ships. And he mocked the Spaniards' supposed power, recalling that "the Great Lord took and gained it from the Moorish and Christian viceroys who held it, ... and we, under his protection and shelter, do not fear the power of all the kings in the world."[96]

In spite of those words a cordial, though tense, atmosphere prevailed. The Dey allowed the Spaniards to land and supply themselves with water and firewood, and he offered no hindrance to their fleet until it sailed away a few days later.[97] This sympathetic and collaborative attitude on both sides, once the trauma of the attack in the bay was over, is an interesting one. Luis Fajardo listed readily and fluently the chief principles employed in traditional Spanish law to justify war in general and war on Muslims in particular. Admirals and captains general of squadrons must have been aware, perhaps with the help of their *auditores*, of the legal framework that protected their jurisdiction at sea and along the North African coast—not only in the more complex decision of whether an embargo against a Christian owner was valid, but also when they seized, or in this case burned, a Muslim vessel. Significantly, the person Fajardo needed to convince of the legality of his action was the Tunisian ruler himself, and the latter, while answering him with equally reasonable positions, still supplied the galleys with their basic needs without hostility or a desire for revenge. Their dialogue may have been amicable because the ransom of seven Turks was also at stake (the fleet obtained almost 800 ducats for them).[98] But that exchange was made in a generous spirit, without seeking the royal license that squadrons required for rescuing captives (though it might have been a form of *alafía*),[99] suggesting that the situation was far from being a clash of civilizations.

96 AGS, GyM, 726: "Cara Çumanday" to Luis Fajardo.
97 AGS, GyM, 726: Diego Vivero to Philip III, 5 August 1609.
98 AGS, GyM, 726: Diego Vivero to Philip III, 5 August 1609.
99 Andújar, "Rescates," 154.

Eloy Martín Corrales has observed that the prolonged corsair conflict between Christians and Muslims in the Mediterranean has kept us from seeing clearly the continuous commercial traffic between North Africa and the Hispanic Monarchy. He insists that exchanges never ceased, whether in the form of ransoms, special concessions linked to support for one side or another in Muslim civil wars (Fajardo's letter mentioned one such case of open protection and collaboration), or imports of North African wheat, on which many Spanish cities depended during times of scarcity.[100] Miguel Ángel de Bunes has stressed the importance of the fortified Spanish enclaves on the North African coast, which served as conduits for exporting goods to the Iberian Peninsula. He also mentions the role of Spanish spies in that traffic, and the still little-studied illegal trade conducted by cities and certain families. (The Medina Sidonias, closely involved in Mediterranean defense, also benefited from commercial transactions that in no way resembled a religious war between irreconcilable parties.)[101] We wonder to what extent the galleys, too, while still acting as the spearpoint against the infidel, might have entered into that porous reality, which included war and misunderstanding, benefiting from the privileges of their jurisdiction and their access to the coast of Africa to make contacts that could help to maintain their crews. We will begin with the question of ransoms.

2.2 *Profiles of a Cross-Cultural Trade: Ransoms*

It is not easy to assess and quantify the ransoming of galley slaves, though according to surviving account books the commonest practice was for rowers to ransom themselves. Azambalí, a Turk, paid 900 reales for his own ransom in December 1605. Amar from Tunis, a galley slave on a flagship, gained his freedom for 660 reales in June 1608 by proving that he was too old and infirm to row.[102] A year later, Solimán from Bône bought his freedom for 800 reales; he was still in good health but "had turned Christian" and adopted the name Cristóbal Sánchez. In 1610, two rowers named Alí, respectively from Alcázar and Tétouan, paid their own ransoms of 870 reales: "The Marquis [of San Germán], being then in the fort of Larache, ordered them freed because he had sent them to King Muley Xeque [Mulay al-Shaykh]" to demand the official surrender of the fortress. Though still able-bodied, they obviously earned their release through this service to the monarchy as envoys and interpreters between the Spaniards and the Moroccan ruler. Juan de Alcoholado, a slave whom Doña

---

100 Martín Corrales, "De cómo el comercio."

101 Bunes Ibarra, "Relaciones."

102 AGS, CMC, 3ª Época, 1436.

Catalina de Armijo had rented to the galleys, bought his freedom for 650 reales, that being the price at which the lady had assessed him.[103]

In December 1615 Juan Fornal, who rowed in a vice-flagship and was probably a Morisco from Murcia, paid 250 reales to be released.[104] We have already mentioned the case of Andrés Hernández, a Morisco from Baeza, who in April 1616 was freed after a legal suit in which the galleys were compensated for his original price, 1,100 reales. Juan Fox, a "Christian slave," had not entered the squadron of Spain after the Moriscos' expulsion, like so many others, but had served in it for more than thirty years; Emmanuel Filibert of Savoy ordered him freed because he was sixty years old, blind, and one-armed, but Juan still had to pay back his assessed price of 250 reales.[105]

The ledgers show, then, a total of nine self-ransomed slaves in nine years at a gain to the squadron of 500 ducats. For North African and Turkish slaves, the main motive seems to have been a combination of old age and infirmity; for some Moriscos, it was doubt about their true religious affiliation when they began to be captured at sea after their expulsion from Castile and Aragon.[106] Aside from these general conditions, permission to ransom oneself was granted only in special situations, possibly through the favorable disposition of ships' officers and a good service record on board. The two rower "ambassadors" from the Marquis of San Germán seem to fit this model, as does Solimán of Bône alias Cristóbal Sánchez.

The case of Solimán/Cristóbal is suggestive. He had been allowed to buy his freedom on the basis of his conversion, hinting that that was a viable option, though Giovanna Fiume has shown that baptism did not require an owner to free a slave.[107] Cecilia Tarruel has clarified that conversion might mask a wish to improve one's living conditions, hopelessness about the prospect of release, or the pressure of one's environment, and that after a slave converted, the decision to free him or her still rested with the owners.[108]

We find a similar case in the galleys. In April 1620, the Council of War studied a petition hand-delivered by the Marquis of Santa Cruz's secretary. The squadron's captain general requested the release of Mostafá, a Moor who had turned Christian and taken the name Juan de Ribera. The marquis had elevated him from his rowing bench to the post of body servant, and he believed that

103 AGS, CMC, 3ª Época, 1570.
104 AGS, CMC, 3ª Época, 1474.
105 AGS, CMC, 3ª Época, 2940–41.
106 Benítez Sánchez-Blanco, *Tríptico*, 261–72.
107 Fiume, *Schiavitù*, 18–19.
108 Tarruell, "Circulations," 210–20.

the slave had cured him of an illness. He proposed assigning another slave to row in Mostafá's place, and the council approved the request.[109] The incident shows that a combination of the aristocrat's efforts, the waters of baptism, and the slave's good service record had combined to set him free.

In rare cases a galley slave might be manumitted through his owner's last will and testament; that occurred more often with domestic slaves whose owners, in the face of death, wished to clear their consciences.[110] Vincenzo Centurione, who for several years contracted out two galleys for the Spanish squadron, arranged for his slaves to be freed after his decease. He made special mention of Miguel Gonzales, a rower in the *San Juan* who claimed to be an Old Christian unjustly treated because his mother had been a mulatto slave.[111]

As a rule, no one could be freed from the Galleys of Spain without paying a ransom or, as in Mostafá's case, earning the gratitude of one's captain general. Occasionally, someone tried. In May 1598 Isuf, a poor slave who had been rowing for thirty years, petitioned Prince Doria for his freedom in exchange for remaining in the prince's service for as long as his master wished.[112] But almost all slaves needed a considerable sum of money to ransom themselves, and we wonder how so many could have saved enough to buy their liberty.

It is possible that the money did not really belong to the slaves and the account books conceal ransoms paid by middlemen, a common occurrence on land.[113] For instance, in 1596 a slave named Barca offered Prince Doria 250 escudos for his freedom; he did not actually have that sum, but a Genoese merchant could pay a portion on behalf of his family, and a "fellow-countryman" freed in Messina could put up the rest.[114] But that did not seem to be the normal case for the Galleys of Spain. The amounts paid were usually much smaller than true captives' ransoms, which ran to several hundred ducados. Nor is it likely that exchanges of captives were involved, since those circumstances were normally noted in the accounts. In September 1615, for example, when Ramadán from Algiers was freed from the vice-flagship, it was recorded that a woman from Barcelona had petitioned the king to exchange him for her husband, a captive in Tunis, for a payment of 1,200 reales.[115] It is plausible, therefore, that

109 AGS, GyM, 858: Consulta del Consejo de Guerra, 27 April 1620.
110 Andújar Castillo, "Sobre las condiciones."
111 AGS, GyM, 846: Petition by Miguel Gonzales, 1619.
112 AGS, Galeras, 5, fol. 30.
113 Vincent, "Procédures."
114 AGS, Galeras, 4, fol. 11.
115 AGS, CMC, 3ª Época, 1454.

the nine slaves mentioned above really did ransom themselves with their own money, and different types of accounts reinforce this impression.

In 1607 the squadron's paymaster entered a deposit by the captain of the galley *San Francisco* of 800 reales found among the belongings of a deceased slave.[116] In 1611, 654 reales appeared among the goods of Azán from Valivadra, a slave in the flagship, who had been killed by a convict rower.[117] When Yzá from Algiers, a slave in the royal galley, died in 1613, an auction of his possessions brought in 348 reales.[118] All three men had enough to ransom themselves if the Prince of Savoy allowed it, and point us toward some references in the ordinances of 1607. That document specified that slaves could improve their situation within a galley by assuming certain posts reserved for them, such as *espalder* (chief oarsman), *mozo de popa* or *mozo de cámara* (ship's boy), or mozo de alguacil (sergeant-at-arms' boy).[119] They were also allowed to set up "taverns" on board and earn what must have been considerable sums, because officers were expressly forbidden from usurping them. Those small businesses were clearly meant to benefit the poorest among the crew through the sale of wine and other supplies, but they were also controversial, in that they raised suspicions that some men were selling the goods, bought on consignment from the squadron, illegally on the side.[120]

The ledgers tell us little about the slaves' economic activities, since financial officers did not usually deal with them, but there are scattered references to crewmens' decisions to exchange some of their food rations for cash. In July 1603 the squadron's paymaster shared out 52 reales among five rowers who preferred to take their entire wine ration for the month of May in coin. The men were one salaried rower, two Christian *corulleros*, and two Muslim first-oarsmen, Amuza from Larache and Hamete from Tétouan.[121] Similarly, in March 1605 a Moorish slave called "Botija" accepted 95 reales in lieu of all his rations.[122] Although these are our only examples, we wonder how many slaves—who might decline to drink wine on religious grounds, for instance—could sell their rations to the onboard taverners without involving a financial officer, thus acquiring some income for improving their living conditions or

116 AGS, CMC, 3ª Época, 1436.

117 AGS, CMC, 3ª Época, 1570.

118 AGS, CMC, 3ª Época, 2941–1.

119 Olesa Muñido, *Galera*, 166–69.

120 Marchena Giménez, "Vida y los hombres," 292.

121 A *corullero* was a trusted rower freed from the benches to act as a porter or stevedore: AGS, CMC, 3ª Época, 397.

122 AGS, CMC, 3ª Época, 1436.

saving for a future ransom. Based on the amount shared among the five rowers, we can estimate that slaves who held special jobs had a wine ration worth about 1 ducat a month, helping to explain the accumulations of cash sometimes found among the belongings of deceased slaves.

Another chapter of the 1607 ordinances sought to regulate the vice of gambling among the rowers. Many of them bet the winter clothing that they were issued every year (two shirts, two jackets, and sometimes shoes and caps),[123] and it seems that the best players were sometimes taken from one galley to another.[124] We do not know just how much money card-playing slaves earned in this way, but we know that others benefited indirectly from gambling. On February 4, 1615, the slave Amarexo from Morocco died aboard the vice-flagship. His possessions were sold in El Puerto de Santa María for 70 reales, and the paymaster kept a complete list of them, a unique precaution that shows us in detail what the slave had owned at his death. Two old wooden boxes, which he must have stored under his bench, contained 30 small collars of heavy cloth, 24 pairs of cotton stockings and 6 of woolen ones, 3 pouches containing 36 small combs, 8 pairs of saddlebags, 2 knives, 4 wooden spoons, and 6 dozen decks of Barcelona playing cards.[125]

Amarexo had clearly filled his own little "cargo hold," and (knives and spoons aside) his seventy-two decks of cards suggest that gambling was a popular business. He also owned an unusual number of stockings. Pantero Pantera, the captain of a papal galley, wrote that "there is no lack of men among the crew who work at making stockings, nightshirts (*camisciole*), dice, toothpicks (*stecchi*), and such things, with which they obtain some money and help themselves greatly, supplementing their small provision of biscuit and water"; perhaps Amarexo had bought his items from more industrious shipmates.[126] He might have obtained all the combs in port or, more likely, by haggling with the small boats that gathered around whenever a galley dropped anchor. We know that such exchanges were common and that Gian Andrea Doria was even asked to forbid them as "harmful to the crews, who barter with ship's biscuit and their own clothing, at great prejudice to themselves ... since convicts and slaves end up thin and stricken with diseases."[127] But the case of Amarexo from Morocco shows that the practice was not always harmful, because some

123 AGS, GyM, 539: letter from Tomás de Aguirre, Santander, 27 January 1599.

124 Marchena Giménez, "Vida y los hombres," 440.

125 AGS, CMC, 3ª Época, 2940–41.

126 Pantera, *Armata navale*, 134.

127 ADP, scaffale 70, busta 25, interno 5: Particulars of the Galleys of Naples by Gian Andrea Doria, 6 July 1587.

rowers could profit from this sort of buying and selling. It also shatters some of our stereotypes about the extreme poverty of these men and their lack of living space—this slave managed to store a great deal under his bench. With a little initiative some of the ill effects of life on board could be overcome.

All these examples show that in studying economic activity in the squadrons we need to consider this kind of small commerce among crew members. Though we cannot calculate its full impact, it was obviously an important counterweight to periodic scarcities of rations, and it added a degree of cross-cultural trade and sociability to life aboard ship. Elsewhere we have studied the case of Hamete, a Morisco from the royal galley who had set up "a little tobacco shop" on board. He extended credit to Christians only if they forswore insulting the prophet Muḥammad, but once he had a dose of his own medicine: a convict, Pedro de Montes, won at cards and invited his shipmates to a drink of wine if they would renounce Muḥammad, giving offense to Hamete and resulting in a harsh exhange of words.[128]

These cases show how galley slaves (like domestic ones), once their work was finished, could engage in trade, save money, and buy their freedom. Aurelia Martín has shown that in many notarial documents of the time, what looks like the freeing of a domestic slave for motives of conscience or friendship actually masks a previous payment by the slave out of savings from his or her labor.[129] Likewise in the galleys, behind records of manumission for reasons of age or illness may lie payments for the slave's assessed price or an exchange for another slave of equal value.

It is also notable that nine years' worth of accounts show only one instance of a slave released in exchange for a Christian captive. We cannot be sure that the records are reliable on this point; every ledger does not show every category, and some ransoms were never noted down. In 1611, Philip III decreed a fine of 200 ducats for any galley officer who freed a slave without permission, but the order must not have been generally obeyed, for it was reissued in 1617.[130] In that year, Catalina Gallardo was allowed to replace the slave Lorenzo Abraham from the *San Martín* with another in order to exchange him for her husband, Blas González, a captive in Algiers; but the transaction does not figure in the account books.[131] There is likewise no record of Pedro Mulato, a slave whom the licenciate Cuerda had sold to the galleys in 1601; in 1617, Cuerda took him

128 Lomas Cortés and Benítez Sánchez-Blanco, "Seconde Inquisition," 83–84.
129 Martín Casares, "Repensar."
130 AGS, GyM, 820: La Junta de Galeras, 30 May 1617.
131 AGS, GyM, 820: Antonio de Aróztegui, 14 April 1617.

back in exchange for another.[132] Just in the period 1617–19, we know that in 1619 the Duke of Maqueda, governor of Oran, received two rowers from the royal galley, Mahomete Ben Buxareb and Mohamete Ben Azen, by exchanging them for two others.[133] Napoleon Canoli, captain of the *San Jorge*, asked permission in 1607 to exchange one of his rowers, Mustafá from Algiers, for another slave in order to free his brother, who had been a captive since 1598;[134] on October 22, 1608, the Council of War agreed, but again the operation is absent from the paymaster's books.[135]

We must realize, then, that the number of slaves ransomed from the galleys was greater than that registered in the accounts, and that some ransoms must have been managed illegally. The average of one documented ransom per year is certainly too low and should be raised, though cautiously. It was still rare to be freed from the galleys in this way (as infrequent as the sale of old and damaged slaves), even if the records were being manipulated. Still, we see that galley officers maintained contacts with North Africa by negotiating some ransoms, and that slaves were not wholly isolated on their rowing benches. They, like other members of the crew, could sustain some relationships with the opposite shore.

2.3 *Purchase of North African Wheat and Control of Maritime Trade*

Like many coastal cities of Castile and Aragon, the Galleys of Spain sometimes imported wheat from North Africa to feed their crews. They did so only on certain occasions, because a number of factors had to align in their favor. Oran was the only fortified port on the coast with a production large enough to satisfy the demand, so purchases could be made only when there was a sufficient harvest and prices were competitive; that happened only a few times in the early seventeenth century, however, and in that period the fleet actually took more grain to Oran than from it.[136] At the same time, the squadron's purveyor had an ample team of commissioners who traveled around Castile assessing harvests and grain prices. Only when crops had been underestimated, or an attack was being organized that required more provisions, would the fleet buy wheat from merchants in Oran.

Beatriz Alonso has shown that in the late sixteenth century the monarchy tried and failed to involve Oran more closely in the normal supplying of the

132 AGS, GyM, 820: Philip III to Emmanuel Filibert of Savoy, 13 February 1617.
133 AGS, GyM, 846: Consulta del Consejo de Guerra, 28 July 1619.
134 AGS, GyM, 677, fol. 681.
135 AGS, GyM, 689, fol. 248.
136 Lomas Cortés, "Galeras de aprovisionamiento."

Galleys of Spain and the armada. In 1597 the squadron's paymaster, Juan Pascual,[137] signed a contract to import up to 70,000 fanegas of wheat, and a year later he signed another for 100,000 more. But the first order was very difficult to fill and the second almost impossible, since it threatened the town's own supplies.[138] Perhaps for that reason, in 1599, when Philip III's visit to Valencia was being organized and the squadron asked for 8,000 fanegas of wheat to feed its crews,[139] Oran could not comply. The town delayed for so long that the fleet's purveyor, unable to wait any longer, began to buy *trigo de mar* ("seagoing wheat," grain sold out of the holds of other ships), although wine and other small amounts of foodstuffs were bought from Oran.[140]

In 1609, after several years of bad harvests, the fleet again tried to acquire a large volume of wheat through Oran. Once more, predictions had been inaccurate and 2,000 fanegas from Cartagena had not materialized; in addition, the ships that would deport the Moriscos needed provisions. The monarchy sent 40,000 ducats to Oran for the purpose.[141] Although we do not know the exact amount purchased, it is recorded that 30,000 ducats were spent and that each fanega cost between 6 and 11 ducats depending on the purchase.[142] We can calculate the total amount of wheat bought at somewhere between 30,000 and 50,000 fanegas. If we add these amounts to the imports in 1597–98 and Martín Corrales's list of the import licenses of Castilian and Aragonese cities,[143] we find that under the reigns of Philip II and Philip III the Galleys of Spain bought and consumed more North African wheat than any other territory under the monarchy.

To a lesser degree, wheat and other goods from North Africa entered the squadron through captures and embargoes carried out under prohibitions against trade with infidels and seizures of Christian corsair ships. Martín de Azpilcueta explained that it was right to pursue those who went to sea to rob, wound, and kill (Christian slaves who served in Muslim galliots did not count, though they were in a state of mortal sin), and in addition all merchants who shipped forbidden cargoes to Africa, whether in peace or in war, should be punished and excommunicated as if they were pirates.[144] According to Miguel Ángel

137 AGS, GyM, 626, 38.
138 Alonso Acero, *Orán-Mazalquivir*, 378–81.
139 AGS, CyM, 539, fol. 194.
140 AGS, CMC, 397.
141 AGS, GyM, 726: Felipe de Porres to Philip III, 22 July 1609.
142 AGS, Estado, 213: Pedro de Toledo to Philip III, 29 October 1609.
143 Martín Corrales, "De cómo el comercio," 151.
144 Azpilcueta, *Manual de confessores*, 400.

de Bunes, prohibited goods were interpreted very broadly and could include not only money and weapons but also any material that could serve the Muslims in defensive or offensive war.[145] Patents issued to captains general of the Galleys of Spain allowed them ample jurisdiction in cases of maritime smuggling and unlawful commerce, giving them another motive for their voyages.

We have limited information about oversight of trade with North Africa, since again only a few cases were recorded when they came to the courts' attention or caused consuls and ambassadors to complain, as happened with the corsair Venart. Here, too, as with the seizure of pirate ships, the Armada of the Ocean Sea seems to have been more active than the galleys. But at certain times under Philip III, the armada and the Galleys of Spain were joined under a single command, so that we can draw on their combined data to assess the situation more fully.

In August 1600 a settee manned by Frenchmen and loaded with leather left the Moroccan port of Salé; it was intercepted a few days later off Gibraltar by a ship of the armada, which presented its case to the Count of Santa Gadea. The settee's skipper tried to defend himself, showing papers that proved how he had conveyed a sum of money from Barcelona to one Juan de Marchena in North Africa and then loaded up with leather bound for Pisa. The count, unconvinced, immediately sentenced the crew to row in the galleys and confiscated the ship and its cargo, ordering them auctioned off for the crimes of illegal export of money and trade with infidels. But that was not the end of the suit, since Juan de Marchena, learning of the seizure, appealed to the Council of State. Marchena, a trader settled in Morocco, was in charge of ransoming captives in his area and, among other business interests, served as the monarchy's agent at the Moroccan royal court. He claimed that the money from Barcelona was intended to free captive Christians, and that in exchange for his services he had a license to trade—an example of how some merchants combined negotiating for captives with lucrative commerce in North Africa.[146] On that basis, he complained that Santa Gadea had taken his ship unlawfully and also had interfered with the king's business. The Duke of Medina Sidonia, who in fact was also involved in such dealings, took up Marchena's defense until, in 1603, it reached the hands of the Council of State's advisor for war.

This case offers several hints about the control that the squadrons exercised over trade with North Africa. Illegal export of money was one of the crimes most often mentioned in our records. Juan de Marchena's settee was seized

145 Bunes Ibarra, "Marco."
146 Andújar Castillo, "Rescates," 138.

because Castilian reales could not be exported to Morocco, and we find a number of other such cases. In 1603 Francisco Gómez, a Portuguese, tried to cross to Morocco carrying twenty-one large sacks of reales and three small ones of escudos.[147] A similar sum was involved when in 1615 the ship *El Amor Verdadero*, anchored in El Puerto de Santa María, resisted inspection and tried to flee. The armada pursued her and fired on her, killing several men. The boarding party found twenty-two large sacks containing the equivalent of more than 30,000 ducats in Christian and Muslim coins.[148]

Marchena's lawsuit casts light on Spanish interests in Morocco, much focused in those years on exploiting the special relationship that the monarchy had maintained with its ruler, Mulay al-Shaykh ("Muley Xeque") since the conquest of Portugal.[149] That tie served at first to facilitate intervention in Portugal's affairs, but later turned to Spain's effort to have Morocco cede the coastal fortress of Larache;[150] in both phases the Galleys of Spain acted as a privileged vehicle for the Spanish-Moroccan alliance. The linkage may have begun when Martín de Arreaga, the squadron's paymaster, was named ambassador to Morocco at the end of the sixteenth century (though he never took possession),[151] and peaked in 1609–10 during the last stage of the negotiations over Larache.

The fact is that the squadron transported much more money to Morocco than it seized from smugglers during those years. That was because in October 1609 the monarchy began to collect 200,000 ducats to finance Muley Xeque's army and compensate him for ceding Larache,[152] and the galleys were charged with conveying the sum to Tangier.[153] The transfer was completed in February 1610, when the Count of Elda received onto his galleys not only 84,000 ducats, 2,000 arquebuses, and quantities of powder and arms for Muley Xeque but also the ruler himself and his court, carrying them to the fortress of Peñón de Vélez at Gibraltar.[154] There, the Moroccan was received like any other ally of the monarchy, with repeated firing of artillery as he sailed into port and thirty more salutes the next day when he set foot on land.[155]

It is clear that the Galleys of Spain had the same kinds of economic relations with North Africa as any other territory of the monarchy; in imports of

147 AGS, Estado, 188: "Juan de Marchena," 7 January 1603.
148 AGS, GyM, 800: Luis Fajardo to Philip III, 12 August 1615.
149 Oliver Asín, *Vida de don Felipe*.
150 Mouline, *Califat*, 311–31.
151 AGS, GyM, 579, 139.
152 AGS, Estado, 219: Duke of Lerma to the President of the Treasury, 30 October 1609.
153 AGS, Estado, 2638, 149.
154 AGS, GyM, 739: Count of Elda to Antonio Aróztegui, 7 February 1610.
155 AGS, GyM, 743: Martín de Tausida to Philip III, 2 March 1610.

wheat, and in collection of monies in Castile and Aragon to pay for the grain and finance Muley Xeque, they handled a larger volume of trade than many other areas. Though the squadron's own needs involved it in only a few ransoms of captives, it is clear that its enslaved crew members could obtain better food and clothing, and even their freedom, through their economic activity. It does not appear, however, that much income came from pursuing smugglers in North Africa, though other interests might have been at work.

Fajardo's fleet stopped at Oran on its way to attack Tunis in 1609, and hearing of an English vessel that was conducting business in the area, set out in pursuit. But Fajardo, after capturing the ship, did not accuse and sentence the skipper but instead, learning that he knew the Bay of Tunis well, asked him to pilot his fleet; on their return, Fajardo set him free and sold him one of the ships captured in the journey for 300 ducats.[156]

It is something of a mystery how the royal purveyors could obtain, year after year, enough ship's biscuit for the galleys by buying "seagoing wheat" from other ships rather than from Oran; it was more expensive, but in certain years a more abundant supply. In 1606, for instance, the Duke of Medina Sidonia, who was in charge of provisioning the fleet, bought more than 5,000 fanegas of wheat in only two months at a cost of 7,000 ducats; it came from eight French and Flemish merchants, and its origin was not specified.[157] Silencing the origin was more common than one might suppose. Perhaps the squadrons wished to stop dealing with merchants who traded with North Africa or came from other forbidden areas, even though those men could sometimes offer advantageous ransoms, sell them wheat, or transport grain or other necessary goods for them. In December 1598, even in the face of a severe embargo, the *auditor* allowed fourteen Dutch vessels to proceed to Sicily to collect the stores of wheat destined for the galleys.[158] The broad jurisdictional powers of a *auditor*, while enforcing respect for the laws of the Catholic king, also gave him latitude to violate them in cases of both individual and collective need (as when the Dutch transports were permitted to sail).

3 Legitimate Trade and Fraud in the Galleys

In October 1601 Empress Maria of Austria wrote to Gian Andrea Doria. She was expecting a ship to arrive in Genoa bearing a crate of her new porcelain, and

156 AGS, GyM, 726: Luis Fajardo to Philip III, 10 September 1609.
157 AGS, GyM, 662, 210.
158 AGS, GyM, 561, 76.

she asked Doria to intervene to keep it from being opened or held up in customs; rather, it should be entrusted discreetly to Cristóbal Fiertempach as soon as it was unloaded. The prince obeyed her request, and in mid-November the crate easily passed customs without inspection.[159] This was not the first time that the captain general of the sea had used his influence to evade customs in favor of the Hapsburgs; in January 1599 he had resisted when the republic of Genoa sought to inspect and charge duties on the baggage of Archduke Albert and his entourage; Doria threatened to divert the ships to the port of Finale, thus damaging Genoa's image, "for it seems to me that this is not the time to care for trivial matters."[160] His strategy worked, and in the end "these gentlemen [of the republic] have behaved so well that they waived not only inspection [of the baggage] but also payment of any duty."[161]

3.1 *Smuggling in the Galleys*

Aside from such special interventions, this type of favor was fairly common and often included an offer to transport goods securely in the galleys. Juan Fernández de Velasco, constable of Castile and governor of Milan in those years, availed himself of the service several times; in April 1600 the Galleys of Genoa brought him a crate from Naples containing thirteen decorated vases for his library,[162] and in June 1602 the Galleys of Sicily shipped to him in Castile three of the four marble fireplaces that Prince Doria himself had commissioned in Genoa.[163] Fernández de Velasco also used his influence over Doria to facilitate orders by his officials, as when in March 1600 he sent Doria a box containing a silver vase that Juan de Mendoza, head of the cavalry in Milan, was presenting to the king.[164] In early January 1600 Doria sent one hundred "lengths of black brocade from Florence" to the Duke of Béjar,[165] and on May 2, he arranged to extract from customs—meeting some resistance this time—a writing desk for the Countess of Benavente.[166]

These favors continued in the succeeding years. In 1601 Doria sent the Countess of Lemos, wife of the viceroy of Naples, a dozen chests, weighing 12 libras apiece, full of the most beautiful damasks that his sister could find in Genoa,

159 ADP, scaffale 85, busta 22: Gian Andrea Doria to Empress Maria, 16 November 1601.
160 ADP, scaffale 85, busta 18: Gian Andrea Doria to the Republic of Genoa, 24 January 1599.
161 ADP, scaffale 85, busta 18: Gian Andrea Doria to Vittoria Doria, January 1599.
162 ADP, scaffale 85, busta 22: Constable of Castile to Gian Andrea Doria, 30 April 1600.
163 ADP, scaffale 85, busta 24: Gian Andrea Doria to the Constable of Castile, 24 June 1602.
164 ADP, scaffale 82, busta 25: Constable of Castile to Gian Andrea Doria, 27 March 1600.
165 ADP, scaffale 82, busta 23: Pietro Serra to Gian Andrea Doria, 8 January 1600.
166 ADP, scaffale 85, busta 19: Gian Andrea Doria to Jusepe de Acuña, 3 May 1600.

with a second crate containing four vases decorated with pearls.[167] A year later his galleys conveyed an ornate silver bedstead as a gift to the Countess of Miranda, whose husband was influential in government,[168] and the same journey may have served to ship a cargo of majolica to Juan de la Serna, the Duke of Lerma's personal secretary.[169]

These services and attentions were crucial to Prince Doria's economic strategy. With his rights, favors, and privileges spread throughout the kingdoms of the monarchy, he had to maintain good relations with its principal ministers; those men would assure him payment and advantageous mediation when difficulties arose in supplying the galleys, enforcing the special concessions granted him by the king, or many other jurisdictional issues, some of which arose in Genoa itself. Although Doria could normally obtain all the franchises he needed from the republic, he sometimes faced customs officials who tried to hold up the export of fresh merchandise. In July 1599, for example, a shipment of meat for the Galleys of Naples almost spoiled for that reason.[170] Resistance might also come from collectors of the tax on wheat, as in January 1600, when they told Doria that his galleys could not be exempt from duties, forcing him to appeal to the Bank of Saint George.[171]

These problems were repeated in every port that supplied the galleys, where there was continuous give-and-take between contracted providers and local governments. Between 1596 and 1603 alone Doria dealt with a long series of conflicts. The Camera della Sommaria in Naples sometimes demanded export fees for his supplies or blocked his privileges, as in 1603, when it demanded the return of his salary as a member of its supreme court, the Consiglio Collaterale.[172] The *Vicaria* of Naples occasionally requisitioned his wheat or kept him from collecting his rents from the region.[173] In Messina, customs men wanted to charge him four tari apiece for the almost 5,500 jars of biscuit that the Catholic fleet took on board.[174] Their counterparts in Palermo filed suit in the Tribunale di Regio Patrimonio (the Sicilian equivalent of the Camera della Sommaria) because the galleys' export privileges caused excessive harm to their profits.[175] And the *alcalde mayor* of Cartagena forbade the export of 100

---

167 ADP, scaffale 85, busta 20: Gian Andrea Doria to Pietro Serra, 5 January 1601.
168 ADP, scaffale 85, busta 24: Gian Andrea Doria to Francisco Tapia, 3 June 1602.
169 ADP, scaffale 85, busta 24: Gian Andrea Doria to Juan de la Serna, 10 June 1602.
170 ADP, scaffale 82, busta 21: Gio Petro to Gian Andrea Doria, 27 July 1599.
171 ADP, scaffale 82, busta 23: Pietro Serra to Gian Andrea Doria, 16 January 1600.
172 ADP, scaffale 85, busta 27: Gian Andrea Doria to the Count of Benavente, 10 October 1603.
173 ADP, scaffale 85, busta 16: Gian Andrea Doria to Philip II, 1 January 1598.
174 ADP, scaffale 82, busta 24: Marquis of Sambuca to Gian Andrea Doria, 22 November 1600.
175 ADP, scaffale 70, busta 24: Domenico Cathaciola and Vicenzo di Lardo, Palermo, 1598.

fanegas of wheat in January 1601 because they were meant for Doria's palace kitchens, not the galleys.[176]

Faced with this array of suits and appeals, Doria did not hesitate to use the trading privileges attached to his office to provide favors for those who could advance his business dealings, both public and private. A prominent instance was the service he provided early in the century to the viceroy of Sicily, the Duke of Maqueda. In 1600–1 the vicereine, the Duchess of Nájera, decided to arm several corsair ships and asked the prince for advice. He helped her first to purchase the vessels, later made arrangements when one of them sank, and assisted again when she sold them after her husband's death.[177] In exchange for these favors, he could exert more pressure to collect on his contracts for wheat, and also to advance a long-standing suit in which he was owed payment on special concessions for royal wheat for the years 1588 and 1594; he also perceived certain back payments.[178] His shipment of majolica to Serna, the Duke of Lerma's secretary, in 1602 seems to have been the return of a favor done the year before, when Serna had intervened with Lerma to release a cargo of wheat held up in Cartagena in 1601. And we can speculate that his favors to the Duchess of Lemos in 1601 were related to pressure that the Sommaria exerted on him that year about the export of some oars and spars on which he had failed to pay the necessary taxes.[179] In short, he implicated viceroys, councillors, and secretaries in the profits he gained through heavy-handed use of the galleys' jurisdiction, through a protected and not always legal trade in luxury items of which he himself was the greatest beneficiary.

In the Dorias' greatest abuse of their privileges in this period, they extracted a group of Flemish tapestries from the charity hospital in Genoa and sent them to Carlo Doria, Duke of Tursi, to decorate his palace in the *strada nuova*;[180] but that incident was not unique. In 1599 several galleys from Naples brought the prince "select grain … wines and damasks and satin, fabrics that it might be best to pass through customs and be assigned a permit so that no problem can arise in taking them home."[181] In 1600 the family evaded customs on an indeterminate amount of silk[182] (an operation they repeated a year later),[183] and imported a silver vase from Naples together with "other items."[184]

176 ADP, scaffale 85, busta 20: Gian Andrea Doria to Francisco Tapia, 13 January 1601.
177 ADP, scaffale 85, busta 21: Gian Andrea Doria to the Duchess of Nájera, 10 April 1601.
178 ADP, scaffale 82, busta 21: Angelo Paganetto to Gian Andrea Doria, 13 August 1599.
179 ADP, scaffale 85, busta 21: Gian Andrea Doria to the Count of Miranda, 19 March 1601.
180 ADP, scaffale 82, busta 23: Pietro Serra to Gian Andrea Doria, 31 January 1600.
181 ADP, scaffale 85, busta 18: Gian Andrea Doria to Pietro Serra, 1 January 1599.
182 ADP, scaffale 82, busta 23: Pietro Serra to Gian Andrea Doria, 16 January 1600.
183 ADP, scaffale 18, busta 41: Tiberio del Pezzo to Gian Andrea Doria, 6 January 1601.
184 ADP, scaffale 82, busta 23: Simone Menocchio to Gian Andrea Doria, 17 April 1600.

These regular shipments of cloth are significant in themselves. Captains general and their purveyors were great buyers of fabric, especially of the types required by the galleys. According to the purveyor Miguel de Oviedo, between January 1598 and May 1601 the Galleys of Spain acquired almost 7,000 quintales of cord for rigging and another 56,700 varas of coarse cotton for sails and awnings.[185] But beside these necessary purchases, there was also a much more luxurious trade. Just the outfitting of the royal galley that conveyed the archdukes in 1599 required the purchase of 2,200 varas of cloth of gold, 5,000 ounces of gold thread, and 5,000 varas of damask.[186] Although that degree of consumption may seem unusual, in fact such sumptuary spending was fairly common in the annual outfitting of the principal galleys, the vice-flagship (called the *patrona*) and especially the flagship (called the *capitana*). In 1603, only to outfit the flagship of the Spanish squadron, the galleys bought 93 libras of Chinese silk, 55 libras of fine Moorish silk, 2 libras of red silk, 740 varas of damask, 5,500 varas of red linen, and about 4,100 varas more of different grades of cheaper wool. The order was so large that a commissioner was sent ahead six weeks earlier to inquire discreetly about prices, since merchants who saw galley officers coming would raise them in anticipation of "the great quantities" they usually bought.[187] Captains general of the galleys had special access to materials like silk thanks to the convoys of vessels that arrived in Messina every year to fill their cargo holds,[188] and since they also maintained a large volume of trade with many merchants, they could acquire these and other luxury fabrics on the most favorable terms.

Other officers of the squadrons, inspired by the example of their superiors (whose activities they helped to conceal), followed the same path. Martín de Quijano, sub-inspector of the Galleys of Genoa at this period, performed similar operations on a smaller scale. Though he lacked Prince Doria's prerogatives, he made up for them with ingenuity, mixing his own goods with those of distinguished travelers. In 1603, for example, he used a voyage of the two princes of Savoy to avoid paying duty on a bedstead he was shipping to Castile.[189] Most of his goods traveled in small parcels, and almost all had been commissioned by family and friends. Though his correspondence is incomplete, it includes several requests for purchases, especially for items of Italian make. In 1594 Melchor de Novar asked him for a few varas of taffeta; Juan de Obregón and

185 AGS, GyM, 582, 99–100.
186 ADP, scaffale 70, busta 24.
187 AGS, CMC, 3ª Época, 397.
188 ADP, scaffale 85, busta 21: Gian Andrea Doria to the Grand Duke of Tuscany, 25 May 1601.
189 AGS, Galeras, 6, fols. 438–39.

Pedro de Muruzábal requested garments for their relatives; Pedro de Quincoces wanted a bedspread, and Juan de Cerón a taffeta one for his own bed.[190] In 1595 Gabriel Sánchez asked Quijano if he could take some baggage onto his galley when the squadron was in Barcelona[191] to avoid paying customs duty, and a letter from 1603 suggests that Martín was even able to sell some taffeta at the court in Valladolid through a certain Francisco de la Serna. Many of these commissions originated in Naples, where Quijano could count on the help of an infantry captain, Rodrigo Messía de Prado. In the spring of 1603 the captain wrote him several letters describing how he sought out the best prices for wine, silk, damask, velvet, bedspreads, and hangings, at the request of both Quijano and his wife (who was his cousin, María de Quijano) and other family members.[192] Some individuals must have owed him a large debt of gratitude, or valued his services highly—in 1598, when Quijano asked Guillermo Berdina to make him a ring in Milan, Berdina sent him one of his own wife's so that he would not have to wait too long.[193]

It is possible that not all this shipping was illegal. Although the galleys' ordinances held that, because of their reduced space, only necessary supplies could come on board and crew members could bring only their "clothing and work outfits,"[194] special permission was sometimes given for ministers or merchants to ship luggage or goods if they paid the required duties. A letter from Gian Andrea Doria's administrator suggests that the prince charged 10 percent interest for conveying money between Castile and Italy, and established the required transport fees.[195] Elsewhere it appears that Doria, in layovers during his journeys, would inquire if any merchandise needed to be taken onto his galleys,[196] and his son Carlo Doria made similar contracts in the following decades.[197]

It is curious, therefore, that in one of his last letters as captain general of the sea Gian Andrea Doria reproaches Pedro de Leiva, captain general of the Galleys of Sicily, for harming the king with his "industries," that is, for using his galleys to trade in personal goods. Leiva retorted in his own defense that everyone else did the same, beginning with Doria's own son, to which the prince replied that

190 AGS, Galeras, 216, fols. 597–646.
191 AGS, Galeras, 4, fol. 108.
192 AGS, Galeras, 6, fols. 442–57.
193 AGS, Galeras, 5, fols. 297–98.
194 Marchena Giménez, "Vida y los hombres," 456.
195 ADP, scaffale 82, busta 23: Pietro Serra to Gian Andrea Doria, 8 January 1600.
196 ADP, scaffale 85, busta 21: Gian Andrea Doria to the Duke of Maqueda, 22 March 1601.
197 San Ruperto Albert, "Emprenedors," 281–82.

it could not be true, for if it were, "I would strangle him with my own hands."[198] After his father's death, Carlo Doria might have seen his way clear to indulge in previously forbidden activities, but letters written only a few months after the rebuke of Pedro de Leiva indicate the opposite.

In June 1602 Carlo Doria set sail for Spain with the Galleys of Genoa. He had orders to join the rest of the fleet on the Andalusian coast to launch a new assault on Algiers, so this was no ordinary journey but an important campaign. One member of the squadron, however, was Domenico Sevo, an agent of Gian Andrea Doria's who had embarked with the sole purpose of selling merchandise at different ports. He brought silk hose, trimmings, collars, bedspreads, cloth called "Japanese" (*Giapone*), and a box of unspecified "stuff." He first tried to sell some in Cartagena, but the layover was too short.[199] In Cádiz his luck improved—while Carlo Doria paid his respects to the Duke of Medina Sidonia, Sevo began to offer his goods in Cádiz and Seville. At least three galley skippers helped him, selling both their leader's merchandise and their own. Sevo managed to dispose of twenty-two bedspreads at 200 reales apiece, the chest of unidentified contents at 40 reales, and the collars and "Japanese" material for more than 300 reales. The decorative trimmings were harder to sell because in Seville, apparently, a more delicate type was preferred, but by August 2, just before the fleet sailed again, Sevo had realized 11,830 reales from all his merchandise.[200]

These letters reveal that Prince Doria not only was aware of how his skippers indulged in trade on the side but even took advantage of the fact to sell his own goods. Another question is whether these transactions fell under the galleys' legal privileges or not. Though we can only guess, it is significant that in the course of five letters Sevo never mentions any deductions for paying customs duties. It is also true that skippers did not always proceed under their leaders' protection; they also risked acting on their own, as we see from occasional cases that came before an *auditor*.

In 1582 a suit was brought against a captain in the Galleys of Genoa, Nicola Garibaldo. Several witnesses testified that in his latest journey to Spain he had brought on board thirty sacks "of a material that looked like earth" (it was gunpowder), saying that it was used in the manufacture of ink and that he planned to sell it in Barcelona. No word was heard of the sale, but a ship's boy in charge of cargo testified that, after returning to Genoa, Garibaldo had asked him to

198 ADP, scaffale 85, busta 22: Gian Andrea Doria to Baltasar de Zúñiga, 20 September 1601.

199 ADP, scaffale 82, busta 27: Domenico Sevo to Gian Andrea Doria, 6 July 1602.

200 ADP, scaffale 82, busta 27: Domenico Sevo to Gian Andrea Doria, 27 July and 2 August 1602.

keep twelve small sacks containing 12,000 reales in silver. Once unloaded, the galley sailed to Sardinia, and though no suspicious goods had been taken aboard before the voyage, on its return trip the skipper had stored eighty-three sacks of grain and one hundred cheeses in the hold; back in Genoa, he unloaded them into small boats under cover of night.

The galley's yeoman of the hold provided more information. The skipper had ordered him to hide fifty-six bales of cloth, some of them silk, under the ship's biscuit, and he knew that other quantities were hidden elsewhere. He had also heard his captain arranging with a scribe to sell the cloth to several Barcelona merchants at 1 escudo per bale, and he further claimed that the captain had brought a large sum of money aboard in sacks that "weighed as much as a man could lift" (600,000 reales and 40,000 gold escudos) and came from a Genoese merchant whose name he did not know but who had paid 4 percent interest on the delivery.[201]

If Doria sued Garibaldo, it was surely because he had gone too far and damaged the prince's own interests. We need only compare the percentage that the skipper supposedly negotiated for transporting the money with the percentage the prince demanded. In any event, his activities show that skippers of galleys, in addition to their official duties, acted by the same logic as any private merchant captain—they tried to avoid traveling with an empty hold and seized on any voyage to load whatever goods they could, on their own or others' behalf. They could usually assume the protection of the squadron's legal jurisdiction.

Other crew members indulged in the same practices. In October 1604 the *auditor* of the Galleys of Spain demanded that the corregidor of El Puerto de Santa María hand over three soldiers from the squadron, arrested as they tried to introduce counterfeit coin on the coast near Santa Catalina.[202] We recall that chapter 10 of the ordinances of the papal galleys forbade the adulteration and counterfeiting of coins in the galleys and the possession of any tools for doing so.[203] Only a few such cases are documented, but we have few records from appeals courts of the galleys, whether about counterfeit coin or, especially, the illegal export of money. For that we can look to different sources, such as chapter 11 of the license granted to the Duke of Lerma for the governance of his galleys in 1616. The provision mentions the great harm caused to the royal treasury by exporting money without a license, and demands that "in the squadron of Denia there not be loaded nor taken from these kingdoms any money from any person, church, monastery, hospital, council, or university,

201 ADP, scaffale 70, busta 25, interno 17.
202 ADP, Puerto de Santa María, 9, pieza 29.
203 ASV, Miscelanea Armadi, 54, fol. 85.

[nor] in any way and for any purpose ... there be taken away or loaded ... any merchandise or contraband ... without having paid the proper duties in the ports."[204] Perhaps the members of the Council of War still remembered the scandal from two years before, when the silk that had vanished from the Indies fleet turned up on the galley *Santa María*;[205] there might also be an echo of the charges brought against captains of the squadron in 1608 for having stolen part of the rations for their own crews. And there had also been the uproar over the Visit of 1591.

3.2 *The Visit of 1591*

The greatest form of corruption in the galleys was not the occasional evasion of customs duties on luxury products, manufactured goods, and fabrics, or the theft of modest amounts of gunpowder by skippers and soldiers. Far more serious was the systematic siphoning off of money from the squadrons' budgets. This type of fraud affected the king's purse most directly, and any crew member might indulge in it to some degree. But it was the financial officers—the squadron members in charge of administering allowances, buying supplies, and distributing them among the ships—who could most easily exploit for their own benefit the economic privileges granted by the king, thanks to the enormous volume of goods they dealt in and the breadth of their client networks. Suspicions about long-standing corruption in the Galleys of Spain led Philip II in 1591 to order the licenciate Juan de Acuña to visit the squadron and report on possible offenses against the royal treasury.

Inspector Acuña wasted no time. Within a few months after his arrival in El Puerto de Santa María, almost every great name associated with the logistical and financial management of the squadrons in those years was confined in chains, accused of stealing from the king's treasury. These included the pursers Tomás de Aguirre and Martín de Durango, the quartermasters Pedro López León and Miguel de Zufre, the purveyor Juan Sáenz de Oyanguren, the paymasters Juan Ortiz de Zárate and Pedro de Quincoces, the inspector Íñigo de Lezama, and the sub-inspector Martín de Quijano himself, together with a few scribes.

204 "[En la] dicha squadra de Denia no se embarque ni saque destos reinos dinero alguno de ninguna persona, iglesia, monasterio, ospital, concejo ni universidad [y que] con ningún color ni para ningún efecto ... se saque ni meta ... mercaderías ni cosas de contrabando, ... sin haver pagado los derechos que devieren en los puertos." AGS, Estado, 1945: "Licencia al duque de Lerma para armar quatro galeras."

205 AGS, GyM, 795: Emmanuel Filibert of Savoy to Philip III, 21 June 1614.

All were accused of serious crimes, the worst having been committed by agents who bought and stored supplies for the squadron. Juan Sáenz de Oyanguren, its purveyor for the coast of Andalusia, was said to have developed a whole network of providers who, in connivance with him, presented invoices that were false or padded with dubious goods and services. The network extended to several ports but was centered on Gibraltar, and several witnesses told Acuña that its members belonged to different professions. There were agents for wine, who researched prices and bought wine for the squadron from private sellers; bakers, accused of cheating the Crown by altering weights and measures of the wheat they received for making the essential ship's biscuit; butchers, who cut underweight portions of fresh meat; traders in cloth and cord, denounced for not having provided full complements of rigging and sails; and other suppliers of coarse wool, tow, suet, and even foods for the sick like chickens, eggs, and sugar. Gonzalo Rodríguez presented a special case. The squadron had no forge of its own in Gibraltar, and Rodríguez was the only blacksmith able to supply the tools, chains, and nails that the galleys needed, so Sáenz had employed him on several occasions. But it was suspected that he had charged for many orders that he had never filled, and it was rumored in the town that he boasted about all the money he was earning, enough that he could soon "reward himself" by buying a vineyard.

Sáenz's possible cheating, however, paled in comparison to that of Miguel de Zufre, a quartermaster in Cádiz. This official, who was in charge of the squadron's storage facilities, practiced a surprising array of deceits to keep part of the supplies for himself. The most common was to remove wheat from its sacks and replace it with rocks and sand. When asked to supply a certain amount of grain, he would declare some of it spoiled and unusable and have those sacks thrown into the sea; but his slaves were told to dispose of the sacks of rocks and sand instead. Each time this happened, Zufre was left with several quintales of grain to distribute among his partners in crime. He did likewise with wine, cheese, and chickpeas, which he later auctioned off in the city.

Miguel de Zufre had even more tricks up his sleeve. According to his trial records, he also cheated with grain in collusion with skippers who shipped it in their galleys, and that crime could be proven. The prosecutor Diego de Barrena showed that in 1588 and 1589 alone, Zufre and his nephew had appropriated almost 8,500 fanegas of wheat from trade with Sicily and Oran. His method was very simple: when ships whose captains conspired with him entered port, they would declare with the help of a scribal accomplice that part of the cargo had been soaked during the voyage and was now useless. Then they either sold the wheat to foreign merchants in the same town or, helped by the paymaster

Pedro de Quincoces, loaded it onto small boats and sold it at different points along the coast.

Not only grain brought into the galleys was manipulated in this way, but also grain that was to go out. Instead of claiming that wheat had been spoiled by soaking, the captains would falsify the capacity of their holds, pretending to transport much more than they actually carried. Zufre, helped by, among others, a renegade skipper named Joan Marroquín, who shipped supplies to Tangier, in just two trips to that fortified port had made 1,400 fanegas of wheat disappear, though the total was assumed to be much greater. He fell back on other deceptions as well, beside the well-known practice of altering the weight and volume of wheat taken from the storehouses. A French baker, Xacome Duarte, once helped him to sell 4,000 fanegas on the private market, after which they split the profits. Large amounts of grain were spirited out of storage at night without leaving any trace in the accounts, and Zufre even managed to sell significant quantities of *mazamorra*, the crumbs of ship's biscuit that remained at the bottom of sacks.

Zufre's actions became so brazen that after Francis Drake's attack on Cádiz in 1587 he claimed that the pirate had burned 3,450 quintales of biscuit, 3,260 fanegas of wheat, and almost 400 casks of stored wine, all of which, in fact, he had stolen and sold himself. In the end, he was tried on nineteen charges, accused of having defrauded the Crown between 1587 and 1589 of 3,750 quintales of wheat, 17 quintales of gunpowder, 20 quintales of cheese, and the abovementioned casks of wine.

Captains and skippers of galleys were usually accused of smaller frauds, along the lines of the smuggling we saw above. Captain Juan Marín's offense, for instance, was to conceal 100 quintales of biscuit out of a shipment of 400, in collusion with the inspector Íñigo de Lezama and the purser López de Zárate. He had also lied when he claimed to have received from Zufre and the purser Aguirre 1,000 varas of coarse cloth and 50 quintales of suet for his galley; those goods had never existed, but, in exchange for the favor, the officials had raised his salary twice in a single year. He does not seem to have made distributions honestly, either. Depending on the circumstances, he appropriated or concealed supplies intended for his squadron and sometimes sold them to his galley's crewmen, sharing the profits with his collaborators.

The findings of the Visit of 1591 did not reflect the severity of the crimes it uncovered, in part because in the course of the trial some of Acuña's own associates were found to be cheating. Someone who had access to them was taking messages to the accused prisoners (three notes, including one written in invisible ink, were found in Miguel de Zufre's possession), and a nun from the Espíritu Santo convent in El Puerto was helping them to communicate with the outside. Those letters went to Alonso de Rosales and often concealed coins (one contained a doubloon worth 4 escudos). Rosales would then order the scribe of Acuña's commission to hasten the proceedings, or he informed the prisoners if they were going to be tortured and later reported on the results.[206] Until his interference was detected, he was probably able to influence the nature of some sentences, though most of them were merely fines.

Juan Sáenz de Oyanguren, after paying his fine, kept his position and years later, in 1610, became an inspector himself, reviewing the accounts of the paymaster Fernández de Villegas.[207] López de Zárate entered Doria's service and in the following years kept the prince informed of the state of his affairs in Italy, particularly in Naples.[208] Tomás de Aguirre, after a stretch in the Galleys of Flanders, resumed the post of purser to the Spanish squadron and occupied it for many years.[209] Martín de Durango remained in his original purser's office, completing forty-two years of service there in 1600.[210] And Miguel de Zufre not only kept his job but soon afterward arranged the appointment of his son Juan as treasurer and quartermaster of Cartagena.[211] In the end, the only significant action that emerged from the Visit of 1591 was the reformed model of management for the squadron introduced in 1592.[212] We should look more closely into the reasons for this relative indifference.

Daniel Dessert explained years ago how the French navy under Louis XIV was maintained in part thanks to a series of families whose members specialized in its administration for generations. Passing on their experience from father to son, they were experts in the logistical and human problems of the enterprise and knew how to handle them efficiently. Blood and kinship became the key to naval management while direct or collateral family ties dominated the profession, making it almost impossible for an outsider to rise through his own merits.[213]

There is no doubt that the purveyors, paymasters, and pursers of the Spanish fleets shared this characteristic with their French counterparts. The great families involved in financial management of the galleys from the late sixteenth to the early seventeenth centuries—the Quijanos, Adanas, Obregóns, Zufres, and

206 AHN, Consejos, 41409.
207 AGS, GyM, 742: Juan Sáenz to Juan de Ciriza, 5 December 1610.
208 ADP, scaffale 82, busta 24: Juan López de Zárate to Gian Andrea Doria, 2 August 1600.
209 AGS, GyM, 975: Tomás de Aguirre to Philip III, 21 June 1614.
210 AGS, GyM, 576, 210.
211 AGS, Galeras, 6, fols. 436–37.
212 Molina Heredia, "Galeras," 605.
213 Dessert, *Royale*, 48–56.

Alarcóns—were related to each other, and Martín de Quijano's letters before and after the Visit of 1591 reveal the internal solidarity that helped them escape punishment.[214] It is equally clear that the monarchy, though it could control them to some degree and had the means to pursue their corrupt practices, was inclined to pardon them, in part because it could not replace them, and in part because the success of naval operations depended to some extent on their efficiency. The power that these officials held over the crews could be decisive at crucial moments, and their personal credit, based on favors to merchants (whether licit or fraudulent), was essential to the ultimate goal of keeping the galleys in good working order, as we shall see in the next chapter.

3.3 *The Galleys of Spain and El Puerto de Santa María*

To grasp the full extent of the influence of these suppliers and other officers of the galleys we must analyze their impact on economic activity along the coast, though that is not easy to do. Because the galleys were so mobile and consumed resources so quickly, a squadron in the course of a year would make purchases at a large number of ports; to draw a map of their client and trade networks and assess the tensions generated by their jurisdiction, we would have to compare each unit's accounts with municipal ones, which are scattered and have not always survived. One place to start, however, is the town of El Puerto de Santa María. Located on lands belonging to the Duke of Medinaceli at the mouth of the Guadalete River (a strategic site near the Gulf of Cádiz, the Jerez wine region, and the commercial emporium of Seville), it became, after the Battle of Lepanto, the home port for the Galleys of Spain.

Our first references to the impact on the town of the squadron's arrival come from 1577. In March of that year its corregidor wrote a report setting forth the chief complaints that the Duke of Medinaceli's magistrates would make against the galleys' jurisdiction from that date and throughout the seventeenth century. Their main tenor was to denounce the continual erosion of the duke's rights caused by the galleys' commercial privileges, whether employed legally or illegally.[215] By comparing those privileges with contemporary account books we can trace the boundaries of this economic relationship.

One of the corregidores' main accusations against the galleys was that they made the town lose sales taxes on meat and wine, though the situation was different for each of those products. The galleys did not consume large amounts of fresh meat, since it was hard to preserve on board, and meat did

214 Lomas Cortés, "Patronazgo."

215 ADM, PSM, 6, pieza 66.

not even represent a large part of the duke's income; therefore, the conflict about it reflects the abuses committed by galley officers with special clarity. Each squadron was allowed to designate one butcher shop for its supplies and buy its products free of sales tax.[216] In El Puerto de Santa María that "shop" was a wooden structure on the riverbank, where the galleys had their meat killed, cut, weighed, and sold—especially beef and veal, together with by-products like leather, lard, and soap. Local officials complained that the business was not only supplying meat for the crews but also selling it to local residents and outsiders, while its lower prices caused unfair competition to the town's other butchers, some of whom even bought there themselves. At the same time, it diminished the duke's income.

Records of two lawsuits from 1581 and 1593, brought by the corregidor and the treasurer of El Puerto's customhouse, provide a clear picture of the problem. The galleys' butcher shop sold meat openly not only to ships' crews but also to anyone who wished to buy it, both on the riverbank and inside the town. It was common to see "Moors from the galleys selling in this town small amounts of mutton and beef, as well as tuna and many other products like soap"—perhaps another way that slaves could acquire funds through petty commerce. Nor was it unusual to find soldiers "in a public street of this city [with] a large basket … in which was … a dead pig missing one leg, and the soldiers were weighing out the meat for certain persons," while "in the square by the forge … there was a galley skipper sharing out a pig, as at other times … [and] he distributed it publicly there without ceremony" and without paying the required taxes. While that meat had been bought in ways that cheated the royal treasury, according to one witness things were even worse, in that many animals had been stolen from local farmers as they drove their herds along the roads, so that some were now refusing to pass near the town.[217]

It is unsurprising, then, that the Duke of Medinaceli made constant demands to have the butchering structure on the riverbank torn down. It appears to have been partly demolished before 1593, but the Count of Santa Gadea—though he was related to the duke, according to Molina Heredia[218]—had it built up again, upon which the customs treasurer, in December of that year, demanded its removal for violating the town's right to collect three different kinds of taxes (*alcabala, sisa*, and *millones*).[219] The attempt seems to have failed, because in 1617 the Council of War was again asked to order the building

216 Sirago, "Flotta napoletana," 111–72.

217 ADM, PSM, 7, pieza 18; ADM, PSM, 8, pieza 14.

218 Molina Heredia, "Galeras," 600.

219 ADM, PSM 8, pieza 16.

taken down.[220] This time it was argued that its position interfered with the loading and unloading of goods at the port, and a royal decree demanded that the duke's taxation privileges be respected, but the squadron's purser, after "taking [the order] in his hand, kissing it, and pressing it to his forehead with proper respect," proceeded to ignore it entirely.[221]

Aside from the "shop's" inconvenient location (and it seemed not to have moved by 1664),[222] what the Duke of Medinaceli really wanted was for the squadron to pay at least some tax, which was very difficult to achieve. In the early years he fought to impose the usual 10 percent duty, arguing that sales to private individuals were not exempt;[223] by 1594 he was trying for only 5 percent.[224] When even that proved impossible, in 1597 his efforts turned to keeping watch over the butchers who bought meat, hides, suet, lard, offal, and other products illegally from the squadron's "shop" and later sold them;[225] but repeated references to this cheating in subsequent decades suggests that it was never wholly eliminated.[226]

Because the squadron's account books dealt with other matters beside these supplies, it is difficult to verify these accusations of fraud. But we do know that although butchers in El Puerto provided meat to the galleys only occasionally, there were other merchants who did so regularly and in great quantities. In these cases the purveyor would buy all the meat for one year from a single seller, so that the privilege was in effect leased out, unlike the case with other products. In 1605 the official supplier became Cristóbal de Ledesma,[227] in 1606 Leonardo Curtis, and in 1607 Juan Pérez. Pérez, in a single year, sold 14,600 libras of meat to the galleys in eighteen deliveries, earning more than 1,000 ducats. At the same period, he became one of the main beneficiaries of the sale of biscuit fragments, *mazamorra*; one of the few products that the galleys were legally entitled to sell, they were often used to feed cattle. We wonder, therefore, if there was some kind of reciprocal arrangement between these suppliers and the galleys, which also helped to stock the "butcher shop" with fresh meat.[228] We would need to compare this information with the rations of meat destined for crew members that year, to see if purchases included an oversupply that

220 AGS, GyM, 823: Consulta del Consejo de Estado, 10 November 1617.
221 ADM, PSM 9, pieza 46.
222 ADM, PSM 9, pieza 43.
223 ADM, PSM 6, pieza 45.
224 ADM, PSM 7, pieza 64.
225 ADM, PSM 9, pieza 22.
226 ADM, PSM 9, pieza 43.
227 AGS, CMC, 3ª Época, 397.
228 AGS, CMC, 3ª Época, 1436.

could later be sold; but, in the absence of such a comparison, we cannot come to any conclusion.

Something similar happened with supplies of fish. The account books register only purchases of cod in season, almost always from foreign ships that were passing through. But as we mentioned above, witnesses complaining about illegal sales of meat in El Puerto also said that galley slaves sold tuna; this puts us on the trail of another suit against the squadron for usurping income owed to the duke. In April 1582 his chief agent claimed that his master's income from duties on fishing had collapsed. Before the galleys had made El Puerto their home, many local boats had taken tuna and other fish and sold it in the town (at one point there had been forty shallops in the fleet). But that was now a thing of the past; many boats had been abandoned, and families that had once lived by fishing were ruined. An investigation was opened, and the resulting trial provided important information. According to witnesses, the collapse had begun six years before, when officers of the galleys had begun to send their own boats out to fish, protected by the squadron's privileges. At the same time, they often seized cargoes of fish from their competitors, giving the crews' needs as their excuse. Altogether they had destroyed almost all incentive to fish, though some offered townspeople a chance to continue fishing as long as they sold their catch to the galleys.

If we are to believe the duke's representatives, the squadron had set up the business very well for its own advantage. The paymaster Pedro de Quincoces and the pursers Francisco de Arriola and Martín de Durango (all of whom would be accused in the Visit of 1591) enrolled local fishermen as soldiers or sailors in the fleet while employing them in their private fishing boats. (Quincoces owned two shallops and Arriola and Durango three each, while others belonged to skippers.) In this way, local men could continue to fish, though with one new condition—they now enjoyed the same privileges as the galleys and no longer had to pay sales taxes to the duke, nor could their catch be seized. Meanwhile, the officers kept part of the profits together with the salaries and rations of those new "crewmen" of the squadron (i.e., the local residents). The other fishermen of the town could not compete in this situation; the fraud had increased the price of an arroba of fish from 9 to 20 reales. This practice, according to the duke's agent, harmed not only the "republic of citizens" but also the royal armadas, which now had to pay more for fish and also had crew members falsely enrolled on their books.[229]

229 ADM, PSM 7, pieza 15.

The most harmful fraud against the Duke of Medinaceli's rights actually had to do not with meat or fish but with wine. A report by the corregidor calculated that between 1584 and 1590 the galleys' purveyor had bought from townspeople of El Puerto more than 112,300 arrobas of wine (slightly over 16,000 a year), of which only one-fourth had been declared to customs.[230] This uncontrolled commerce diminished the duke's revenues, but above all it kept him from exploiting fully the tremendous potential of shipping wine from his vineyards to the Indies. At the end of the sixteenth century, El Puerto de Santa María had more than 180 taverns, thanks to its strategic location at the mouth of the Gulf of Cádiz, from which sherry, the prized wine of Jerez, was exported.[231] It was said that the Duke of Medina Sidonia, by selling his casks of wine by that route, brought in double what they would have earned in Andalusia. But, as a report in 1592 made clear, Medinaceli's attempts to do the same was thwarted by the dealings of the galley's captain general and financial officers. The Count of Santa Gadea himself had stolen a march on the duke, "load[ing] one or two ships every year at his own risk with wine and other goods for the Indies" and benefiting from his jurisdiction within that enclave.[232]

The squadron's ledgers reveal to what extent El Puerto's manpower and wealth depended on trade in wine. In 1603 alone (a normal year without major campaigns), the squadron bought 7,800 arrobas of wine from more than fifty residents;[233] these figures accord well with the complaint registered in 1590 if we remember that at that date the Galleys of Spain consisted of about thirty vessels but had only eleven left at the beginning of the seventeenth century. It is unsurprising, then, that in those years income from brokers who sought out wine for the galleys increased dramatically, while the duke's men saw the expansion of that profession as aggravating the problem—both townspeople and outsiders "bribe them [the brokers] very well to conceal their sales ... and the truth rarely comes to light." As a result, there were "many frauds and deceits that the brokers carry out ... with the king's ministers who come to them with their deals and schemes ... which is very inconvenient for the treasury." It seems that townspeople hid their harvests in their cellars when prices went down and pretended that officers of the galleys had bought them, so that the duke's goal was "to keep the king's ministers from making agreements ... for they buy everything on offer by saying it is for his Majesty, and though it is obviously done for the sake of their deals and schemes that is impossible to

230 ADM, PSM 7, pieza 19.
231 ADM, PSM 7, pieza 64.
232 ADM, PSM 7, pieza 76.
233 AGS, CMC, 3ª Época, 397.

prove; and with this they [residents] do not pay tax on what they sell, for they say it is on orders from his Majesty." The duke's side demanded of the court that at the end of each harvest a registry and inventory be made of every house and storeroom in the town, and that early in each year the squadron communicate to the corregidor the amount of wine it planned to buy; further, that the magistrate of El Puerto be present at each transaction to oversee prices and amounts, even those legally free of tax, as a way of palliating "the greed of the king's ministers, which increases daily."[234]

Medinaceli obtained a warrant from the treasury that ordered the squadron's purveyor to declare every purchase made in El Puerto, but it did not help much. At the close of the sixteenth century, the licenciate Tomás de Angulo proved that wine was still being sold illegally to galley officers. In a trial of eighteen town residents, he showed that at least 1,720 arrobas of wine had been sold to different members of the squadron without prior declaration or payment of the required taxes.[235] It began to be common, therefore, that instructions issued to El Puerto's chief treasurers and scribes include a reminder that financial officers of the galleys should be pressured every year to allow inspection of their ledgers, so that those could be reconciled with customs records.[236] The effort yielded few results, however, as the officers continued to avoid cooperating.[237]

There seems little to support the accusations, repeated throughout those years, that embargoes by the galleys, purchases on credit, and delayed payments of debts were bankrupting producers of wine.[238] On the contrary, it appears that, as with meat and fish, townspeople took advantage of the galleys' jurisdiction, especially their officers' exemption from paying "tributes, tolls, or any other duty on the provisions and supplies and other things that they buy for them, nor are those who sell to them required to pay them."[239] Residents could avoid those taxes as well, creating a lucrative business between themselves and the galleys, with the connivance of customs officers and to the detriment of the duke's income. A complaint in 1581,[240] and an accusation in 1586 by Seville's chief scribe against El Puerto's head magistrate and some of its councillors, charged them with exporting wheat and biscuit illegally without

234 ADM, PSM 8, pieza 15.
235 ADM, PSM 8, pieza 13.
236 ADM, PSM 9, pieza 22.
237 ADM, PSM 8, pieza 5.
238 ADM, PSM 8, pieza 5.
239 ADM, PSM 8, pieza 9.
240 ADM, PSM 7, pieza 2.

the proper registration or permit.[241] We find two familiar names among the customs officers in 1593: Juan Mosquera Figueroa (doubtless a relative of the squadron's *auditor*) as executor, and Joan Marroquí, the skipper who had helped Cádiz's quartermaster steal wheat from North Africa, as the collector of pilotage fees.[242]

This last detail is revealing. The Duke of Medinaceli complained that aside from usurping his sales taxes, the squadron harmed maritime traffic in El Puerto by engaging in pilotage, the system of towing ships across the mouth of the Guadalete River. We have no data on the history of this concession, but in 1579 its owners sued because the arrival of the galleys had diminished their income. An original sum of 460 ducats a year had dwindled to only about 70 ducats,[243] largely through interference by the galleys, which piloted their own vessels. Aside from this unfair competition, "for fear of them [the galleys] ships avoid this port and go to others, because [the galleys] regularly steal rigging and sailors from them and do other damage, the greatest and most inconvenient of which [is] the general embargoes of ships ... because foreigners do not come so as not to be embargoed ... and locals cannot sell their products."[244]

Although the embargoes could be harmful and off-putting, it is only fair to recall how much business derived from provisioning the galleys. Between June 1602 and August 1603, for example, the squadron's paymaster registered a total of no fewer than forty-two shipments, of which at least twenty were handled by skippers from El Puerto de Santa María. Most involved short journeys that connected the squadron to suppliers in Sanlúcar, Seville, or Las Aceñas de la Cartuja, where a bakery made most of the ships' biscuit. These vessels carried wheat, artillery, gunpowder, money, wood, and wine. In addition, there was the work of loading and unloading, transportation to warehouses, and, above all, the products bought directly from local residents.[245]

Although most of the duke's complaints involved trade in meat and wine, the galleys' purveyor maintained close, stable commercial relations with many men and women of El Puerto. The squadron was an important client of the local bakeries and often ordered large quantities of biscuit. In 1608, seven bakers

241 ADM, PSM 7, pieza 22.

242 ADM, PSM 8, pieza 19.

243 ADM, PSM 7, pieza 8.

244 "[P]or temor dellas dexan de benir navíos al puerto y ban a otros, porque de hordinario les toman xarcias y marineros, y hacen otros daños, [siendo] los envargos generales de navíos ... el mayor ynconveniente de todos, ... porque no bienen los estranjeros por no ser envargados, ... y no pueden vender sus frutos los vecinos." ADM, PSM 7, pieza 31.

245 AGS, CMC, 3ª Época, 397.

agreed to produce 6,150 quintales at a price of 97,000 reales, and year after year the bakery owned by Alonso de Luna and Alonso Martín billed the squadron for thousands of ducats. They were not alone. A shoemaker, Juan de Jaén, made hundreds of shoes every year for the rowers,[246] and a cooper, Sebastián Rodríguez, sold thousands of barrel hoops (6,000 between 1603 and 1605). The commonest contracts in the ledgers are for small but very frequent transactions with all sorts of providers: scribes, landlords, haberdashers, dyers, wineskin makers, blacksmiths, carpenters, woodcutters, weavers of esparto grass and wicker, locksmiths, haulers, silversmiths, and even a few painters and sculptors who decorated ships' figureheads and flags. Altogether, they numbered about 150 in a population of slightly over a thousand. (There might have been more, but the books often omit the seller's origin or the details of a sale to more than one person.)[247] Much of the business of El Puerto de Santa María was obviously done with the galleys, a fact that could result in tensions over jurisdiction.

The Duke of Medinaceli had two principal aims, to control the sale of wine and to avoid embargoes. He always instructed his agents to maintain "friendship and good relations" with the captains general of the galleys, their purveyors, and "persons close to them ... because in this way and with a little cleverness many [problems] will be lessened, if they cannot be entirely solved."[248] Some of the duke's men took this advice literally, like Diego López, head treasurer of the ducal rents and therefore the person in charge of collecting sales tax. After his arrest, he confessed "the friendship he had with the [squadron's] purveyor ... [with whom] he often went fishing, and they visited each other on special occasions. ... [and] they and their wives would go to the riverbank on summer evenings." Oddly enough, his friend the purveyor never visited him in prison, and after a calm period it seemed "a very obvious thing" to "have lost [for this reason] the friendship of the *Adelantado* [the Count of Santa Gadea]."[249]

Aside from the dangers of too-close friendships, experience showed that a minimal level of mutual understanding was the best way to ensure that "the chief ministers and their lieutenants and officers do justice without offending or extorting anyone."[250] As the duke explained to his new corregidor in 1592, "The greatest difficulties in governing El Puerto de Santa María are the encounters with the captains general of the galleys ... who greatly exceed their jurisdiction and commission, causing great damage to mine and to my property,"[251]

246 AGS, CMC, 3ª Época, 1436.
247 González, *Censo de población*, 84.
248 ADM, PSM 7, pieza 31.
249 ADM, PSM 8, pieza 38.
250 ADM, PSM 7, pieza 13.
251 ADM, PSM 7, pieza 75.

for they are "skilled in their good treatment of my vassals in the matter of buying their crops and paying for them well (and they must not allow my taxes to be evaded) and in many other things that always ensure friendship and pleasant relations."[252]

There was even a permanent ducal commission for dealing with the situation, made up of the corregidor, the commander of the fortress, the duke's treasurer, and his chief scribe. Its only mission was "the defense of my jurisdiction ... in matters of captains general of the sea and the galleys,"[253] more specifically to make them understand that "they have no right to do anything or take a hand in that city [El Puerto] and its jurisdiction any further than they have in Sanlúcar, Cádiz, and other seaports." It seems that after several years in which the galleys had made El Puerto their home port, their captains general had come to believe that their jurisdiction extended to the whole town; and the truth is that, with the help of their *auditores*, they had become highly effective in countering actions by the corregidores. The duke finally became so impatient with the problem that he sought out corregidores who would be less flexible and less obedient of the law: "So what we seek is to deny him [the Count of Santa Gadea] the bad habit he has acquired of usurping my jurisdiction, so he will see there is someone who will oppose him and face off with him ... as a legally trained corregidor would not."[254]

That remedy turned out to be worse than the disease. Soon after the first of those "lay" corregidores, Alonso de Cornejo, arrived in El Puerto, it began to be rumored that he "associates with fallen women, with whom it is said he has misbehaved," and, above all, that he was incapable of defending the duke's interests before the *auditor* of the galleys because "he is not an attorney and has no experience of what must be done."[255] It seems that by the late sixteenth century so many townspeople had been made unofficial "crew members" of the galleys that any attempt to settle a dispute immediately met with "conflicts of jurisdiction" between the two legal systems. In 1594 Philip II ordered that the "membership" in the galleys, as soldiers and sailors, of all residents of El Puerto be canceled, on the grounds that "by living exempt from the justice of El Puerto ... they are emboldened to commit crimes."[256]

Apparently, it was impossible to keep *auditores* of the galleys from meddling in the town's legal affairs.[257] Although every resident was subject to civil

252 ADM, PSM 9, pieza 22.
253 ADM, PSM 7, pieza 70.
254 ADM, PSM 7, pieza 75.
255 ADM, PSM 9, pieza 49.
256 ADM, PSM 8, pieza 21.
257 ADM, PSM 9, pieza 67.

justice, crimes related in any way to supplying the galleys, an activity in which many townspeople took part, fell under the captain general's jurisdiction.[258] New legal infrastructure was built, in the form of a prison, to punish the many "public sins by murderers, blasphemers, thieves, cohabiters, ruffians, and other persons of ill repute … [resulting from] the Galleys of Spain wintering here."[259] The Medinaceli family never managed to collect sales taxes on provisions bought for the galleys on its lands, even after obtaining royal decrees in 1594, 1617, and 1619 that ordered the squadron's officers to pay them.[260] Still, the symbiotic relationship between the squadron and the town's income was probably greater than the dukes liked to admit, and dated back a long way. In 1568, when an outbreak of plague kept the galleys from anchoring in the river, that income suffered a severe blow—all the fresh bread and biscuit had to be thrown away because there was no one to buy it.[261]

According to a registry from March 1599, the Galleys of Spain employed 1,387 men among officers, soldiers, sailors, and rowers.[262] Because about the same number of families lived in El Puerto de Santa María at the time, we can understand the significance of the galleys' arrival at the mouth of the Guadalete. Even more in that port than elsewhere, the prolonged presence of the squadron, with its large population and its prerogatives, made it difficult to assimilate its crew members in a jurisdictional sense. They influenced every aspect of daily life in El Puerto, as we see from the rapid turnover of corregidores and ducal treasurers, whose correspondence with the Duke of Medinaceli is full of conflicts with officers of the galleys. But all this was really the result of successful social and economic integration. In spite of the duke's complaints, many residents learned to exploit the jurisdictional advantages of the galleys' privileges in ways that improved their professional and commercial lives. Eventually, the distinction between crewmen and townspeople grew less clear. Ties of mutual interest caused the duke's income to decrease, much as the process of devassalage did—his former vassals kept their properties and professions in El Puerto but now obeyed a different authority, one that assumed the right to judge any criminal or economic offenses they committed. The case of El Puerto de Santa María illustrates how the galleys' economic privileges in provisioning and subsistence could alter the economic life of coastal towns. This generated jurisdictional disputes that may have been even more dangerous

258 ADM, PSM 9, pieza 60.
259 ADM, PSM 9, pieza 46.
260 ADM, PSM 9, pieza 52.
261 ADM, PSM 8, pieza 46.
262 AGS, GyM, 541, 148.

than those produced by occasional landings of soldiers, as their implications were much more profound and potentially more harmful to the interests of local authorities.

The risk resided not only in the squadron's fiscal exemptions that lowered local incomes but also in the frauds that ran along a parallel track. Many merchants gained by it, but the biggest winners were the crews. (All ranks took economic advantage of this favorable jurisdiction to the extent they were able.) Soldiers and slaves sold small items cheaply, both aboard and ashore, to make temporary improvements in their living conditions or save for their ransoms. Captains and skippers smuggled manufactured goods, money, and gunpowder, often in collusion with financial officers and even captains general. The latter used their jurisdiction to weave a dense network of contacts based on special favors, which often involved cheating on customs duties. But it was above all the purveyors, quartermasters, and other financial officers who were most clever at exploiting not only those deceptions but also the systematic theft of provisions and the funds meant to purchase them. Helped by the very local authorities who should have pursued their crimes, and by many merchants and captains, they developed a wide range of corrupt practices that were never seriously pursued by the Crown no matter how flagrant they became. A crucial factor in maintaining this corruption was the involvement of the families who managed the squadrons' logistics over generations, thanks especially to the patronage they enjoyed over all ranks of crew members.

We must consider whether this habitual corruption, in all its dimensions, helped to support and preserve the crews. Many members certainly gained more immediate and tangible benefits from this "lucre" than from captures of pirate ships or even from embargoes. Those practices, at least for the Galleys of Spain, normally did not yield much profit in prize money (which was distributed late and unevenly) or more efficient recruitment of rowers. Both those resources came not directly from warfare at sea but from a combination of more complex factors. Embargoes did not bring the squadrons much income either (in the form of auctioned ships or newly acquired convicts), because of diplomatic pressure by consuls and ambassadors. It is not strange, therefore, that the Galleys of Spain should cultivate smuggling much more than they condemned it, or that they had more to gain by trading with North Africa than by capturing ships along its coasts. The galleys' earnings from exporting grain, from ransoms, and from interference in North African civil strife outstripped their profits from corsair warfare. And this was true even though such warfare was in theory the spearpoint of the crusade, the preferred vehicle for a religious war between two supposedly irreconcilable opponents that left no room for collaboration or understanding.

Officers of the galleys, in their unceasing search for provisions, established a broad range of relationships and strategies, both legal and illegal. All of these, however, were simply new ways of exercising the commercial rights of the ancient admiralties, which captains general inherited along with their jurisdiction. It is clear that the establishment of permanent squadrons of galleys, and the definition of their officers' responsibilities, at the end of the sixteenth century did more than change the administration of civil and criminal law in many coastal ports; they also influenced the development of commercial activities and the legal mechanisms for resolving conflicts connected to them. In the late 1500s, galley tribunals controlled by their *auditores* consolidated a new model of justice whose jurisdiction extended not only to coastal trade but to seafaring itself. We cannot assess the full extent of its influence over maritime commerce, but the trials we know of almost always involved summary solutions, with armers and captains then forced into long waits after appealing to the Council of War. Still, the spread of these new tribunals into every squadron must have influenced contemporary thought about the freedom of the seas, and their existence reconfigured the jurisdictional map of the Mediterranean. To complete our analysis of all the ways in which captains general ruled their squadrons, and how their competencies and faculties were expressed, we must examine not only the fleets' external features but also their internal ones.

CHAPTER 3

Resistance, Consensus, and Solidarity

García de Toledo, captain general of the Galleys of Naples, wrote a report to King Philip II that described the greatest difficulties he had faced throughout his years as leader of the squadron. In an attempt to give a Stoic tinge to his discourse, he associated every problem with one of the four elements in nature. The greatest obstacle was water, whose instability made all movement on the sea uncertain. Fire was a danger because ships were made of wood and cloth, while air imperilled any kind of maneuver—sometimes the wind did not blow at all; at other times it blew too hard. Finally, earth was represented by the rocks and sandbanks on which ships could run aground. The writer noted that at sea "you must defend yourself against many [dangers]," whereas on land there was only one: the crew members themselves, "who are looking you in the face day and night to seize the first occasion they can, and having performed their work all their lives, they well know how to act."

These reflections are valuable on several levels. They offer a glimpse into an officer's interior world and betray the psychological pressure, even for an captain general, of serving on the deck of a galley under the eyes of men hungry for any sign of weakness or opportunity. They reveal the ever-present threat of insubordination, mutiny, or flight, especially by rowers condemned to long sentences or slavery. An officer must fear his entire crew: "When you do not pay them it seems you cannot punish them, [and] everywhere you go they stir up trouble."[1]

These observations betray a significant aspect of the internal governance of a galley, and will form the basis for the final section of this book. We shall explore how the jurisdiction derived from ancient customs of the sea, and the ordinances we have described, were applied aboard the galleys themselves, and we shall draw some conclusions about cooperation and conflict among the various social, juridical, and religious groups who lived together within those small territories.

1 Fernández Duro, *Historia de la Armada*, 2:409.

1 Escapes and Mutinies

García de Toledo speaks of how an alert rower could take advantage of an officer's inattention when a ship was anchored close to land, and seems to be referring to the danger of escape. For Pantero Pantera this threat reflected poorly on the work of petty officers such as *cómitres* (rowers' boatswain) and *alguaciles* (sergeants-at-arms), who either failed to guard their rowers well—especially those serving life sentences, who were more likely to try to flee—or dealt out unjustified, arbitrary punishments. Sometimes discipline was applied unevenly, and there might also be personal quarrels or alliances between these officers and certain crewmen. Pantera claims that superiors might impose harsher punishments on some rowers than on others (in the form of beatings, confinement in chains, or hard labor) in order "to extract something from them," particularly money. He gives no specific examples, but we can imagine gambling debts, unpaid bills for purchases, and bribes offered in exchange for better treatment or for turning a blind eye to illicit economic activity.

Rowers sometimes escaped during brief absences from the ship to find water or firewood, but Pantera notes that the greatest peril came at night, when guards were careless or did not keep the lanterns alight along the rowers' benches. Most escapes were the result of such imprudence and were not violent, though there were exceptions—a few slaves from the *Santa Lucía*, who a few years later entered the papal galleys, had murdered the officer who was guarding them as they gathered wood in a remote spot.[2] We will now consider how rowers could escape without being betrayed by their mates, how frequent those attempts were, and what legal consequences they brought.

1.1 *Escapees*

In his study of the *Libro general de forzados* (General book of convicts), Manuel Martínez shows that in the eighteenth century, 4 percent of convicts in the galleys tried to escape at one time or another.[3] We have no similar registry for the early seventeenth century, but we can trace the phenomenon through bounties awarded by a galley's paymaster for "finds" (i.e., captures). The first period for which we have data is June 1602 to August 1603. In the first of those months, a slave named Alcácer escaped from the *Santa Bárbara* during a layover in Seville, Amete Zarzaña disappeared from the *San Jacinto*, and an unidentified

2 Pantera, *Armata navale*, 124–26.

3 Martínez Martínez, *Forzados*, 98.

slave fled from the flagship, also in Seville. In 1603, two escaped slaves from the *San Jorge* were recaptured.[4] To these five slaves we should add the number of convicts, but the data are difficult to interpret. We know that two escaped in 1602 near Cartagena and that a third was retaken in 1603 after a brief flight, but from this point on the picture is less clear because the escapes listed were from prisons on land. In 1602, two men escaped from prison in Seville and another four from El Puerto de Santa María; in 1603, seven more escaped from the latter town. But we do not know if they were convicts condemned but not yet embarked, or men who had fled the galleys, been captured and imprisoned, and had escaped once more (a not unusual occurrence).

Unfortunately, we have no information for the second half of 1603 and all of 1604, so the series resumes in 1605. In early January, an escaped slave, who had probably fled the year before, was located in Cádiz, and in March bounties were paid for the seizure of two more. One slave was captured in Utrera in June, and two more escapees were retaken swiftly by several residents of El Puerto de Santa María in November. In the same year, one convict escaped in March and another in June, bringing the total for 1605 to eight rowers. The numbers fell slightly in 1606: two slaves were arrested in Jerez in April, and before the month was out another "disappeared" prisoner was found. A slave was taken in Rota in July, then in early autumn the skipper of a merchant ship trapped another, and several soldiers seized a convict, giving a total of six men for that year. Two escapes by slaves took place in 1607, a single individual from the vice-flagship in August and two men in the winter. For that year, flights by convicts were more common—seven bounties were paid to residents of Sanlúcar, Seville, Jerez, and Barcelona who caught them, so the annual total was ten men.

The records for 1608 contain fewer details, so we can confirm only that two slaves who had escaped from the flagship were arrested in Jerez and Medina Sidonia, respectively. There must have been some convicts as well, because elsewhere a payment of 3,000 reales is noted for their capture. Since the standard reward for capturing any escapee—slave or convict—was 100 reales, that sum suggests that a large group had fled; but the note also mentions "other things," so we cannot estimate the number of men involved.[5] The year 1609 yields no data at all; there was more activity in 1610, but details become scarcer, and we learn only that five slaves escaped. A miscellaneous order records several payments (including one for renting a ship), but we do not know the

4 AGS, CMC, 3ª Época, 397.

5 AGS, CMC, 3ª Época, 1436.

number of recovered slaves and convicts, or if any were among the escapees of that year. In 1611 the picture is slightly clearer, and we find seizures of six slaves and three convicts who had fled.[6]

There are no records for 1612–13, but sometime in 1614–15 a bounty was paid for four slaves from the *San Martín* recaptured after their escape.[7] For the three-year period 1616–19, we learn only that in 1617 an escaped convict managed to reach Cáceres, where he was arrested but fled once more. His was not a unique case; in November of that year, two slaves seized in Ronda also managed to escape from jail. There are no more data for the remainder of the period, however.[8]

It is hard to determine whether the small number of escapes in these years reflects improved guarding of the crews or simple carelessness by the paymaster, who, as we know, was not always scrupulous about recording all the squadron's economic transactions. Therefore, it is best to focus on the years 1602 to 1608, which cover the final year of the more careful paymaster Juan Pascual and the first ones of his successor Juan Fernández de Villegas (before the latter was accused of fraud). During those six years of fairly complete records, we find forty-six excapes by rowers of the squadron, divided about evenly between twenty slaves and twenty-six convicts. These numbers might be slightly smaller if we knew that the two slaves who escaped in December 1607 were the same ones captured in Jerez and Medina Sidonia in 1608. But aside from this uncertainty, it appears that in the early seventeenth century an average of six or seven rowers managed to escape from the Galleys of Spain every year. Our data are too imperfect to allow a calculation of what percentage of all rowers they represented. Most often, the escapees seem to have been single men, at least once they reached land. The less common cases of pairs of fugitives might involve two slaves, two convicts, or one of each, as we see from the escapes from the vice-flagship in 1607.

Another question is how successful these escapes were, measured either by distance or by time lapsed until capture. As to the first of these, the rower who covered the most ground was the convict who reached Cáceres in 1617; another, named Mexía, managed to return home to Almodóvar del Campo in 1600.[9] Slaves obviously had a more difficult time, since most of them were caught somewhere near Seville or El Puerto de Santa María, but there were notable exceptions. Morisco slaves who managed to escape often went undetected

6 AGS, CMC, 3ª Época, 1570.

7 AGS, CMC, 3ª Época, 1454.

8 AGS, CMC, 3ª Época, 3324.

9 AGS, GyM, 572, 301.

"because, since they are Spanish-speaking, they handle the language easily."[10] They were therefore more like convicts, who could forge the friendships needed to orchestrate their flight and then conceal themselves on land; they shared a cultural background with soldiers, sailors, and officers. Although slaves lacked that advantage, they still managed to escape successfully from time to time. Amete Zarzaña enjoyed his freedom for ten months, from June 1602 to March 1603, though we do not know where he escaped from or where he was caught. It seems that two unnamed slaves who fled in 1602 were not retaken for several years: in 1609, after Pedro del Castillo, an assistant sergeant-at-arms in the galleys, had trapped them in one of his sweeps, two residents of the village of Orce in Granada were sentenced to pay their assessed sale price for having let them escape. The sentence might have come down some time after the events, but appeals to the Council of War usually did not take so long; those two slaves, perhaps Moriscos from Granada, might have been at large for a long time, which is surprising when we think of how few possessions escaped galley slaves must have taken with them.

In April 1598, Gian Andrea Doria authorized several soldiers to seek out two fugitives from the royal galley who had apparently been caught once and placed under a priest's supervision. But on arriving, they found that the priest, in an act of conscience, had let the men get away and that in their haste they had left all their goods behind. Doria suspected a less-than-pious motive, and asked his men to tell "the good priest" from him "that I believe that he let those men escape from there not out of charity but to steal their clothing. This makes me think that he is one of those priests who is not good, and if I cannot punish him because he is not under my jurisdiction I will at least report him to his bishop." This was not the only instance in which priests and monks were accused of sheltering runaways, though it may have been the most dramatic. What interests us here is that the belongings in question were no more than two shirts, three coats, three caps, and three pairs of trousers (the change of clothing that rowers were usually issued as winter approached).[11] Once these fugitives had lost them, we can imagine how difficult their newfound freedom must have been.

We have to wonder whether many of these escapes were motivated by the causes that Pantera outlined in 1614. The records show that violence was not usually involved (at least, no instance of it appears for the Galleys of Spain), while there were many accusations against the men in charge of guarding the

10 Lomas Cortés, "Armada de Felipe III," 218.

11 ADP, scaffale 70, busta 24: Gian Andrea Doria, 28 April 1598.

rowers.[12] Almost every escape was followed by punishment of those men, such as the sailor Francisco Rida and the soldiers Francisco Ferrer and Martín de Oviedo, accused of letting two slaves get away from the *San Jorge* in 1603. Juan Velasco, a corporal of a galley, had to replace the slave Alcácer on the rower's bench after the latter's flight in 1602.[13]

The *alguaciles* were no more fortunate. One of their duties was to guard the most dangerous convicts and slaves, who were to be kept in chains and, as Gian Andrea Doria explains, to be visited "more than once a day, and be so well guarded by day and by night that not only are they unable to escape but cannot even speak to anyone, because they have plenty of allies."[14] The prince, like Pantera, believed that the greatest risk of flight occurred at night and that to avoid it suspected men were to be always securely chained and kept from communicating freely with the rest of the crew. Therefore, if a rower escaped, the responsibility fell on the officer who had failed in his duty.[15] That was the fate of the sergeant-at-arms of the galley *Spínola* who, accused of having allowed the convict Cristoforo Carcano to escape in May 1604, then vanished himself without a trace. For Gian Andrea Doria, there might be two reasons for his actions, "that he was in agreement with him [the convict], or for fear of being punished," although he was inclined toward the first; he knew from experience that in the galleys any crewman could be "favored and helped by others" as long as he was able to "spend."[16]

Doria's statement is significant. We have explained elsewhere how, by mixing convicts, slaves, and salaried rowers on the same bench, officers tried to prevent the formation of close friendships that might lead to disciplinary problems; that made it harder to develop any kind of collective feeling or esprit de corps.[17] But this same information shows that rowers with resources, or those who could gain the friendship or connivance of an officer, could overcome that obstacle. Those relationships could turn dangerous, however. If collaboration with *alguaciles* was possible, so was collusion with other petty officers (in 1609 Pedro García, a forger rowing in the Galleys of Portugal, was on the point of fleeing with the help of an Italian gunner)[18] and, above all,

---

12 Martínez Martínez, *Forzados*, 99.

13 AGS, CMC, 3ª Época, 397.

14 ADP, scaffale 85, busta 20: Gian Andrea Doria to the governor of Porto Ercole, 15 January 1601.

15 Martínez Martínez, *Forzados*, 390–93.

16 ADP, scaffale 85, busta 29: Gian Andrea Doria to the Count of Fuentes, 5 May 1604.

17 Lomas Cortés, "Esclave captif," 23.

18 AGS, GyM, 726: "Don Luis Bravo de Acuña, cavallero ...," 13 June 1609.

with fellow rowers. In 1618 Diego López, a convict in the Galleys of Denia, escaped from his bench. The *auditor* promptly blamed the *alguacil* and the three sailors who had been guarding the rowers on the night of his disappearance, but he extended the blame to several other rowers as well. Ruggiero Ferrero, Antonio Melone, and Andrés Gaspar, the convicts who had sat immediately in front of, behind, and beside López, were sentenced to two additional years in the galleys because in such a confined space they must have known of the planned escape. They were as guilty as the fugitive and should receive as heavy a punishment.[19]

This strategy was undoubtedly meant as an object lesson for the rest of the crew, and it sought to destroy any possible ties of comradeship and solidarity they might develop. Sometimes envy or friction with one's neighbors on the benches could frustrate a plan for escape. Francisco Dávalos was a Sicilian renegade who for a long time passed as a Turk in the unhappy galley *San Jorge*; when he finally gained permission to be ransomed in exchange for a captive from Algiers, he was betrayed and accused because it was rumored "among the Moriscos, convicts, and free men" aboard ship that he was a charlatan who only pretended to speak Turkish like a native.[20] Still, cooperation among rowers was always present and at times was directed not to the flight of one or two rowers but to mutiny by a whole crew.

1.2 *Mutineers*

In May 1616 two Catalan galleys spied a North African galliot off the coast of Los Alfaques and set out in pursuit. But when they had almost overhauled her, most of the sailors and foremast hands of one galley, believing that the Moors would resist being boarded and would open fire, ran and hid under the rowing benches, getting in the way of the rowers and the soldiers who were preparing to board. In the confusion the sailors had stopped hauling on the sails, and the mainsail began flapping over the deck, hampering the soldiers even more; the rowers slackened their speed, until the prize pulled away and was lost. Because of the "little skill and valor [the men] had shown," the galleys' *auditor* brought a case against all those who had behaved "in a cowardly manner."[21]

Cowardice was one offense associated with insubordination aboard the squadrons; Marchena Giménez adds that a second one was failure to be paid.[22] Since it was a serious charge, *auditores* would choose to bring a lawsuit rather

19 ADM, AH, 256, ramo 2–4.

20 Lomas Cortés and Benítez Sánchez-Blanco, "Seconde Inquisition."

21 AGS, GyM, 812: the Duke of Alburquerque to Philip III, 14 May 1616.

22 Marchena Giménez, "Vida y los hombres," 305–6.

than leave it to the summary punishment that naval custom demanded. Above and beyond questions of ordinary discipline, the greatest danger aboard a galley was mutiny. The risk was easier to control in Christian squadrons, where slaves were kept in separate units and most of the rowers were convicts, but in Ottoman ones, where most of the benches were filled by captive Christians,[23] the rowers formed a tighter and potentially more seditious collective. It would be wrong to assume that convicts were less dangerous because only a few were serving life sentences or because they suffered less than slaves. Although organizing a mutiny was more serious than attempting to desert, convicts did attempt it from time to time. In March 1599, Gian Andrea Doria resisted freeing a French rower, Honoré Vincens, even though the Peace of Vervins required it, because a few months earlier Vincens had tried to rouse the rowers of the flagship to mutiny.[24]

Though we have no details of that incident, we know it was related to an attempted mutiny aboard the galley *Spínola* in early August 1598. The disturbance began at nightfall while the ship was completing a short sail between the arsenal in Genoa and the quay at Pegi. A convict named Claudio, who was in charge of the tavern on board, was selling small amounts of cheese, bread, and pears to rowers who wanted to supplement their rations. It all seemed to start with a joke. During the trip, the stern rowers had proved more vigorous than those in the bow, so the convict Gio Spagnolo, the lead rower on the stern benches, decided to mock his mates who sat forward by throwing the bread he had just bought from Claudio, challenging them "to pick up the bread like [the] starving men" they were. The victims retorted that "the bow rowers had more bread and other things than those in the stern," and, before the *alguacil* could take control, a food fight broke out, Claudio's lean-to was overturned, and the confusion aroused the captain's suspicions, "especially when he saw the rowers happier than usual."

The next morning a soldier named Juan Domingo confirmed those fears. During the melee he had crouched next to a crossbow slit on the port side; he had noticed that while bread flew through the air, a Neapolitan convict named Grattapane, the galley's *corullero* (a favored rower of the *sotacómitre*, of the rowers' boatswain's assistant),[25] had covered himself with a boatcloak and hidden himself. There, he was soon joined by Pietro Catalano, a convict who was a musician, who pretended that he needed to sleep. Domingo, suspecting that the two might be planning to escape, approached their hiding place to

23 Panzac, *Marine*, 34–37.
24 ADP, scaffale 85, busta 18: Gian Andrea Doria to the Duke of Guise, 20 March 1599.
25 Olesa Muñido, *Galera en la navegación*, 1:166.

await developments. He did well, because at around two in the morning the two convicts began to converse. Catalano wanted to know why the "business" had not been done, and Grattapane replied that the captain had had all the weapons carried aft so that no one could get at them. Catalano complained that they might have attempted it in any case by seizing wood from the railings, and that it was a mistake to postpone the operation because they might be discovered. But Grattapane would not be moved: "Without arms nothing good could be done, and ... they had to await a better occasion." His companion finally agreed, after pointing out that they should change their signal: "He did not like to throw bread because it seemed too obvious." Like a good musician, he would have preferred a blast on a horn—then, if things went badly, they could throw it down on deck and in the confusion no one would know who was responsible.

Juan Domingo heard no more of the conversation, but he did not need to. The next morning he told the whole story to his captain and was soon seen leaving the ship in the direction of Doria's palace. The prince did not act at once, however. The reason is not clear, but perhaps he wished to give the tale-teller an alibi—the case should not seem to be brought immediately after Domingo had disembarked. On 13 August, the *auditor* began his questioning, which produced no ready answers. All the convicts whom Domingo had named denied taking part in the fracas, offering an impressive array of alibis. The Sicilian Marco Gionta, probably a benchmate of Grattapane's, said only that he "did not meddle in anyone else's business."

The *auditor* was not convinced. Juan Domingo, after returning from his interview with Prince Doria, had been assailed by questions from Grattapane and other convicts about his absence from the ship. The *cómitre* had apparently told Grattapane that he expected "a great dust-up with his Excellency," which put the whole group on the defensive. Catalano, when questioned, admitted having spoken with Grattapane that night, but only "about the queen's arrival" (the journey of Queen Marguerite was being planned) and whether she would be distributing any largesse. Grattapane confirmed the story and denied having pressured the soldier in any way. On 15 August, the *auditor* declared the interrogations complete and ordered all the accused to be strung up for an hour.

That public spectacle served as an object lesson to everyone on board; being strung up was one of the harshest punishments. A man would be hung by his hands (or other limbs) from the mainmast. The time he spent there varied, as did the severity of the torment. Sometimes he was left simply to bake in the sun, but he might also be hauled up and then dropped suddenly almost to the deck. It is easy to imagine the effect of this practice on the other rowers as they heard the cries and groans of their shipmates and saw how some tried desperately to resist, especially when they were hauled up for the second or third time. That was what happened to Claudio the taverner. Burned all over by the sun, he was cut down in a state of "delirium" to be bathed in water and vinegar. Another, seeing he was about to be hauled up again, pretended to be seized by a fit, but when the ship's barber said that he was only shamming, the punishment was repeated. When Gionta refused to confess, they tried hanging him "by three limbs," then recited a Credo before beginning a new round of haulings. Finally, after four or five days of torture, almost all the men began to confess—except Claudio, who held out. On 19 August, Gionta admitted that the night before the melee Catalano, who was being led unchained from one galley to another, had seized a chance to speak to Grattapane. It seems the latter had talked to the mate in charge of the forward hold, where most of the weapons were kept, and they had agreed that the next time the galley tied up at the quay in Pegi, the men would try to seize them.

To hide the attempt on the weapons, a diversion would have to be created. That would be the role of Claudio, the convict who ran the tavern, together with Spagnolo and another Neapolitan convict named Angelo. The stern oarsman would give the signal by throwing the bread he had bought from Claudio toward Angelo, who would be prepared to respond and encourage his fellow rowers to join in. Finally, Claudio would make sure that every possible projectile was within reach so that in the confusion the arms could be carried out of the bow. There, Grattapane and Catalano would be waiting to receive them and distribute them among the other conspirators, among them Gionta himself. Although the first part of the plan, the food fight, had gone well, they could not seize the weapons, which had unexpectedly been shifted to the stern hold. Later, Catalano was transferred to the royal galley and rumors about the betrayal began to circulate, so no mutiny was attempted again.

After this confession, all the dominoes began to fall. Grattapane finally admitted that before the trip to Pegi he had gone to the rail to relieve himself and had met Catalano there. As Catalano seemed distracted, he had asked what was on his mind, and the musician had replied "that he was thinking about his ill fortune, not able to earn a penny," and was wondering how he could regain his freedom. In this way, "discoursing about their enslavement, they [decided they] would try to raise a mutiny aboard the galley" and realized that they were at a good moment for it, as most of the soldiers were new recruits and, when the galley made its expected traverse from Genoa to Pegi, it would be only lightly guarded. They decided that the next morning they would speak with certain convicts about arousing the rowers, to convince them to take part and wield weapons if they managed to steal them. Catalano, in the trial, accused Grattapane of having been the only instigator and of having involved him only because they were rivals for the same woman. He claimed not even to have been aboard the *Spínola* that day—in fact, other interrogations tried to establish if he had been or not. After several days of torture, he admitted that he knew about the plan and would have participated, but he still refused to say any more or to betray any of his companions.

The squadron's *auditor* passed sentence at the beginning of October. Although the intent to mutiny had been proven, he believed he was faced with "a simple agreement with little basis and not well deliberated." He therefore condemned Spagnolo and Angelo to three additional years in the galleys, while giving life sentences to Grattapane, Catalano, Giova, and Claudio. He still thought that some of them—Grattapane, in particular—deserved to be hanged; in fact, he recommended to Gian Andrea Doria that he "make some kind of strong demonstration of it, by having one of them die as an example to the rest," in the presence of the whole squadron so as to awake "terror in them all." But he preferred that sentence to be handed down in the form of a special agreement, so as to preserve the respect owed to the captain general as head of the squadron's jurisdictional universe.[26]

This measure was normal in the governance of the galleys. Just as in any kingdom of the Hispanic Monarchy during the prolonged absence of the king, squadrons of galleys were used to the fact that their captains general were not aboard continuously, especially while the fleet was in its winter harbor. Therefore, serious problems were held over until the captain general could arrive, just as disputes were not presented to the king until he arrived in a city to convene Cortes. Gian Andrea Doria defined this practice perfectly when he commented on the report that contractors of the Galleys of Naples had sent him in 1587: "They were there continually desiring his very fortunate arrival to present their disputes, and to find relief for many offenses."[27] The practice arose from a wish for justice, which was the principle that the *auditor* upheld in 1598, that it must be clear who dispensed punishment and mercy in the squadron, and to whom its members owed fealty, devotion, and obedience.

This attempted mutiny in 1598 gives rise to other questions, first of all, about the characteristics of the conspirators. A *cómitre* favorite, a taverner, a musician, a mate with access to the hold—almost all of them belonged to the small subset of privileged rowers aboard the galley, the ones who through their service and talents had earned a higher status that removed them from

26 ADP, scaffale 70, busta 25, interno 2.
27 ADP, scaffale 70, busta 25, interno 5.

the benches and gave them a slightly easier life. Those convicts were the elite among the rowers, enjoying greater chances of success and influence over the others. Still, although they were better treated and even befriended by their superiors (the *cómitre* himself had alerted Grattapane that Doria was planning something), they still dreamed of escape and even attempted it. Given their standing among the crew, we may imagine how the other rowers felt when they saw their leaders hauled up on the mainmast and envisioned their own fate if they followed them. We do not know what ultimately happened to Grattapane and the other members of the plot. The trial records contain no reference to the interrogation and sentencing of the mate who would have opened the hold, or of others mentioned during the trial, one Mattuccio and a French convict called Honorato, who was certainly the Honoré Vincens who was not amnestied in 1599 because he had rebelled. Pietro Catalano might have had occasional contact with henchmen in other galleys, and perhaps the mutiny was meant to be wider (Vincens rowed in the flagship), but this is mere speculation.

The attempted mutiny of 1598 reminds us that for the period and the squadrons we are studying, there are no references to participation by slaves. The exception that proves the rule may be found in an appeal to the Council of War in October 1607, when its consultant reviewed a sentence by the *auditor* of the Galleys of Portugal. A renegade Muslim, Diego López, had converted to Catholicism and left North Africa to marry and settle in Lisbon. He had been denounced for receiving into his home "some Moors who had escaped from the galleys," for which the *auditor* had sentenced him to ten years as a rower, five absolutely and five more at the captain general's discretion. The Count of Elda had exempted him from the second period (another instance of how *auditores* respected and deferred to the jurisdictional authority of captains general).[28] We do not know if López was deliberately concealing fugitives in his house or simply welcoming those who disembarked to conduct some business but intended to return. Without further data it is hard to classify the episode, but the *auditor* who sentenced him must have believed in his guilt, suggesting that former Morisco slaves were able to organize and count on some outside help. In the absence of more information, and to gain some notion of attempted mutinies by rowers of Muslim origin, we can turn to cases of Moriscos convicted to serve in the galleys.

The naval campaign of 1602 included Fray Mateo de Aguirre's plan to conquer Algiers[29] and produced two episodes that reveal the presence of Moriscos

28 AGS, GyM, 677, fol. 624.

29 Rodríguez Joulià Saint-Cyr, *Felipe III*.

on board. The viceroy of Majorca had commissioned a galliot from an armer with a corsair's patent; it was meant to serve for four months in the fleet that would attack Algiers.[30] During several layovers between Cartagena and Cádiz, it was reinforced with all the petty officers and rowers it would need and was also boarded by Fray Mateo and two Muslim envoys, Mahamet Benamar and his son Alí.[31] Those two passengers were meant to remain anonymous until the ship reached the North African coast, but that proved unrealistic in the confined space on board. The rowers soon learned of the plans against Algiers and reacted in two different ways. It seems that several convicts demanded payment for their silence, but others wanted to go much further and start a mutiny to keep the galley from reaching its destination; and one of the ringleaders, according to Mateo de Aguirre, was a Morisco. The attempt failed, however, and the Morisco and another convict were soon swinging from the yardarm.[32]

The second incident took place in Denia. The viceroy of Valencia stated that during that same galliot's layover there on 19 July, a soldier was seen to disembark and ask a Morisco for the shortest route to towns where New Christians (i.e., converted Muslims or Moriscos) lived. He did not get very far, however. We know that soldiers often aroused suspicion when they set foot on land, and he must have been under observation by the authorities, since they quickly detained him together with the Morisco he had questioned. The latter lost no time in confessing: the soldier had told him that he too was a Morisco, from Seville, and that the galliot was full of men on their way to conquer Algiers. He wanted to warn his fellows in Valencia that the king was preparing to "remove the Moriscos from this kingdom [of Valencia] to send them to the galleys, and that in Castile the Old Christians were enlisting in an army that would come to this kingdom to slit the throats of any New Christians who remained." The "Morisco" soldier denied it all, claiming to be the son of a Basque and a gunner in the Galleys of Spain.[33] Unfortunately we do not know the end of the story, but these two accounts of conspiracies involving Moriscos in the royal squadrons suggest that they were trying to reveal the purpose of the mission to Algiers or even prevent it. The attempted mutiny in the galliot, and the case of the Morisco "gunner," might have been inspired by fear or some other scruple. The Count of Benavente seemed inclined to set the soldier free, which suggests that he did not take the report very seriously.

30 AGS, Estado, 190: Fernando Zanoguera to Philip III, 19 May 1602.
31 AGS, Estado, 191: 12 June 1602.
32 AGS, Estado, 190: Fernando Zanoguera to Philip III, 2 August 1602.
33 AGS, Estado, 190: the Count of Benavente to Philip III, 3 August 1602.

We should not assume that convicts were invariably seditious or always trying to exploit weaknesses in their officers, as García de Toledo described them in his report to the king. We have already mentioned the conflict that arose in November 1606 when the governor of the castle in Lisbon tried to free two convicts from the galley *Santiago* who had been sentenced after having mutinied aboard a vessel in the fleet. At around noon, shouts were heard from the galley tied up at the pier, alerting soldiers who were playing cards on the pier nearby. Before the true cause was known, many people on shore thought that convicts aboard had started a mutiny. From a distance, it was clear that they had pulled down the awning over the deck and were waving their jackets raised on pieces of railing, shouting "Guards ahoy!" and "Come help the galleys!"

Although a few soldiers were on guard in the galley, many more of them were ashore (as the *auditor* was able to establish), and those were trying to find their way back. But when the first boats reached the galley and reinforcements arrived on deck, they found a strange situation aboard. It was true that some convicts were brandishing pikes, swords, and especially pieces of rail and that they had divided into groups. About twenty soldiers were confronting them with pikes and arquebuses, but they were not guards from the galley, and one convict kept saying, "Gentlemen, we must not rise up against the king!" It was finally understood that several of the viceroy's soldiers had tried to free their two comrades by force but had not removed their chains, so that as they tugged on them, they dragged other convicts along. The *cómitre* had tried to stop them by calling on the stern oarsmen from nearby benches to pull on the chain from the other end. Then, the viceroy's assaulters had injured the mate and an oarsman, provoking the convicts to hurl themselves on some of the soldiers, seize their pikes and swords, and form groups to defend themselves. What people on shore had seen and heard was the prisoners' call for help. In this case, they had armed themselves with wooden railings not to rebel but to protect and defend their shipmates and the whole galley.[34]

Although escapes from the galleys were common, it is significant that mutinies and rebellions aboard the squadrons were rare. One explanation might be the officers' efficiency in guarding the rowers and keeping them divided from each other, the relatively small number of slaves, and the dissuasive effect of public punishments, but other hypotheses are possible. Xavier Gil Puyol, considering the absence of revolts and revolutions in seventeenth-century Castile, suggests that confidence in royal justice and the stability of juridical culture in large swaths of Castilian society served to absorb many types of conflict and

34 AGS, GyM, 662, 1–3.

violence. He also notes the importance of mediation in resolving local disputes and confrontations, and the monarchy's ability to find consensus with local communities.[35] Perhaps those same elements were present in galley squadrons, and the absence of serious mutinies responded to the same conditions as in other territories under the monarchy. In seeking answers, we can now examine how not only justice but also mercy and pardon were meted out aboard the galleys.

2 Internal Justice, Mercy, and Solidarity in the Galleys

In October 1601, after the attempted surprise attack on Algiers ended in disaster, Gian Andrea Doria was stripped of his captaincy general of the sea. As soon as the news was known, most of the crew of the royal galley were seized by uncertainty. The prince had been the ship's almost exclusive patron, and with his departure the future of dozens of aspirants, favorites, sailors, salaried rowers, soldiers, and officers was left hanging—the royal galley would revert to an ordinary one and lose many of its men. Doria, eager to "pay all those who have served in my time," immediately began to negotiate with the court for the back salaries and stipends of the officers, aspirants, guards, and servants, while trying to extract a pledge to relocate them all to other squadrons.[36] He ordered his officers to reassure their men and promised them that, as long as the vessel stayed afloat, they would receive their due, even if it came from his own pocket.[37]

His negotiation did not bear fruit at first, but soon afterward a few officers such as Martín de Quijano began to receive grants in recompense for their services.[38] Although many aspirants and favorites had been paid large salaries that perhaps could not be maintained, in June 1602 Doria extracted a pledge from the Duke of Lerma, through his agent at court, that all those who wished could transfer their assignments to the kingdom of Naples.[39] As for the convicts, he asked for information on those who had completed their sentences or were about to do so, and offered a salary to any who wished to remain in his service as rowers (presumably in the Galleys of Genoa); the rest were transferred to

35 Gil Pujol, "Más sobre revueltas," 374–83, as part of a larger state of the question of rebellions in the seventeenth century.
36 ADP, scaffale 85, busta 22: Gian Andrea Doria to Martín de Quijano, 25 December 1601.
37 ADP, scaffale 85, busta 23: Gian Andrea Doria to Pietro Serra, 5 January 1602.
38 ADP, scaffale 85, busta 23: Gian Andrea Doria to Martín de Quijano, 2 January 1602.
39 ADP, scaffale 85, busta 24: Francisco Tapia to Gian Andrea Doria, 2 June 1602.

the Galleys of Portugal.[40] It is surprising how many salaried rowers the prince had in the royal galley: 143 in 1600 and 1601, according to a contemporary reckoning. Many were, in fact, convicts who had chosen to remain with him after serving their sentences in the preceding years, but there were also sailors and steersmen from many places of origin in Castile, France, and Italy; the prince also owned nineteen slaves who came from Fez, Tétouan, Chercell, Algiers, Bizerte, Djerba, Negroponte, and Istanbul.[41] He brought all of them with him, together with a few crewmen that the monarchy had no desire to transfer. Among them were the German guard of the captaincy general of the Sea, forty soldiers whom he offered to continue employing as his household and personal guards, in spite of the high cost of doing so.[42] He extended the same offer to two slaves, "the best of the royal ship," and two convict musicians—a trumpeter and a virtuoso called Catalano.[43]

The dearming of the royal galley shows the level of commitment that Gian Andrea Doria felt toward his men, from officers to rowers, and the extent of his patronage of them. Such bestowal of favors, and negotiation on the crew's behalf, was key to maintaining discipline as well as the bonds of reciprocity and consensus needed for good governance. Other officers under Doria served as his intermediaries, connecting him to the needs of his men and carrying out his policy of assistance.

2.1 *The Captain General's Mediation and Mercy*

We are now acquainted in general terms with the jurisdictional privileges that galley crews enjoyed when they went on land. These served as a public, external incentive for men to enlist and remain loyal, and were doubtless the most visible form of protection that captains general could offer their people. We have also seen how, in spite of strict rules of discipline, some escape valves were available to crewmen both aboard and ashore—permissiveness in the matter of gambling was one of the most obvious. Likewise, internally, there was a degree of support for rowers, particularly slaves, through their economic and commercial activity on board ship and the possibilities for ransom. We have noted several cases of slaves who either found enough money to ransom themselves or, in the opposite case of extreme poverty, wrote to their captains general seeking help and mediation in gaining their freedom.

---

40 ADP, scaffale 85, busta 23: Gian Andrea Doria to Martín de Quijano, 21 January 1602.

41 AGS, Galeras, 78: "Buenaboyas de la Galera Real."

42 ADP, scaffale 85, busta 23: Gian Andrea Doria to Pietro Serra, 27 December 1601.

43 ADP, scaffale 82, busta 27: Domenico Sevo to Gian Andrea Doria, 13 July 1602.

One of these petitions, penned by the convict Domenico de Vicenti and addressed to Carlo Doria in 1609, offers a glimpse into the phenomenon. Domenico suffered from two conditions common to many convicts. First, although he had finished serving his sentence,[44] he had spent two months in a vain attempt to be freed; second, his poverty prevented him from bringing a formal suit. As a first step, he had "made a plea to his superiors for the freedom he was owed," but they had "replied that he should appeal to your Excellency." We see that galley officers themselves could advise the poorest rowers to seek justice through the captain general's favor, provide them with the means to do so, and convey their requests. De Vicenti not only made this plea but added a second one: "to let [him] be released without paying, since he has nothing to give as the usual 'glove money' to the officials."[45] We remember how Gian Andrea Doria once observed that a rower could be helped if he was in a position to "spend"; obviously, it was hard to find support without funds for suborning the right people (*paraguanti*, or "glove money," being the Italian term for a bribe to a royal minister). Even in these cases, however, one could appeal to the captain general of the squadron over the heads of the officers who controlled the crews' everyday lives. Nicola Garibaldo's trial for smuggling began with an accusation that he abused his slaves,[46] and in 1609 Pedro García, a forger whom we met above, caused severe trouble for the inspector of his squadron when he denounced him for robbery and other illegal actions.[47]

Rowers in possession of funds could use them for ends other than escape. In 1609 Lope de Sancho, Miguel Bellido, and Juan Albariel, Moriscos condemned to the galleys by the Inquisition, spent their money to buy one Muslim slave apiece to row in their stead (a fourth shipmate, Francisco Fernández, had tried to do the same). It seems that "because they were rich they wanted to buy them ... and they were good rowers," so neither the captain general of the Galleys of Catalonia nor the captain of the *San Sebastián* made any objection. The Moriscos had the freedom of the ship "with a single ring around one foot" while they served their sentences, a practice to which the Holy Office in Barcelona had objected.[48] But rowers of any economic status had access to mechanisms for negotiating their complaints and demands, and at least some of them must have trusted in the value of petitions for mercy and justice. That did not entirely exclude other means of procuring their freedom. Pedro García first

44 Martínez Martínez, *Forzados*, 43–45.
45 AGS, Galeras, 215, fol. 291.
46 ADP, scaffale 70, busta 25, interno 17.
47 AGS, GyM, 726: "Don Luis Bravo de Acuña, cavallero ...," 13 June 1609.
48 AHN, Inquisición, libro 741, fols. 334–37.

tried to escape but then offered his services to the king by revealing corruption among officers in his squadron.

Nor was he the only one to take that path, with greater or lesser success. In February 1602 a Morisco convict on the *Santa Bárbara* reported to the inspector Juan Ruiz de Arce that a fellow Morisco, Francisco Pacharo from Chelva, had confessed to him on his deathbed that a revolt was being planned in Valencia: that summer 80,000 men would recover 20,000 arquebuses they had stored in a cave in Chiva, and would start a war. Ruiz de Arce did not give much credit to the tale, but the convict had supplied a list of conspirators that needed investigation;[49] therefore, the accuser was taken from his galley and sent to Valencia, where Archbishop Juan de Ribera was waiting to interrogate him.[50]

Anselmo Dondano, a convict from Savoy who rowed in the Galleys of Genoa, was less fortunate. In March 1604 he confided to his officers that he had found certain papers, which seemed to contain plans for an attack on Genoa by the Duke of Guise. Since Gian Andrea Doria was absent, the captain of the galley alerted Doria's administrator, Pietro Riccardo, who acted as discreetly as his master had done on hearing of the intended mutiny in the *Spínola* in 1598. At midnight, four of the prince's German guards seized Dondano (we see that they were still in Doria's employ two years after the royal galley had been dearmed). To disguise the motive, they took three other convicts as well, and once in the palace they confined each one separately, keeping them awake all night so that Dondano would not be the only one to show signs of interrogation. But the ruse was soon revealed: the prisoner claimed not to know whom the papers belonged to, only that "they had been thrown under his bench." When Gian Andrea Doria learned of the episode, he called the prisoner "a madman or a rogue," concluding that he had written the papers himself; as he later explained to the governor of Milan, Dondano had offered a "service" to the republic that he might later use to request his freedom.[51] It seems that it at least released him from the rowers' bench, because he spent two months in prison before Doria handed him over to the republic, after telling him in person "that if they give him any more [papers] he should report it at once, so we can see who gives them to him."[52]

Prince Doria did not attend to accusations by his convicts only in especially serious cases like this one. As he explained in a letter to the Prince of Avellino

49 AGS, Estado, 189: Juan Ruiz de Arce to the Duke of Medina Sidonia, 21 February 1602.

50 AGS, Estado, 192: the Count of Niebla to Philip III, 13 August 1603. See Catalá Sanz and Urzainqui Sánchez, *Conjura morisca*, 11–42.

51 ADP, scaffale 82, busta 30: Pietro Riccardo to Gian Andrea Doria, 29 March 1604.

52 ADP, scaffale 85, busta 29: Gian Andrea Doria to the Count of Fuentes, 27 May 1604.

in January 1601, he did not normally intervene when a case first arose aboard his galleys but allowed the *auditor* of each squadron to proceed as the law required. If the parties did not agree, however, the case would be passed up to the *auditor general* of the fleet, based with him in Genoa. At that point, by his authority as captain general of the sea, he would review the appeals of cases from all the squadrons.[53] That was the occasion on which the prince might be consulted and informed about requests by his rowers (for ransom, freedom, and so forth) and could use his position as an arbiter to confirm a sentence or grant clemency.

The episode of a convict named Giuseppe Questa will illustrate how Doria might review sentences passed by *auditores*. In 1598 Questa wrote to Doria about his history: A few years earlier, after an attempted escape, he had been forced to pay back a sum of money that the prince himself had given him "as an act of mercy." But since the failed escape had earned him a longer sentence, he was asking the prince at least to return his money, to ease his living conditions a little.[54] What makes the case even more interesting is that at the same time, in a coordinated effort, his brother Lorenzo Questa wrote to the prince asking for his own freedom. He adduced the fourteen years that his brother had served of his sentence, and the fact that his aged mother and his daughter lived in extreme poverty with no means of support. He threw himself on the mercy of the prince, who considered the case but did not grant the request, because there had been no official shortening of the sentence.[55]

Unfortunately, we do not know if Questa regained his confiscated funds, but we can see how with a family member's help he managed to appeal to the prince by two different channels. That suggests that some convicts had at least rudimentary legal knowledge and drew on it in trying to solve their problems peacefully—without abandoning more radical solutions altogether. We have a few examples (though too few to be called a trend) of the sequence "attempt to escape/appeal to the captain general." Perhaps rowers, after serving many years of their sentences, learned to adapt to certain legal forms, with some help and guidance from officers who wanted to minimize escapes and maintain order. That would encourage good habits of mediation in the face of conflict, interpersonal violence, or injustice, in much the same way that officers trained prisoners from the beginning to adapt to the harsh conditions of their service.

We must consider how often these appeals were successful. We have already noted how, faced with a chronic shortage of rowers, officers often forced

53 ADP, scaffale 85, busta 20: Gian Andrea Doria to the prince of Avellino, 16 January 1601.
54 ADP, scaffale 70, busta 24: "Giusepe Questa, figlio di Gio Batista. ..."
55 ADP, scaffale 70, busta 24: "Ricorre a V.E. il padre Lorenzo Questa. ..."

convicts to remain at their benches even after having completed their sentences.[56] But we have paid less attention to cases in which prisoners obtained their freedom before their time was up. We refer here not to exceptions such as ransoms, invalidism, or exchanges for slaves but rather to instances in which a prisoner was freed through the intervention of a tribunal or a private individual.

First we must identify the various tribunals that sentenced convicts to a particular squadron. The Galleys of Genoa, for example, received most of their convicts from the Senate of Milan, but also from different vicaries and the barons of Lombardy, the Lords of Genoa, the Duke of Parma, the Duke of Mantua, the magistrate (*grasciero*) of Piombino, the Lords of Lucca, and in lesser measure the Vicaria of Naples.[57] Prince Doria therefore had to consider petitions for clemency from these tribunals, because to deny them could complicate the future flow of convicts into the squadron.

To assess how often Prince Doria received appeals from these entities we can take the year 1600 as representative. In January, the Marquis of Cusano, a Milanese aristocrat, informed Doria that he had decided to pardon a convict known as "Il Balabene" who had been sentenced to the galleys a few years earlier.[58] In March, Cardinal Madruzzo wrote to him from Rome requesting freedom for Vincenzo, a convict from the flagship, who had served only three years of a ten-year sentence for homicide.[59] In April, the *confaloniere* of Lucca asked him to free Giovanni di Antonio because the man had almost completed his sentence,[60] and in August the Duke of Parma reported that after receiving many appeals to free Anibal Baretta, he had decided to do so and hoped that Doria would expedite the matter.[61]

The most frequent and insistent petitions came from the governor of Milan. In January, he requested freedom for Bartolomé Vergara, a convict in the royal galley, because he had been rowing for many years.[62] A new petition arrived in May, motivated by a conflict with the vicar of the bishop of Tortona: the governor had sent one Alejandro de Inicia to the galleys before the vicar could confirm the order, and to avoid problems he wanted to have him back again.[63] In June, at the request of the Senate of Milan, he interceded on behalf of Mario

56 Heras Santos, *Justicia penal*, 315–16.
57 ADP, scaffale 70, busta 25, interno 12.
58 ADP, scaffale 82, busta 23: Marquis of Cusano to Gian Andrea Doria, 15 January 1600.
59 ADP, scaffale 82, busta 23: Cardinal Madruzzo to Gian Andrea Doria, 25 March 1600.
60 ADP, scaffale 82, busta 23: the *confaloniere* of Lucca to Gian Andrea Doria, 17 April 1600.
61 ADP, scaffale 82, busta 24: Ranuccio Farnese to Gian Andrea Doria, 5 August 1600.
62 ADP, scaffale 82, busta 25: the Constable of Castile to Gian Andrea Doria, 22 January 1600.
63 ADP, scaffale 82, busta 25: the Constable of Castile to Gian Andrea Doria, 10 May 1600.

Guatordio,[64] and in August did the same for Gio Maria Savo. Savo had served only five years of his ten-year sentence, but when the governor had visited Genoa someone (apparently, "a person who could not be denied") had "sought him out urgently," and therefore after a positive vote by the treasury and the Senate, "I have resolved to show him mercy, with the condition that he serve the rest of his time in Flanders in the armies of His Majesty at his own expense, and secure his pledge with the sum of three thousand *scudi* to accomplish it."[65] Finally, in December, he requested "grace and mercy" for Juan Serrano Aguilera, a fourteen-year-old who had been sentenced for homicide.[66]

Gian Andrea Doria granted all nine petitions, but not without complaining to the governor about the number of his requests and especially for having offered him an "equivalent recompense" in the form of new convicts, "which will not be a poor one and will not be long delayed, since we have a large catch" of highway robbers. A prisoner could be exchanged for a slave, but not one prisoner for another.[67] He sent a similar complaint to the confaloniere of Lucca, claiming that the convicts arriving from that jurisdiction were beginning to be "not very useful, because of the many clemencies that are offered to those serving long sentences." But Lucca was not listening and almost immediately sent two more notices, requesting freedom for Vincenzo del Mancino[68] and Gaspar Beretta.[69]

As the confaloniere admitted in a later missive, all those pardons resulted not from close consideration of each case but from the sheer volume of appeals for clemency on behalf of convicts.[70] One such plea was made by the wife of the convict Miguel Morata, a former bandit. In 1607 she spent eight months in Madrid until finally Antonio Aróztegui, secretary to the Council of War, sent a formal notice to the captain general of the Galleys of Portugal asking if her husband could be freed. The wife even obtained a grant of 50 reales from the council to pay for her return home, because she had been through so much "trouble" during that period.[71]

---

64 ADP, scaffale 82, busta 25: the Constable of Castile to Gian Andrea Doria, 17 June 1600.

65 ADP, scaffale 82, busta 25: the Constable of Castile to Gian Andrea Doria, 4 August 1600.

66 ADP, scaffale 82, busta 25: the Constable of Castile to Gian Andrea Doria, 15 December 1600.

67 ADP, scaffale 82, busta 25: the Constable of Castile to Gian Andrea Doria, 10 May 1600.

68 ADP, scaffale 85, busta 20: Gian Andrea Doria to the *confaloniere* of Lucca, 16 February 1601.

69 ADP, scaffale 85, busta 20: Gian Andrea Doria to the *confaloniere* of Lucca, 18 February 1601.

70 ADP, scaffale 82, busta 30: the *confaloniere* of Lucca to Gian Andrea Doria, 5 January 1604.

71 AGS, GyM, 677, fol. 570.

An additional resource was the Council of War and the various territorial councils, which also acted as ultimate courts of appeal. In July 1619 alone, the following petitions passed through the hands of the council's secretary: Ana Hernández, mother of the convict Juan de Figueroa, asked that his sentence be reduced from life to a limited time; he had been rowing for eight years, since the age of thirteen. Juan Cabrera, a convict in the *San Jorge*, had served six years of his eight-year sentence and claimed to be "broken and useless." Nicolás Gentil, a pilot and skilled mariner in the same galley, had been sentenced to three years without position or salary after his ship was lost. Juan Caballero, inspector of the Galleys of Portugal, had been condemned by his captain general to lose his rations and stipend. Captain Domingo de Acosta demanded that the *auditor* of the Galleys of Spain recuse himself from a certain investigation. Antonio Cabia, a reserve *cómitre* in the galley *San Francisco*, demanded his back pay. Sebastián Rico, *cómitre* of the Spanish flagship, had been shot in the arm during a skirmish with a Turkish ship and requested extra funds to support his household. Francisco Maza, captain of the *San Juan Bautista*, sought promotion to sergeant major of the Galleys of Spain. Melchor de Torres, "officer of the court of the *auditor* general of the galleys and the fleet," demanded the salary owed him for having served temporarily as a prosecutor. The paymaster Fernández de Villegas had a long-running dispute with the *Junta de Galeras*, which oversaw the Galleys of Spain, for his management of their budget. Juan de Falces, of the Galleys of Sicily, and Francisco de Vargas both requested a supplement to their pay. Cristóbal Fontanet, a soldier in the Galleys of Catalonia, wanted a promotion to lieutenant. Juan Gómez, a soldier in the Portuguese vice-flagship, sought an increase in the supplement he already had. Two gypsies, Sebastián García and Sebastián Hernández, had been sentenced to row for three years for stealing a pig; they claimed to have been beaten for no reason, and asked to be freed. Juan Griego, captured from an Algerian galliot, thought that he should be released for being a good Christian. The father of the former chaplain of the Galleys of Portugal hoped to collect the back salary of his deceased son in order to pay a granddaughter's dowry. Miguel González, a slave already mentioned, also petitioned. Francisco Antonio de León, a convict in the royal galley, asked to be freed after sixteen years of rowing; his shipmates Claudio de Baudio, Juanelo de Lofredo, and Juan Caballero made the same request. Antonio Lauro, a convict in the Galleys of Genoa, claimed he had been wrongly registered in the squadron's books as a slave. And finally another gypsy, Francisco Palomero, convicted to a life sentence, demanded his freedom after thirty-two years at the oar.[72]

---

72 AGS, GyM, 846.

In the space of only a few weeks the secretariat of the Council of War received twenty-five petitions from crew members of every squadron of the monarchy, from convicts requesting their freedom to naval and military officers appealing their sentences or seeking royal favor toward a promotion, a raise in salary, or other forms of patronage. To these we must add the pleas for clemency that some convicts sent to religious institutions. In April 1600, the Dominicans of the Predicadores convent in Valencia interceded for Juan Terán, convicted to the galleys without pay for having stabbed a man.[73] And in February 1602 the confraternity of Santiago el Menor in Piacenza convinced the Duke of Parma to free Antonio Francesco Riva from the Galleys of Portugal.[74] Other petitions were addressed to the ecclesiastical tribunals that had issued the sentences and even to the Pope.[75]

In short, it is clear that in the galleys of the Hispanic Monarchy a widespread juridical culture drew on every possible avenue for justice and clemency. Petitions were forwarded continually at every level, from each *auditor* court up to the Council of War. And though it might appear that pardons from the latter institution were not easy to obtain—since it was always conscious of needing to keep the rowing benches staffed with experienced men—there was better luck in the territorial, seigneurial, and ecclesiastical tribunals, where the principle of maintaining the squadrons' interests was attenuated or even absent.

Captains general had the option of opposing these pardons, even by seeking the king's backing. The Duke of Tursi attempted it twice in 1620, first when the Senate of Milan requested freedom for the forger Juan Domenico Scio,[76] and again when the Council of Italy asked him to pardon a pimp, Juan Bautista Gabrietti.[77] Both petitions were denied. When central councils of the monarchy ruled against captains general in favor of prisoners, crewmen must have felt renewed faith in royal justice. That fact, together with their captains general's patronage, offered petitioners a broad range of possibilities for channeling their demands and resolving their conflicts, in ways that were legal and guaranteed. It is fair to conclude that the absence of mutinies in the galleys of the Hispanic Monarchy during these years might obey the same motives that avoided rebellions in other territories. To better

73 AGS, GyM, 571, 185.
74 ADP, scaffale 82, busta 27: Ranuccio Farnese to Gian Andrea Doria, 19 February 1602.
75 AGS, Galeras, 230, fol. 346.
76 AGS, Galeras, 230, fol. 364.
77 AGS, Galeras, 8, fol. 5.

understand how peace was maintained in the galleys, we must analyze the role of officialdom in building consensus.

2.2 *Auditores, Inspectors, and Other Officials*

It is not easy to study the daily administration of justice aboard the galleys. Reasons include the summary nature of judgments and the paucity of documentation, which preserves only the most serious cases that carried more weight in the judicial process. We are not certain, therefore, of the extent to which *auditores*' courts were able to manage tensions among the crew. We can examine recorded deposits of *penas de cámara,* fines imposed for especially serious offenses, but just as we have seen with account ledgers, many paymasters were unsystematic in noting down these types of payments. During the period under study, in fact, we have full accounts only for the three years from November 1616 to October 1619.

In addition, the data are sketchy. The largest fine during this time (1,309 reales) was imposed in December 1616 by the Marquis of Santa Cruz on two soldiers, Pedro de Silva of the flagship and Pedro de Rojas of the *San Martín*, for an unreported crime. The next notation, in January 1617, records a death sentence decreed by Emmanuel Filibert of Savoy against Pedro Antolín, a soldier of the royal galley. In July of that year Álvaro Martín, a soldier in the *Toledana*, was made to pay 24 reales to the tribunal for an unnamed offense. In June 1618, Santa Cruz sentenced two soldiers to pay 55 reales. Manuel Alberto, skipper of the *San Jorge*, was fined 200 reales in October, presumably because of the "loss" of his galley mentioned above. And in November four crewmen of the royal galley—the captain Gregorio Buriel, the corporal Juan Leonés, and the soldiers Mateo de Torres and Antonio de Silita—were sentenced to pay 700 reales. The year 1619 brought two sentences. The *alguacil* of the *San Juan*, Pedro Cifuentes, was fined 294 reales, and a convict from the *San Pedro* named Juan, whom a court in Vélez-Málaga had sentenced to pay 176 reales before he was taken on board, was cited because he still owed that sum.[78]

We find, then, that in the space of three years the court of the Galleys of Spain imposed only eight fines, for a total of 2,900 reales. The *auditor* may have handed down more sentences, because we know that in 1619 the pilot of the *San Jorge* appealed his sentence of three years without position or salary (presumably, for the loss of the ship, the same offense for which his captain was fined). Further, the accounts record only payments actually made, so that more people might have been assessed fines but have simply been unable to pay.

78 AGS, CMC, 3ª Época, 3324.

Still, we can form some hypotheses. It is notable that only skippers and soldiers were fined (the exception, for the convict in the *San Pedro*, was imposed at the request of a different tribunal). That fact, and the amounts involved, suggest that at least two fines represented the assessed price of one or more escaped rowers, while others corresponded to graver offenses like murder or damage to royal property. It is also possible that some fines included fees to scribes who penned documents in the appeals. But even then, and assuming there might be other unpaid amounts, this three-year sample suggests that the *auditor* of this squadron only occasionally levied fines on crew members. Again, we find a tendency toward summary justice, expressed especially through an immediate economic penalty.[79] But we cannot rule out the possibility that captains general, who, after all, could appoint and dismiss *auditores*, might have a policy of assisting the accused, benefiting some soldiers and sailors, whose pay was usually scant and often delayed.

The most significant aid that *auditores* could offer the crews, however, even beyond the protection they provided against other jurisdictions, was their testamentary function. As Alessandro Farnese explains in his ordinances of 1587, one of the chief duties of the office was to administer the estates of deceased soldiers. By hearing eyewitness statements from a soldier's shipmates and chaplains, the *auditor* tried to determine the man's last wishes to the extent possible; he also had to inventory his possessions and preserve them until his heirs could claim them, after settling any legitimate debts the man had left behind, if his funds were sufficient.[80]

The *Junta de Galeras* accepted these same rules for the monarchy's squadrons and applied them to all Christian crewmen. Chapter 12 of the conditions for contracting galleys, drawn up in 1601, called for preserving for three years not only the goods a man possessed at his death but also his back pay, while a search was conducted for his heirs. Only if none were found by the end of the period could his possessions be sold at auction, with the stipulation that profits be devoted to ransoming captives.[81] We unfortunately have little information about this practice. Unlike the possessions of slaves, which were usually looted by their ships' officers and rarely auctioned by the paymaster (as we saw in the last chapter), the goods of other rowers, sailors, and soldiers were kept in the custody of the *auditor* or his designated official, and we have been unable to locate the relevant testaments.

79 Martínez Martínez, *Forzados*, 91.
80 Casado Moreno, "Ordenanzas," 449.
81 AGS, GyM, 579, fol. 491.

One will that has survived was dictated by the convict Lelio Merenda aboard the galley *Duquesa*, belonging to the Duke of Tursi, which was quarantined in Palermo's arsenal in April 1624 during an outbreak of plague. The dying prisoner, in the presence of his *cómitre*, the chaplain of the flagship, and one Francisco Brochero, named as his sole heirs Ginés de Torres and his son Pedro—curiously, omitting his wife. He expired "fairly quickly, without having made any other will." Because of the plague in the city, no notary could be found to certify his death, so that later the three witnesses had to retell their story before the *auditor* Antonio Gabriel, *pretoris* of the squadron.

We know of this case thanks to the suspicions of the *auditor*, who initiated a trial in the belief that Lelio had actually not died but escaped and that the witnesses were giving false testimony.[82] It offers us a glimpse into how wills were recorded in the galleys, and how cautious *auditores* were in accepting the deceased's last wishes as genuine. Recording them correctly was supposed to involve the royal scribe from the *auditor* court. The case of Juan Hurtado, captain of a galley in the squadron of Spain, gave rise to a conflict. When he wished to make his will, he feared that "the deposition was invalid because the scribe was not a public and official one," so he consulted a second scribe in El Puerto de Santa María before his death in 1616. When Hurtado's executors tried to have the second will read, the *auditor* refused, because "the testator was captain of a galley and the affairs of a galley's people fall under the jurisdiction of the *auditor*, and as such must be handled by his scribe because they belong to his tribunal and none other"—that was the precedent in other cases. The local corregidor, however, protested that "when the galleys are in this port or in any other where there are public, official scribes, by the laws of the kingdom any wills and contracts made with them by people from the galleys must be considered valid." The galley's scribe "can attest only to the judicial acts that pass before the *auditor* in the course of his trials," with recognized exceptions: "When ... they are at sea, or on some deserted shore, or on the Barbary Coast or in other places where there can be no public scribes." Besides, although Hurtado was a member of the squadron, "on his death he lost the privilege of military law that he had enjoyed." There were apparent precedents, moreover—the cases of the inspector general Alonso de Velasco, who dictated his will in El Puerto, and the purveyor Felipe de Porres, who died intestate and whose inheritance was recorded by a scribe from the same town.

82 AGS, Galeras, 8, fols. 344–46.

Although the *auditor* defended himself with a report we will examine below, in the end the Marquis of Santa Cruz decided to close the matter and defer to the corregidor of El Puerto this time, because the situation had become less clear. It began to be known that several years before, the *auditor* had ordered Captain Juan Ruiz to be violently seized. (He had learned that the captain had dictated his will before a public scribe, and had threatened to demote him to rower if he did not revoke it.)[83] This new dispute with the corregidores of El Puerto shows us another dimension of the jurisdictional conflicts that arose as the authority of *auditores* was still being constructed and its relationship to land-based justice worked out. *Auditores* obviously set great store by their areas of authority; they were one of the special privileges that attracted men to serve in the galleys, and promised some kind of positive and noncoercive relationship between the *auditor* and members of the crew. In the judge's care for the estates of deceased rowers, he and other officers presented themselves to the men as guarantors not only of their basic rights but also of their possessions and last wishes, while those convicts, sailors, and soldiers faced multiple difficulties and had no public scribes to assist them.

We find an enlightening example in a letter that the Duke of Tursi wrote to the inspector Martín de Quijano in April 1603. Shortly before, on his deathbed, Captain Pedro de Eguera had entrusted Quijano with his whole worldly estate (3,000 reales) and made him promise to manage it until his nephew and heir reached adulthood. Quijano had done so for a while, but Tursi, after asking his father, Prince Doria, for permission, had assigned his two administrators in Genoa, Francesco Roberto and Pietro Serra, to take over; that freed the inspector from the task of investing the money until the child was old enough to receive it.[84] The incident illustrates the many-layered nature of this policy of assisting the men—even at the captain general's level there was concern for protecting men who had served in one's squadron. And Roberto and Serra were not just any agents, but the principal managers of the Dorias' fortune. In the face of such favor, officers would feel renewed trust in their captain general protection, thus strengthening the bonds of reciprocity and mutual interest between them, bonds essential to creating the consensus required to govern the "Babylon" that was a squadron of galleys.

Officers of the galleys, freed from responsibilities of this type, could extend some help in turn to other members of the crew. Quijano, the inspector, was

83 AGS, GyM, 858: "Relación del corregidor del Puerto de Santa María."

84 AGS, Galeras, 6, fols. 487–88.

solicitous for maintaining good relations with his captains. In 1603, when Captain Juan de Verio left the squadron as his company was being reorganized in Milan, Quijano asked him to recover some gold buttons, valued at 500 reales, that he had pawned (we do not know if aboard his own ships or in a coastal town).[85] It seems he also helped Captain Ponz, who did not want some soldiers of his company to be taken off the rolls (some were ill in Savona, while others had gone to "confess" in Alessandria), and he sometimes mixed the captain's letters with the squadron's official correspondence so that they would arrive more quickly.[86]

Captains, relieved of some duties by financial officers, could concentrate on maintaining cohesion among their soldiers, as when two of Captain Ponz's men were accused. The scandal broke out aboard his galley in March 1603. It seems that a *buenaboya* named Dominguillo had given two of Ponz's soldiers, Pedro del Castillo and Juan García, 6 libras of smuggled gunpowder to be sold in Elba and Piombino, but the plan had been discovered. The squadron's officers assumed that the men had made other such attempts before, counting on the silence of their shipmates, so they accused they entire crew. The lack of privacy aboard weakened the crew's protests, but Ponz hastened to take their part. He claimed that they slept far from the hold where the powder was stored, and could not have collaborated if the man who guarded the powder had done his job. With this explanation, Ponz appealed to Quijano for help, while making him a significant offer—all the soldiers in the company offered to repay the price of the stolen powder out of their own pockets, so that their companions would not be consigned to the rowers' benches as punishment.[87]

2.3 *Solidarity among Soldiers, Sailors, and Rowers*

Solidarity among shipmates was the norm. When in 1619 Pedro Beltrán, *alguacil* aboard the galley *San Francisco*, was put in irons after two slaves had escaped, he asked Melchor de Borja, captain general of the Galleys of Denia, to let his friends take up a collection to support his appeal to the king. He presented a robust list of the names of his shipmates and the amounts they had pledged. In his own galley eighteen soldiers, fourteen *buenaboyas*, seven sailors, the drummer, the steersman, and the chaplain offered whatever they could, for a total of 733 reales. But contributions came from other ships in the squadron as well. Thirty soldiers from the flagship gave 423 reales, and five men of the vice-flagship also reached into their pockets. Only two sailors from the

85 AGS, Galeras, 6, fols. 478–79.
86 AGS, Galeras, 6, fols. 464–65.
87 AGS, Galeras, 6, fols. 472–73.

Santo Domingo took part, but even so, the end result was significant. Thirty-five men from Beltrán's own galley added to the pot, with contributions ranging from 4 reales from each *buenaboya* to 38 reales from the drummer Juan Bautista. From other ships in the squadron, a total of thirty-seven men, especially soldiers, joined the effort, paying 20 reales apiece. In all, Pedro Beltrán's "friends" in the squadron provided him with 1,560 reales.[88]

This type of collection was common during musters, with the funds devoted most often to care of the sick and injured in the squadron's hospitals. Although patients were most often cared for in a hulk,[89] it was not unusual to rent houses on land for the purpose. In El Puerto de Santa María, for example, the Galleys of Spain paid a token annual rent for houses ceded by the monastery of Santa María de la Victoria. They kept a small staff there, the first physician of the squadron, the hospital's steward, and the senior monk, who received and administered the modest amounts that were assigned. The ledgers for 1603 show that the monk recorded sixteen payments for a total of 3,840 reales, a trivial sum in relation to the squadron's annual budget, and in comparison to other military units.[90] Except for small amounts for maintaining the building (the ceiling was repaired in 1603), most of the money went toward the "care and comfort" of the patients. The cures were supplied principally by an apothecary from El Puerto de Santa María, Francisco Maldonado, who provided medicines in exchange for almost all of the hospital's budget (2,200 reales in 1605, 3,000 in 1606). Any remaining funds bought sugar, almonds, eggs, and chickens (the standard diet for the sick), almost always from Antonio Alfenio. In fact, however, 1,200 reales from the budget for 1603 were spent on rations for soldiers and sailors, recorded separately, so that receipts and expenditures were rarely in balance.

For this reason, charitable donations were essential if the hospital was to function. The monk was in charge of collecting them, and at each pay period he passed the hat among seamen and salaried rowers.[91] His largest windfall usually came in July and added up to several thousand reales (more than 4,400 reales in 1607). In fact, these alms formed such an important component of the annual budget that the hospital often proceeded on advances made by the paymaster against future donations.[92]

---

88 ADM, AH, ramo 2–5, 25 January 1619.
89 Gracia Rivas, "Sanidad," 172.
90 Storrs, "Health, Sickness," 346.
91 Rodrigo Alfonso, "Hospital," 309–10.
92 AGS, CMC, 3ª Época, 397, 1436.

Aside from this collective solidarity, individuals also stepped in to offer aid. When the quartermaster Mateo de León died indebted (in the last chapter we saw that his two female slaves were sold at auction), his friend and guarantor Miguel de Vilar, skipper of a Galley of Spain, was imprisoned. With the Crown demanding a payment of 300 ducados, the brothers Juan and Antón Agustín—pilot and skilled seaman of the flagship, respectively—offered 1,000 reales in cash in exchange for his freedom; the balance of the debt would be deducted from his back pay. It seems that Vilar and the Agustíns were cousins,[93] but guarantors did not have to be family members. After several slaves escaped from a Galley of Denia in October 1619, a *buenaboya* offered himself as guarantor for part of the fine imposed on the three sailors arrested for failing in their guard duty.[94]

How could salaried rowers have enough money to donate to collections and even give financial support to their friends? Boatswains, *cómitres*, were key players here and formed one more link in the long chain of favors that was forged in the galleys. Beside maintaining discipline among the rowers, these officers were intermediaries when others sought workers for "extraordinary" duties. They knew which men were strongest or most trustworthy. Sometimes, they chose slaves to haul water or wood; at other times, they contracted freemen for day labor. In February 1602 Gian Andrea Doria asked the *cómitre* of the royal galley to find *buenaboyas* who might want to leave the galley for at least a month and earn some extra money for "digging my vineyard, for which I will give them my usual sum, but they must pledge to each other not to run away."[95]

Rowers could benefit from friendships not only with their *cómitres* but also with their captains. In October 1600 the *auditor* of the Galleys of Genoa brought suit against Captain Alessandro Mutio and other officers of the vice-flagship *Spínola* for having freed a rower named Saba' without permission. Apparently, he was a poor man who "didn't have a cent," but it was known aboard that "several times Saba' had begged Alessandro to help him." Somehow, his pleas persuaded both Mutio and another "gentleman" of the galley to seek a way to ransom him. Finally, the skipper of a ship from Sestri Levante offered to mediate, with the result that without permission and for an unknown sum Saba' was released in Genoa. For several weeks, he was seen wandering unchained around the city, seeking passage to North Africa, while presumably living at the home of the man who had freed him.[96] Such "galley friendships,"

---

93 AGS, GyM, 677, fol. 680.

94 ADM, AH, ramo 2–5, 22 October 1619.

95 ADP, scaffale 85, busta 23: Gian Andrea Doria to Pietro Serra, 7 February 1602.

96 ADP, scaffale 82, busta 24: Cesare Massa to Gian Andrea Doria, 5 October 1600.

as Doria called them,[97] which could sometimes be close, arose from inevitable contacts aboard ship. Although we have little documentation of relationships between slaves and convicts, we have much more for ties between slaves and officers.

In 1592 Miguel de Zufre had to respond to the findings of the licenciate Alcázar after the Visit of 1591. A chief witness on his behalf was the captured slave Jerónimo Pérez, a mulatto whom the quartermaster had made his assistant; he was found to be living in sin with a woman from Cádiz.[98] In June 1590, when the corregidor of El Puerto de Santa María arrested Romanico, a *cómitre* in the Galleys of Spain, and charged him with sodomy, he found him to be a former slave whose officers had trusted him enough to elevate him from the rowers' benches. The corregidor offered to pay his assessed price of 300 reales if his shipmates would surrender him to be burned at the stake, but it seems that they managed to free him.[99] If a slave could achieve the respected status of *cómitre*, or live as an ordinary citizen of Cádiz while helping officers of the fleet with their affairs, it is unsurprising that some might even be assigned to guard duty at night. In 1600 Cesare Massa complained of that after two prisoners had escaped from the galley *Doria* while only one sailor was on guard: "It is of little benefit to assign slaves, because they do not apply … care and diligence."[100] In the same year, the Count of Santa Gadea noted in a letter that when galleys of the Marquis of Santa Cruz were sent to Lisbon, men were so few that "they divert slaves to guard duty."[101] Perhaps the most picturesque example of the trust placed in slaves took place in 1604. While Philip III was holding Cortes in Valencia, the Duke of Lerma "conspired with Don Carlo [Doria, the Duke of Tursi] to play a joke on the court that accompanied His Majesty. They decided to send a frigate loaded with sailors and slaves, all dressed as Moors, to disembark near Oliva and frighten all the wagons and servants who were marching toward Denia, and so put the whole Court to flight."[102]

If slaves could attain unheard-of positions of trust aboard, that was even more true of convicts, who sometimes enjoyed the same type of "social" promotion. In January 1599 Diego Sánchez de Marchena, after twenty-four years of service, asked the purser Martín de Durango for his freedom. He actually

97 ADP, scaffale 85, busta 23: Gian Andrea Doria to Diego Pimentel, 10 November 1602.
98 AHN, Consejos, 4041.
99 ADM, Puerto de Santa María, 7, pieza 60.
100 ADP, scaffale 82, busta 24: Cesare Massa to Gian Andrea Doria, 10 December 1600.
101 AGS, GyM, 567, 163.
102 ADP, scaffale 82, busta 30: Gio Antonio Marini to Gian Andrea Doria, 24 January 1604; Cabrera de Cordoba, *Relaciones*, 207.

did not wish to leave the galleys, where he had served as executioner, but after demonstrating for years that he was "good at his job," he hoped to earn a salary as a freeman and support his children. In 1600 the Council of War granted his request and gave him 50 escudos,[103] proving that in the galleys a man could begin as a rower but could, over time and by gaining his officers' trust, forge a career in service to the monarchy.

A striking story is that of Rodrigo Moreno. In February and March 1607 he came to court to present documents to Aróztegui, the secretary, hoping to have them considered by the council. The first one was drawn up on behalf of all the convicts in the Galleys of Spain who had been sentenced to life or to several decades as rowers; they pleaded for their freedom on several grounds, but especially illness and old age.[104] The second petition came from Gonzalo Solís, a former lieutenant and veteran of Flanders who had been rowing for nine years. With only one year left of his sentence, he asked to be freed because he was poor, wounded in the arms and legs, and above all dishonored by having ended in the galleys after more than twenty years' service in army regiments and the *Casa de la Contratación* (which administered trade with the Indies).[105] But the most revealing petition of all those that Moreno presented to Aróztegui was his own. This "representative" of the convicts had once been a convict himself. It seems that after his four-year sentence in the Galleys of Spain he had accepted an offer to continue as a salaried rower, spending fifteen years in that capacity. When his grateful officers proposed making him a soldier, he then served three years in the ranks. But during his slow, difficult ascent, Moreno had never forgotten where he came from, and he helped other convicts whenever he could. This was his third approach to the court with appeals from his former shipmates and himself. Moreno had "given his youth" to service in the galleys and, like Diego Sánchez, did not wish to leave them, but he had not yet received his soldier's pay and was still owed many years of rations as a *buenaboya*. Nonetheless, the council did not offer him any redress.[106]

Loyal service could also lead a man to freedom fairly swiftly, though not without risk. When Lieutenant Solís submitted his petition to Moreno for the Council of War, he mentioned one of the most interesting periods of his irregular life, his second stretch as a rower. Years before, while rowing in the galleys of Federico Spínola, he had been unchained and armed so that he could fight in an engagement in the English Channel. Apparently, he had been captured

103 AGS, GyM, 577, 10–11.
104 AGS, GyM, 677, fol. 36.
105 AGS, GyM, 677, fol. 124.
106 AGS, GyM, 677, fol. 61.

by the Dutch, and had managed to escape and return to Castile, but once there had violated the terms of his banishment, which earned him a new sentence to the galleys.[107] Such cases were more frequent than one would suppose; captain's general often promised liberty to rowers who showed genuine courage in combat. Luis de Torres, a convict serving a life sentence in the Galleys of Portugal, earned his pardon in that way. During an engagement in the Algarve, he was unchained and allowed to arm, then leapt onto the enemy vessel, receiving several wounds. On that basis, and after thirteen years of rowing, he was freed "so that others may be inspired on similar occasions," though he was banned from returning to Antequera, where he had committed his crimes.[108]

In the armies of the Hispanic Monarchy, professionalization of command structures supported the troops and added to their effectiveness in combat. The entire edifice rested on loyalty, which was created, preserved, and enhanced through rewards. According to Davide Maffi, in practice this meant that captains general based their authority in large measure on distributing favors and honors; these descended from the top of the pyramid to its base and, though usually small, could increase over time through promotions and other means. The ultimate goal was to renew continually the fealty of each fighting man toward his commander.[109]

Galley squadrons reproduced this system while adapting its benefits to the greater legal, social, and professional diversity of those who manned the ships, especially rowers. Rowers could not expect financial aid or a pension; nor could they, as officers often did, appropriate the salary of a nonexistent seaman. But they could hope for lighter duties, a ransom, a review of their sentences, or even a pardon. Men could be promoted from salaried rowers or *cómitres* to soldiers or pilots, depending on their skills. Though the galleys seemed divided into strict hierarchies of convicts, sailors, and officers, all more or less privileged, integrated, or marginalized, in fact each sector held the possibility of change (through service, money, or influence of friends), irrespective of a man's original position.

The galleys also reflected the structure and organization of Mediterranean societies on land, extending them but adapting them to their special circumstances. The reduced space on board made everyone share the same discomforts and eliminated the limits and barriers that existed elsewhere, making it possible to form relationships that would have been unheard of ashore.[110] For example, a Flemish convict rowing in the Galleys of Genoa in 1599 was able to

107 AGS, GyM, 677, fol. 124.
108 AGS, GyM, 677, fol. 393.
109 Maffi, *Baluardo*, 191, and *En defensa del Imperio*, 322–23.
110 Judde de Larivière, *Naviguer*, 47.

speak in person with Nicholas Damant, chancellor of Brabant and president of the Council of Flanders, during the voyage that brought Queen Marguerite to Valencia; Damant later asked Gian Andrea Doria to grant the man's freedom.[111] Galleys were among the few spaces that reflected the cultural and religious diversity of the Mediterranean, especially through their large complement of slaves. We wonder whether captains general used this circumstance as one more mechanism for protection, patronage, and the creation of loyalty.

3 Religious Belief

On August 14, 1600, captain general García de Toledo sailed out along the Calabrian coast with six galleys. He had received several reports about the presence of three galliots from Bizerte, and since his flotilla had left on Assumption Eve, he expected the Virgin's help in capturing the enemy. His prayers were answered. At dawn on August 15, they spotted the Tunisian ships, which immediately took flight. Toledo, with his fellow captains, decided which galliot was the leader, and each skipper set off in pursuit of his assigned prey. The chase stretched into several hours, as often happened, and García de Toledo could not overtake his galliot until nightfall, when he faced an unexpectedly fierce adversary. The Tunisians' fire was so intense that it killed nine soldiers and sailors and wounded another thirty-two, but worst of all, three rowers were among the dead. Those losses produced such disorder in the benches that the galley lost speed, resulting in the Tunisians' escape.

Fortunately, two of the Neapolitan galleys had captured an enemy ship, which turned out to be the leader, seizing about one hundred slaves and freeing many captive Christians from their chains.[112] García de Toledo, his pride wounded, tried to repair his reputation and justify his actions. He set the Christian captives free with great pomp in a public ceremony in Messina. Meanwhile, the other two captains, "men very close to him," fought to be recognized as the first to overhaul the prize,[113] a condition for being awarded the "jewel," one's first pick of the captured slaves. Captain Pedro de Chaves insisted that he had been the first to touch the galliot's stern, destabilizing it enough to allow him to fire his guns and begin boarding; he himself had planted on the enemy deck a flag with an image of the Virgin, to whom he attributed his victory.[114] His

111 ADP, scaffale 82, busta 21: Nicholas Damant to Gian Andrea Doria, 20 May 1599.
112 ADP, scaffale 82, busta 24: García de Toledo to Gian Andrea Doria, 16 August 1600.
113 ADP, scaffale 82, busta 24: Captain Bermúdez to Gian Andrea Doria, 18 August 1600.
114 ADP, scaffale 82, busta 24: Captain Chaves to Gian Andrea Doria, 18 August 1600.

rival, Captain Bermúdez, could do little to counter that dramatic symbolism but insisted that his own galley, outstripping the others, had been the first to touch the enemy stern and draw level with the galliot's starboard side while letting off a volley of arquebus fire. That action had slowed the ship's way and allowed his colleague, who came from behind, to attack and board her.[115]

3.1 *Catholic Belief*

The tale of how the flagship from Bizerte was captured gives us some insight into how religious belief was lived and expressed aboard the galleys. First, we must stress the importance of worship of the Virgin Mary, which operated on two levels. When Pedro de Chaves raised his galley's Marian flag to mark his victory, we glimpse how that image could be employed for political and personal ends. In Chapter 1 we described how the people of Naples reacted in October 1618 when the Duke of Osuna raised the Virgin's standards over the ships in his fleet. He intended his order to manifest the oath he had taken "as to the article of the Conception of the Virgin ... showing myself truly and specially devoted to her."[116] He thus presented himself publicly as a defender of the faith that was growing in weight and influence in Spanish politics, while at the same time he offended Neapolitan religious groups headed by Cardinal Caraffa. Those men were scandalized at how the crewmen of the fleet were obliged to swear an oath to the Virgin of the Immaculate Conception, while the black flags that flew from their masts bore both the image of Mary and the arms of the House of Girón.[117]

Osuna achieved the dual goal of renewing his ties to the discourse and political program of the monarchy (in fact, his family had made that pledge long before) and of consolidating his position vis-à-vis his rivals. This was not the only time he had used his leadership of the fleet toward those ends. Only a few months earlier, in August, he had attracted notice by delaying his ships' sailing until after the feast of the Blessed Ignatius of Loyola and donating a silver lamp in person to the Company of Jesus.[118]

While Pedro de Chaves's objectives in 1600 were more modest, they were not so different from Osuna's. Although we know nothing of Chaves's early years, he appears in May 1599 in Barcelona petitioning the Count of Lemos, just named viceroy of Naples, for the command of a new galley—his current one, the *San Felipe*, was old and almost useless. Further, he was competing in

115 ADP, scaffale 82, busta 24: Captain Bermúdez to Gian Andrea Doria, 18 August 1600.

116 ASV, Segretaria di Stato, Avvisi, 8, fols. 450r–451v.

117 Linde, *Don Pedro Girón*, 308–10. See Le Flem, "Arithmétique navale."

118 ASV, Segretaria di Stato, Avvisi, fols. 58r–65r.

this request with another captain, a "young man" like himself, named Bermúdez. That presented a problem. Chaves had just arrived from Cartagena with his wife and children after having sold "everything he owned," so he needed the viceroy's patronage not only to advance in the service but also to establish a new social position for his family in Italy.[119] Luckily, Lemos decided to favor the two captains equally (after all, his own situation was not so different), and he gave each of them command of a new galley.[120] Against this background, it is easy to understand why, only a year later, these two captains showed such zeal in capturing a prize, probably the first one that presented itself since they had been favored by Lemos. Both men needed to prove their worth and position within the squadron, so Chaves did not hesitate to use every means at his command to outshine his rival. In linking his victory to the Virgin, he was aware of the influence of such a gesture; his own captains general had used the same resource in constructing their discourse and justifying their actions.

Chaves did not triumph, alas. After an inspection of the spur at each galley's prow, it was determined that Bermúdez's account was the more plausible one.[121] But the squadron's captain general had used the same stratagem—the Virgin's protection—when his ships sailed out just before Assumption Day. The gesture was connected not only to political and symbolic goals but also to sailors' unceasing search for mediation and protection in the face of all the uncertainties and misfortunes of life at sea.[122]

Not by chance was the brotherhood of Our Lady of Miracles in El Puerto de Santa María made up of soldiers, sailors, aspiring officers, and captains of the Galleys of Spain. In southern Andalusia a devotion to that Virgin was linked to the discovery and evangelizing of America, highlighting the importance of sailing and sailors in the propagation of the faith. Her feast day in August was an occasion for crewmen to seek her succor with greater fervor during the season of campaigns. In 1615 they reached into their pay to donate a silver lamp costing almost 10,000 reales to her shrine,[123] and early in the century they spent hundreds of reales in pledges to her. These sums were distributed to several foundations. The monastery of San Francisco received similar amounts—1,500 reales in 1605, in two payments on August 11 and 29, perhaps corresponding to the departure and return of an expedition to Oran.[124] The principal beneficiary

119 Varachaud, Franceschi, and Zysberg, "Qui étaient les capitaines?"; Cabanous, *Mer*, 57–60.

120 ADP, scaffale 82, busta 21: the Count of Lemos to Gian Andrea Doria, 15 May 1599. See Favarò, *Gobernar*, 77–82; Enciso Alonso-Muñumer, *Nobleza, poder y mecenazgo*, 222–23.

121 ADP, scaffale 82, busta 24: Gian Andrea Doria to García de Toledo, 18 August 1600.

122 Civale, *Guerrieri*, 118–27.

123 AGS, GyM, 846: "La cofradía de Nuestra Senora de los Milagros ...," 19 July 1619.

124 AGS, CMC, 3ª Época, 1436.

was the brotherhood of Our Lady of Charity and Piety—formed by the squadron itself in 1576[125]—which in 1614 alone took in more than 7,000 reales from alms collected among the crews. In those same years, there were smaller donations to the sacristan of Our Lady of Mercy in Barcelona and the monastery of San Diego in Cartagena.[126] Clearly, many men in the squadron were actively seeking consolation and spiritual protection through donations and endowments, although the recipients rarely received the full amounts pledged.

The galleys' brotherhood could probably count on a fairly stable income; we can trace through its account books how captains made substantial loans to help individual crewmen, charging them to the brotherhood's funds. But many sailors' endowments and donations were hard to deposit. In 1607 the friars of the San Francisco monastery sued the financial officers because, over the years, galley crewmen who confessed and received the sacraments with them had run up a debt of almost 9,000 reales. The friars asked that such alms not be debited to the mens' pay but be drawn on profits from *mazamorra*, the sale of superannuated slaves, or prize money, sources that, as we know, were problematic in themselves.[127]

The men's wives also took part. On days like August 5, the Feast of the Virgin of the Snows (patroness of marital devotion), they gathered to pray "to God for the ministers of the Catholic King" and for their husbands, as the Marchioness of Santa Cruz and her ladies did during the Relief of Genoa in 1625.[128] There were also moments when naval battles took place near the coast and people gathered to watch and pray. In 1618, during a battle "so fierce that it frightened many people who were watching from the Rock of Gibraltar ... the Holy Sacrament was displayed in all the churches" of the city "while prayers were said."[129]

The Marian calendar also reinforced this mediation, as the most auspicious dates for sailing and combat were chosen from it. We have already seen how García de Toledo did so in 1600. It is surely no coincidence[130] that all the captains general who facilitated the expulsion of the Moriscos from the kingdom of Valencia in 1609 began their embarkations on the eve and feast day of the Virgin of the Rosary, patroness of the Christian victory at Lepanto.[131] The Marquis of Villafranca acknowledged in 1611 that the fleet sailing to occupy Larache

125 Marchena Giménez, "Vida y los hombres," 418–20.
126 AGS, CMC, 3ª Época, 1454.
127 AGS, GyM, 677, fol. 674.
128 ASV, Segretaria di Stato, Avvisi, 11, fols. 227r–231v.
129 ASV, Segretaria di Stato, Spagna, 60E, fols. 218–20.
130 Lomas Cortés, *Proceso de expulsión*, 100–24.
131 Rivero Rodríguez, *Batalla de Lepanto*.

the previous year had waited until November 20, the Feast of the Presentation of the Virgin, to ensure a "good outcome" for the expedition, and that as a result "Our Lady, on the eve of her feast day, granted him that fortune."[132] Prayers uttered aboard the galleys had also begged for divine intervention. To ensure that "God would direct [the taking of Larache] as His own cause, so that His holy name may be praised there," Villafranca asked the chief purveyor, as an exceptional favor, to loan him the utensils for mass that had been in storage since the royal galley was disarmed in 1601. Those fifteen pieces (which included a cross "with its crucified Christ and Calvary and two images on the sides, all of silver," a box for the sacred implements, chalice, paten, oil vessels, and bell of the same metal, a missal, and several lengths of velvet and linen for the altar and the chaplain's robes)[133] would connect the crew spiritually with the just cause in which they were engaged. Each galley also contained its own holy objects, received on the day of its launching.

In his gloss on a narrative by Pere Joan Comes, Capmany i Monpalau explains how in Barcelona each galley, after being baptized with the name of a patron saint and blessed, would perform the ritual of "saying the good word," an auspicious prediction. At the launching of the *Santa María* in 1424 a sailor had cried, "May God preserve her to fight the Turks and the French!," to which all those present had responded, "Let it be so!"[134] Later on, captains general could change a ship's dedicatee. Juan Riambau, quartermaster of the Barcelona shipyards, explained in 1599 that of recently launched galleys the *San Pablo* had become the *Esperanza*, the *Santiago* was renamed the *Bazana*, the *San Telmo* was now the *Fama*, the *San Francisco* the *Fortaleza*, the *San Pedro* the *Quimera*, the *Santísima Trinidad* the *Ocasión*, the *San Juan* the *Ventura*, the *San Andrés* the *Victoria*, and so on. Sometimes the change was meant to exalt the family of the armer, but new names most often referred to the cardinal or theological virtues, alluded to a successful mission, or announced a victory (or the hope of one). Works of humanism or Antiquity underlay this symbolic structure, in which the monarchy also participated. Riambau notes that the king had ordered every galley to bear on its stern a carved "wooden escutcheon with the name of Jesus at the center."[135]

If to all this we add the blessings and pious donations that the armadas received, we see that religious expressions, for various reasons, played a significant role in organizing campaigns and the ways in which sailors faced them

132 AGS, GyM, 742: the Marquis of Villafranca to Juan de Ciriza, 20 November 1610.
133 AGS, GyM, 741: Miguel de Oviedo to Philip III, 7 October 1610.
134 Capmany i Monpalau, *Memorias históricas*, 1:48–50.
135 AGS, CMC, 2ª Época, 816. Édouard, "*Argo*."

or justified them after the fact. But we should not confuse the special circumstances of such events with the everyday spiritual climate aboard the galleys or in port. As the friars of the monastery of La Encarnación in El Puerto de Santa María knew all too well, very little charity was forthcoming from officers or crew. In the whole period under study, they were paid only for a few masses in memory of the quartermaster Mateo de León.[136]

3.2 *Vice among the Crews*

The friars' quarrels with soldiers and sailors of the squadron went back to the earliest years of their presence in the town. In January 1574, not long after Augustinian friars had founded La Encarnación, they complained of their precarious situation to the Duke of Medinaceli. Shortly before, the duke had given them an old abandoned convent in the center of town; it was meant as the site for a new congregation that would elevate the lamentable spiritual life of residents along the river where the Galleys of Spain dropped anchor. But crewmen had not been received there with open arms. Homeowners in nearby streets complained to the corregidor that the presence of the new institution had the friars "lording it over" them, their wives, and their daughters. The squadron's people joined the outcry, claiming that the abandoned building had been used as a hospital for ailing seamen, a function that the monastery had abolished. But the friars told another tale of what had gone on inside the building, stating that the "hospital" was no more than an improvised brothel: "We will not refrain from telling how this church and house had been profaned and what abominations were committed here … as is well known to all." The trade had been so attractive that owners of many houses rented them out "for twice their worth to the bad women and prostitutes who come when the galleys are in port, and because [their houses] are close to them people give more than they should, and they know that since there are men of religion here they should not accept such people."[137]

The problem was not easy to solve. In November 1619 the governor of El Puerto, in one more attempt to quell the defiance and licentiousness of soldiers from the galleys, followed one of them at night: "While visiting certain houses he entered that of a public woman, and as he was lying with her the governor visited that house as that of a bad woman, and he found the soldier in bed with her." The governor declared that "it was up to him to punish public disorder and sin," and when the soldier went for his sword the official "seized

136 AGS, CMC, 1ª Época, 1927.

137 ADM, Puerto de Santa María, 6, pieza 38.

him by the neck" and managed to take him to prison. But the next day several other soldiers went in search of the governor, "telling him that he was a swine and that if he interfered with the soldiers they would cut off his nose and ears." Threatened with being denounced to the city council, they retorted, "The council is garbage."

The episode proved once again that "the soldiers live impure lives, with great risk that there will be serious disturbances when their leaders cover and protect them; and because of their bad behavior the town is ruined and some residents are trying to leave it."[138] But prostitution, like gambling, was an evil tolerated for the sake of the greater good (maintaining group cohesion and, to the extent possible, avoiding other threats to crew members' discipline and behavior). A report presented to Pius V in 1571 named prostitution as the greatest problem on board ship, because of its inherent scandalousness but, above all, because of two other issues derived from it. Since space was so limited on board, there was room for few loose women and "not all [the men] could have them," causing them to quarrel with each other; even worse, some in their frustration would "commit other abominable sins" that made "men too effeminate to fight."[139] We know that this crime almost led a *cómire* to the stake in El Puerto in 1590. Gianclaudio Civale has studied the issue.[140]

Two further problems were associated with crewmen's deprivation (the "bad humors" they suffered) during long sea voyages. Gian Andrea Doria spoke of the first to several confidants in 1601: "When women become pregnant (perhaps the air of this place favors it) and their husbands are a long time at sea, when on their return they sleep with them [the women] miscarry; it happens to them all and it has happened to me. ... We all told Don Carlos [Doria, the Duke of Tursi] that it would happen if he slept with his wife, but being young and in love he paid no attention,"[141] and wishing "to sleep or spend the night with his wife while she was five months pregnant,"[142] he paid her "so many favors" that he provoked an abortion.[143] The second issue was jealousy. Pedro de Leiva, admiral of the Galleys of Sicily, claimed in 1598 that he had to make frequent stops at his crewmen's home ports because otherwise "there is no doubt that most of these people would desert me rather than lose either their wives or their daughters"[144]—a situation that could lead to outbursts of violence, like

138 AGS, GyM, 858: "Sumario de lo que contiene la ynformaçión ynclusa fecha en el Puerto."
139 ASV, Miscelania Armadi, 2:116, fols. 139–41.
140 Civale, *Guerrieri*, 111–14.
141 ADP, scaffale 85, busta 22: Gian Andrea Doria to Jusepe de Acuña, 20 October 1601.
142 ADP, scaffale 85, busta 22: Gian Andrea Doria to Baltasar de Zúñiga, 5 October 1601.
143 ADP, scaffale 85, busta 22: Gian Andrea Doria to Diego Pimentel, 5 October 1601.
144 ADP, scaffale 70, busta 24: Pedro de Leiva to the Duke of Maqueda, 20 October 1598.

the one committed by Giovanni de Luca that we saw in Chapter 1. Permissiveness toward prostitution, then, could help to avoid certain problems on board, but it could also encourage them. We recall how in 1598 the musician Catalano attributed Grattapane's betrayal of him to a dispute over a woman; since convicts could rarely leave the ship, she must have boarded for one reason only.

Chaplains were not very effective in controlling these vices. In theory their job was to help tend the sick, administer the sacraments on board, and teach the soldiers good Christian habits—one more way of attaining victory.[145] But another duty was to act as a sort of sheriff to enforce "spiritual" punishments for the convicts. The one meted out to Antonio Boni serves as a perfect example. This twenty-two-year-old convict had been sentenced by the diocese of Savona to five years in the galleys for having practiced "many magical and superstitious experiments … to gain the love of women … and men respectively, and for having used … intestines of animals … with a certain powder, and with ample abuse of the holy mass, invocations of demons … and divers diabolical and dangerous superstitions … teaching them to other people and exhorting them to learn them." Under interrogation, he had even claimed that no harm could come to him "because God was his cousin and the Devil his grandfather." In the galleys, he had to receive "the crown of the Most Blessed Virgin Mary" every week, was put on bread and water on Fridays, and was obliged to confess at least on Christmas, Easter, Pentecost, and All Saints' Day.[146]

But as an accusation against the chief purveyor Miguel de Oviedo revealed in 1611, chaplains were far from modeling good Christian behavior for their crews. They were neither visiting sick convicts nor hearing deathbed confessions nor administering the sacraments. The problem was most acute during sea voyages, because many chaplains simply failed to report for duty when the galleys were leaving port. The senior chaplain of the Galleys of Spain, Hernando de Chaves, had called them to account many times; finally, in early 1611, exasperated with the situation, he had threatened excommunication for all those who did not fulfill their responsibilities, which included making daily visits to rowers to monitor the health of their souls and reciting the Hail Mary with them both in port and at sea.

It seems, however, that those efforts originated not with the senior chaplain but with an order from the Marquis of Villafranca to expel Diego de Cáceres from his chaplaincy. There were two grounds: Cáceres had not tried to save the souls of the seamen in his charge, and he had behaved improperly during the

145 Lavenia, *Catecismo*, 25–26.

146 AGS, Galeras, fol. 360.

occupation of Larache a few months before. During that expedition, a man had died, Francisco Jordán, "a cooper from the galley *San Pedro*, a young man who had no home or residence but usually worked in the galleys." It seems that at death's door he had willed a sum of money meant for fifty masses for souls in Purgatory, but without specifying "where they should be said." Cáceres, who was present, decided to share out the bequest among the squadron's chaplains, "because they are poor and because it belonged to them, since as has been said he [Jordán] died in … the land of Barbary." Villafranca viewed this as theft, especially since the chaplains were not doing their jobs. Hernando de Chaves, in defense of his chaplain, maintained that Villafranca simply wanted to benefit the main church of El Puerto de Santa María, and in revenge had not only eliminated Cáceres's position but had written to the collector of the archbishopric of Seville asking him to accept the bequest.

Chaves accused Villafranca of trying to provoke a jurisdictional conflict between Seville and the chaplaincy of the squadron.[147] But it is curious that the captain general should try to excommunicate chaplains who did not attend to their duties. Behind that façade, the real clash of wills was that between the respective jurisdictions of the captain general and the senior chaplain, both trying to control a crucial aspect of the policy that supported men in the galleys. (We recall how in 1625 a suit against the chaplain of the Galleys of Sicily also involved possible fraud in certifying the death and testament of a convict.) In the last instance, it was a question of chaplains' loyalty. Captains general could react forcefully to anyone who challenged them. Villafranca sent several soldiers to break into Hernando de Chaves's house and rouse him from bed, and would have put him in prison but for the mediation of Martín de Quijano. Shortly afterward the Marquis wrote to the Council of War claiming that since Chaves did not go aboard any galleys himself, he was no witness to his chaplains' performance or lack of it, that the galleys needed someone more learned who would attend to the matters that daily "come up … with these wicked people," and that it would be best to pension off this "broken-down, decrepit" priest and have him leave the squadron. He intended to name a new chaplain whom he could trust.[148]

3.3 *Captains General and the Inquisition*

Control of the office of senior chaplain was crucial because, at least during Hernando de Chaves's time, that priest also served as the Inquisition's commissioner aboard the galleys and in El Puerto de Santa María.[149] It is significant

147 AGS, GyM: Miguel de Oviedo to Philip III.
148 AGS, GyM, 759: the Marquis of Villafranca to the Council of War, 18 November 1611.
149 AHN, Inquisición, libro 585, fol. 403r.

that an official "in the galleys of His Majesty acts as the commissioner of the Holy Office," because those agents served as delegates in the Inquisitors' districts, reinforcing the notion of squadrons as territorial entities. Commissioners received accusations and took witnesses' testimony;[150] we know from the instructions to Andrés de Alva, who held that post in the galleys in 1573, that he performed those functions, with one specification. The commissioner should attend to those "who sail in them [and] accuse others in the same galleys of blasphemy"; he should hear their cases but then inform the Inquisition tribunal in the port where the galleys were anchored. Therefore, those cases could fall under more than one tribunal. The Galleys of Spain, for instance, normally used the Castilian tribunals of Murcia and Seville. That was where testimonies would be corroborated and trials continued, following two principles. If, when the report, was received, the post of inquisitor of the sea was occupied, as happened in 1573, the tribunal had to respect his jurisdiction and ask permission to ratify testimonies from crew members. If the sin was not a grave one (for example, in a case of blasphemy), it should impose only "spiritual penances such as the fasts, pilgrimages, and prayers that you think fit, without arresting them, warning them that from now on they should abstain from saying such words, and with this you will order them to return to the galleys."[151]

This passage refers to one of the commonest sins committed by Christian rowers aboard the galleys. Blasphemy or a mere accusation of it, like an accusation of conspiring to mutiny, could lead to the Inquisition's removing a convict from his bench and (if the victim were lucky) imposing a sentence to be served on land. Luis del Valle, a convict rowing on the *Leiva*, tried to bring this about when he was accused of blasphemy and reconciled by the Inquisition in Murcia in 1575.[152] Not content with that, he repeated his behavior in 1576, when he appeared before the Seville tribunal.[153] One year later, his blasphemies were again noted in Murcia, but the Supreme Council finally ruled that "from now on you will pay no attention to what he says and writes, and will tell the captains that whenever he blasphemes and speaks about religious matters he should be severely flogged."[154] That was not the only such warning in 1577. In December, all the tribunals were advised that the convict Juan de Alvarado, "who has done penance in other inquisitions," tried to "exempt himself from work, and to avoid his [duties] had the idea of speaking great heresies and ...

150 Bethencourt, *Inquisición*, 81.
151 AHN, Inquisición, libro 578, fol. 157r.
152 AHN, Inquisición, libro 578, fol. 343r.
153 AHN, Inquisición, libro 579, fol. 18r.
154 AHN, Inquisición, libro 579, fol. 119r.

most bold blasphemies before the Inquisitions of Seville, Granada, and Murcia," so that in the future "you must pay no attention to anything this man says to you ... he must serve in the galleys without ever leaving them, and you must warn the captains that when he speaks any heresy or blasphemy he must be severely flogged."[155] These stern words do not seem to have done much good because Alvarado continued to deploy his strategy, resulting in a new appeal to the Holy Office in Seville in 1578.[156]

Aside from these isolated cases, captains general most often informed the Inquisition when they had captured renegade Christians at sea. It seems that some of those men were able to leave the galleys after abjuring *de vehementi* (strongly suspected of heresy): Lucas Arregoçes in Murcia in 1576,[157] Niqueta Griego and Bartolomé Genovés reconciled in Seville in 1579 (a case in which the captain of the vice-flagship ended up in prison),[158] and a Morisco and a Frenchman whom the Murcia tribunal had removed with other renegades from the Galleys of Spain in 1590. All served out their sentences in different monasteries.[159]

As a general rule, however, captains general did not often send men to Inquisition tribunals. Only three petitions by high officials were recorded in the last fifteen years of the sixteenth century, aside from the case of Guillermo de la Fuente, a gunner from the *Marquesa*, investigated in 1585 for suspicion of possible Jewish ancestry.[160] Gian Andrea Doria inquired in 1583 about the merits of a case against three Turks who rowed in his galleys,[161] and in 1588 Carlo Centurione sent two men to the Inquisition in Murcia.[162] And in 1591 the Count of Santa Gadea wrote to the Jesuit provincial requesting a priest who could convert several English convicts "who with a true heart, not a false one, wish to join our Catholic faith." Santa Gadea obviously had a personal stake in the outcome.[163]

Pedro de León described how Jesuit priests in Seville succeeded in their spiritual and physical care of rowers from the Galleys of Spain:

> Aside from the many confessions ... that we heard from convicts, all of them [were] moved to confess and take communion in a body among much joyful noise from minstrels ... we have seen the great fruits gained

155 AHN, Inquisición, libro 579, fol. 118r.
156 AHN, Inquisición, libro 579, fol. 168v.
157 AHN, Inquisición, libro 578, fol. 374v.
158 AHN, Inquisición, libro 579, fols. 228, 232, 248.
159 AHN, Inquisición, libro 581, fol. 309v.
160 AHN, Inquisición, libro 580, fol. 319v.
161 AHN, Inquisición, libro 580, fol. 216v.
162 AHN, Inquisición, libro 581, fol. 217v.
163 AHN, Inquisición, libro 582, fol. 2r.

> by them all, both soldiers and convicts. ... There were some conversions of convict Moors and Turks, who have learned the catechism and converted. In my time [there were] six Moors and Turks in our house, and to baptize them we took them in rich clothing to the principal Church in procession, with musicians and trumpet players and a large following ... [and] we returned to the galleys with the same following, where they acclaimed us with volleys and music. ... Once there, when all was calm, I would preach to them ... and the Moors and Turks who were there would be confounded and sometimes others would convert, from seeing how their companions were celebrated and how, after having been baptized, they lived as good Christians.[164]

No doubt spurred by Santa Gadea, the Jesuits increased their visits. In 1591 and for the rest of the decade permission was given for several campaigns of support and conversion, directed particularly from the recently founded English College (Colegio de los Ingleses) in Seville toward English convicts. Their main purpose was to obtain confession and penitence from all those men "of the sect of Luther and Calvin" who, because they were in the galleys, could not attend the Holy Office in person; the fathers would ratify their testimonies and request their release from the rowers' benches so that they could appear before the tribunal of Seville. There, sincere converts could be reconciled "without [wearing] the habit or having their goods confiscated, being assigned some spiritual penances," and the others absolved "*ad cautelam* [with caution] ... without reconciliation," under orders to be "instructed in the faith" and returned to the galleys.[165]

This solution did not wholly satisfy the captains general, however. In 1598 a correction was made, and the Jesuit Richard Walpole and the Supreme Council

164 "Allende de las muchas confesiones ... que les hacíamos a los forzados, moviéndose todos a confesar y haciendo comuniones generales con mucha fiesta de ministriles, ... se ha visto el mucho fruto que se ha hecho en todos, así en los soldados como en los forzados ... . Resultaron algunas conversiones de moros forzados y turcos, los cuales se han catequizado y convertido. En mi tiempo, seis moros y turcos en nuestra casa, y después, para bautizarlos, los hemos llevado muy bien aderezados de vestidos ricos a la Iglesia mayor en procesión, con menestrales y trompetas y mucho acompañamiento, ... [y] volviamos a las galeras con el mismo acompañamiento, adonde nos recibían con salvas de tiros y música ... . Llegados allá y sosegados les hacía plática, ... y los moros y turcos que allá estaban se confundían y algunas veces se convertían otros, así por ver las fiestas que les hacían a sus compañeros como por ver que después de bautizados vivían como buenos cristianos." León, *Grandeza*, 57–58.

165 AHN, Inquisición, libro 583, fol. 257v.

were told that men had to be absolved or reconciled "without removing them from the galleys, finding a way to instruct them on board as well as possible."[166] Though each captain general could decide for himself, those visits by Jesuits brought gifts of food and medical care that saved the squadron part of the limited annual budget for its hospital; in the end, however, any outside presence was problematic. As the contractors of the Galleys of Naples declared in 1587, the arrival of persons "to bring inquisitions into the galleys" was troublesome because they "not only inquire but also instigate."[167] Gian Andrea Doria himself hated to have to receive such visitors politely, "for you know with what intent these men usually come here."[168]

The Marquis of Santa Cruz would have agreed. In 1563, after he had let a group of convicts recover in the Jesuit hospital in Seville, Father Sancho López denounced several Dutchmen among them to the Inquisition as Lutherans. Unfortunately, their trial did not focus on these rowers' actual religious practices, but tried to identify their Lutheran contacts in Flanders.[169] For Santa Cruz, in any event, the result was the same: he lost several rowers to the Inquisition, to the detriment of his galleys' performance.

Not all officers saw the Jesuit presence aboard the galleys as positive. Martín de Quijano, for one, mocked them in 1594 in a letter to his brother-in-law, the purser Francisco de Aduna; although the letter has not survived, we can surmise its tenor from Aduna's reply:

> Your sister and I have had a very good time reading it, and it pleased us greatly to learn of the special incident of the Jesuit fathers' visit … . I would have shown it to the Marquis to give him a good laugh, and plan to do so when I have the chance, not … just once, twice, or thrice but three hundred times. … You must have very good shoulders to have borne two little candles, and not the holy kind either. … Now as a penance you will have to have the sweet name of JHS [both 'Jesus Christ' and 'the Society of Jesus'] always in your mouth, four holy beads on your rosary, and a few theological arguments in your head.[170]

---

166 AHN, Inquisición, libro 583, fol. 262v.

167 ADP, scaffale 70, busta 25, interno 5.

168 ADP, scaffale 85, busta 34: Gian Andrea Doria to Regent Castelet, 9 September 1605.

169 AHN, Inquisición, 2075, expediente 48.

170 "[N]os ha dado boníssimo rato a su hermana de Vuestra Merced y a mí el leerla, y es tanto el gusto que nos dio el saver el particular subçesso del viaje de los padres de la Compañía … . La hubiera mostrado al marqués para que se riera un rato, como lo pienso hazer en teniendo lugar, y no … una vez, ni dos, ni tres, sino trezientas … . Muy buenos ombros tiene Vuestra Merced, que sufría dos candelillas y no benditas … . Bien podrá agora en

If the galleys had had little contact with the Inquisition up to that point, beginning in the early seventeenth century they had even less. There was one petition from Juan de Grimaldo in 1600,[171] and several rowers were handed over to the Murcia tribunal in 1603,[172] but after that officers of the galleys scarcely communicated with the Holy Office again. Perhaps, as the number of galleys in the squadron shrank and fewer men were needed, Inquisition cases fell in proportion; if thirty ships had generated few cases, a mere ten ships would present hardly any. But the general impression is that captains general showed little interest in controlling their rowers' Christian orthodoxy. Not only did the Inquisition's presence in the galleys impinge on their absolute authority, but removing rowers from the benches interfered with the squadron's performance. It also set a bad example, in that men could assume that an Inquisition trial might free them from rowing for a spell. (The Holy Office tried repeatedly to combat that type of excuse.) And since crewmen were condemned to the galleys already, the Inquisition was not really necessary. When in 1615 Emmanuel Filibert of Savoy was appointed the new captain general of the sea and (on his request to Philip III) the Inquisition of the Sea was reestablished, we understand that he was simply exercising a prerogative and not responding to an actual need.

A separate question is whether he exercised the privilege not in pursuit of greater Christian orthodoxy on board but for a different end. Rafael Benítez Sánchez-Blanco and I have explained how, in the years when the Galleys of Spain had their own inquisitor, their tribunal showed little interest in punishing renegades and Moriscos for practicing Islam. It cared much more about fighting for broader jurisdiction, which would allow it to conclude trials and pronounce sentences without appealing to other tribunals.[173] It is tempting to speculate that behind that attitude lay an effort to remove the squadron from the influence of the few tribunals that still had the power to keep galleys from sailing and arrest their crewmen—because their jurisdiction was of a different order, and they were not subject to captains general. If the captain general of the sea had full control over an inquisitor of the sea, he could seem to respect the authority of the Holy Office while still keeping his rowers on board; that allowed him greater freedom of movement while making his jurisdiction even stronger.

penintençia contentarse con llevar siempre en la boca el dulçe nombre de JHS, quatro quentas benditas en el rosario y algunos puntos de theología en la caveça." AGS, Galeras, 216, fols. 637–39.

171 AHN, Inquisición, libro 584, fol. 17v.

172 AHN, Inquisición, libro 584, fol. 298v.

173 Lomas Cortés and Benítez Sánchez-Blanco, "Seconde Inquisition."

During those years the inquisitor of the sea, Martín de Vivanco, chose to open only a few cases in which rowers volunteered to confess their sins, but he ignored any accusations they made against their shipmates. His prudence shows how thoroughly Emmanuel Filibert of Savoy controlled the institution; he and his officers also ignored any heterodoxy among their Christian rowers so long as a galley's order, discipline, and seamanship were unaffected. A Valencian Morisco named Pedro Roget, alias Hamete, was serving a life sentence but made every effort to live in his galley as a good Muslim. He performed his ablutions like a "Moor," ate meat on Fridays and other Christian fast days, boycotted masses by chaplains and sermons by preachers, taught lessons on Islam from books he had on board, contradicted his *cómitre*, and argued about religion with Old Christian convicts—he was thought of as an actual *faqih*, an expert in the faith. He enjoyed great religious freedom, having been sentenced in 1606 and having served under three different captains general by that time. Such men were a problem only for chaplains, who tried in vain to tame them, but chaplains, too, had to please their superiors in the end.

If Moriscos' practices were tolerated, even more were those of North African slaves. Roget spoke in his confession about one aboard the *San Francisco* who also taught Islam and was taken for a *faqih*. As Vivanco complained when he demanded wider jurisdiction, after the expulsion of the Moriscos the Hispanic Monarchy still contained a space in which Muslims could exercise freedom of conscience, performing their rites as circumstances allowed, displaying their loyalty to Islam, and actively resisting their chaplains and inquisitors. But that resistance did not undermine the efficiency of the squadrons or challenge captains general and their military objectives; they reflected a more quotidian sort of conflict, like the ones that had arisen in many territories of the monarchy before the expulsion of 1609. In this sense as well, galley squadrons reproduced elements of the society that surrounded them. The same dynamic had played out among nobles in Aragon and Valencia who, in exchange for loyalty and cooperation from their Morisco vassals, declined to hold them to strict Christian orthodoxy on their own lands.

The same could be said of chaplains, who were poorly paid and often uneducated; like parish priests of churches in former Muslim territory, they found their ministry very difficult and often shirked their duties.[174] In the galleys, the Inquisition scarcely functioned, and chaplains lived alongside many North African Muslims. It is reasonable to conclude that religious permissiveness was one more way of building consensus aboard the galleys. This occurred in spite

174 Benítez Sánchez-Blanco, *Heroicas decisiones*, 314–25.

of the weight given to expressions of Catholic religiosity, both the kind that many Christian crewmen lived daily, and the more political and symbolic variety deployed by officers who were experts at using religious displays to advance their careers.

The minimal interest that captains general showed in their men's spiritual lives forged one more link in a long chain of favors and contributed to a policy of cohesion among the various collectives that made up a galley's crew. Captains, at the tip of the pyramid, had to find a balance between punishing men and satisfying their demands, especially those of the rowers, in the context of the squadron's needs and while interacting with decisions by other tribunals. Although men might occasionally escape, this strategy (sometimes using unorthodox means) managed to avert serious mutinies that could lead galleys into the hands of their enemies. In practice, governance aboard the galleys often differed profoundly from the grandiloquent reports issued by their leaders and the avowed principles of a crusade.

Conclusion

In 1616 the Marquis of Santa Cruz heard the case of Captain Hurtado's will and ruled for the corregidor of El Puerto de Santa María. The *auditor* of the Galleys of Spain, the licenciate Vázquez de Andrade, complained in a legal brief that the ruling infringed on the jurisdiction of the captaincy general of the squadron. He alleged that the royal scribe of the *auditor's* court was empowered to draw up wills and other legal documents for crewmen from the galleys and execute them in case of death, without violating royal laws or the jurisdictions of public scribes in coastal towns.

Vázquez de Andrade based his argument on the notion that "it is established and clear that Your Excellency, as captain general of the galleys, holds full jurisdiction from His Majesty *mero y mixto imperio* [by delegation of absolute power] … and that such [jurisdiction] is delegated to me as the *auditor general*"; therefore, the Marquis of Santa Cruz must not forget that "what Your Excellency governs is a Republic, which moves from place to place under your orders" and therefore "has its ministers for the affairs of the captains, soldiers, sailors, convicts, and officers who travel in them [the galleys], with a judge, scribe, and *auditores* [assigned to] them in the royal books, with their salaries which His Majesty pays for their work. And since this jurisdiction is clear, His Majesty has granted to it everything that is necessary in law, without which it cannot be exercised."

For this reason, the scribe of the galleys was not like those other "royal scribes who move around the kingdoms," who in the past had come into conflict with public scribes in cities and towns; he was scribe to "this republic of galleys" and enjoyed more rights than those of El Puerto de Santa María. There, the local landlord, the Duke of Medinaceli, "had bought all the jurisdictions," whereas the galleys' scribe "was named by Your Excellency" and therefore by the king. The *auditor* acknowledged that often, through ignorance, certain doubts could arise; but, to clarify matters, he recommended consulting the rules in the "military laws issued by the Duke of Parma and Plasencia, lieutenant governor and captain general of the states in Flanders by [order of] our lord the king, which laws must be kept and observed in all the states of His Majesty in Spain," one of which was the galley squadron.[1]

1 AGS, GyM, 858. Licenciate Vázquez de Andrade, 31 December 1619.

Vázquez de Andrade was reflecting on the *iurisdictio* and full power of the captain general, based on the dual civil and criminal imperium granted by the king, confirmed by the doctrine established in Farnese's ordinances and the texts of Mosquera de Figueroa, and carried out in daily practice by *auditores* who refused to accept any higher authority. In so doing, he showed how the squadron faced the same essential problem as any other governing institution in the early modern age—how to define the legitimacy of its power and the limits of its jurisdictional reach.[2]

This evolution paralleled that of the viceroyalties, and we can affirm that just as every viceroy, in the territory he governed, assumed the office of captain general, captains general of the galleys were the viceroys of their squadrons. The analogy played out on several levels. We find it in the liturgies and ceremonies that accompanied them in the public sphere, internally through formulas that recognized their authority (oaths of fealty, public displays on entering port or after a victory, etc.),[3] and externally through their identification with the principles and objectives of the monarchy.

The most revealing resemblance, however, may be the way in which the "territory" of the galleys adopted the exact model of governance of the king and his council, copied in turn by each viceroy and his *audiencia*.[4] In other territories, this innovation was meant to articulate and reinforce the power and "presence" of the absent monarch; it reinvented an ancient special commission that, stabilized and transformed, produced friction with the institutions of various estates within society. In the galleys, its origin was somewhat different. It sprang from the modernization of naval structures and the need not only to create governance for the institution but also to rule a new society (made up of both military men and civilians) in a force that had once been intermittent or temporary and was now permanent.

Once again, the chosen strategy was to adapt an ancient office, that of captain general, which was known and respected in the institutional structures of the coastal regions, though it was not free of controversy. Those difficulties did not arise because the new institution altered the traditional distribution and balance of power, tilting it toward the monarchy. Rather, it revealed the evolution of a long-standing situation—the presence of galleys in port and their crew members on land—that had formerly been occasional but now was continuous. The increased number of ships and their men's unbroken terms of service refocused the issue and called for a new configuration of their contacts

2 De Benedictis, *Politica, governo e istituzioni*, 263–65.

3 Rivero Rodríguez, *Edad de oro*, 182–89.

4 Pardo Molero and Lomas Cortés, *Oficiales reales*, 15.

with society. These changes had an internal dimension (the need to maintain efficient discipline among the crews) but especially an external one—a new set of corporations, the galley squadrons, had to be integrated and accepted as another form of territory, while learning to coexist with a jurisdiction (the admiralties, whose powers had once been even broader) that was of ancient origin but capable of innovation in its self-definitions and objectives.

The creation and progressive consolidation of the galley courts represented the definitive face of these changes. In invoking Roman legal doctrine to define themselves, they were again mirroring viceregal policy. It was necessary to do so because these courts were in constant conflict with local justice as it defended the laws and privileges of "the governed" (as in the case of Hurtado's will), and also because they interfered in maritime and port-based trade. This intromission into the markets arose because the ancient rights of the admiralties over captured prizes, smuggling, and other aspects of maritime commerce lived on among the privileges of captains general. Further, the galley squadrons soon became an offensive weapon in the Hispanic Monarchy's trade wars, enforcing the ban on commerce with North Africa and embargoes against other nations. Extending royal authority beyond immediate coastal waters, thanks to the squadrons' permanent nature and the actions of their courts, transformed the previous context by introducing a new tribunal that was unique in the brief and summary nature of its proceedings and dangerous in its coercive capacity. At the same time, the exercise of its customs privileges and ability to buy supplies "at the king's prices" gave rise to disputes with local authorities; the fiscal exemptions it enjoyed had a negative impact on many other rights and offered many opportunities for corruption.

These changes were also expressed internally, emphasizing even more the corporate nature of the galley squadrons. Pantero Pantera claimed that every galley was like a human body whose soul was divided into the same types that Aristotle had described. The rowers, sailors, and soldiers stood for the vegetative and sensitive soul of the galleys that permitted their movement and the rest of their natural operations, while the captain general was their rational soul, designed to direct the entire body toward happiness.[5] Doubtless, the people of each galley were divided into the same categories as any other society of the time, and obeyed the same hierarchical principle by which each man's position was defined by his privileges or lack of them; if he had none, it reflected his degree of integration or marginalization and his legal capacity. But the cramped physical space in which these divisions existed tended to blur

5 Pantera, *Armata navale*, 179.

certain distinctions and gave rise to a variety of contacts based on either economic interests or so-called "galley friendships." As a result, there were many examples of solidarity and especially patronage that extended to every collective on board; they arose from a policy of assistance that was highly structured and based on principles of fealty and obedience, directed from above by the captains general in their role as arbitrators.

In the last analysis, this reality kept that society from being wholly static and allowed for limited movement. A slave, through his service aboard a galley, could improve his living conditions or gain his freedom through the same channels that domestic slaves used on land; a convict could see his sentence commuted or shortened and even begin a new career as a soldier or sailor. Gian Andrea Doria once claimed that at different points in his life his service on board had let him escape from his family, flee from the plague, support his children, and pay his daughter's dowry.[6] We can assume similar motives for many other sailors, soldiers, and aspirants to service, but there was also the attraction of the privileges attached to their way of life.

While enlisting as a soldier could take a man to faraway places, enlisting as a sailor in a squadron that patrolled his home coastline could lead him to a privileged position in his community. In the first place, it exempted him from local justice in the region where he continued to live, while supplying comrades who could help him out of difficulties. Second, it allowed him to continue any economic activity without having to pay taxes to his former landowner. Having a squadron as a client could open the door to enjoying the squadron's own exemptions, while new business opportunities would arise as the squadron spent its money in local markets. Even though officials in El Puerto de Santa María complained that economic and criminal abuses by crewmen of the Galleys of Spain were depopulating their town, we wonder if local residents were really leaving the area, or if the laments simply meant that these deep commercial intrusions were "depopulating" the jurisdiction of the Duke of Mediaceli.

It would be wise to set aside for a moment the view of life in the galleys as horrific, and consider whether in some ways it might even have been attractive. We should analyze how the right to resist, which exists in every political and social universe, could be exercised. In fact, in some contemporaneous galley squadrons there were cases similar to magnicide. In 1602 Cesare Magalotti, captain general of the papal galleys, died of multiple stab wounds to the chest and abdomen by a Turkish slave elevated to seaman, who was then accused of being a fanatical traitor.[7] We have seen attempts at mutiny in a few Spanish

6 ADP, scaffale 82, busta 21, Gian Andrea Doria to Gio Petro, 30 July 1599.

7 Guglielmotti, *Storia*, 7:147–48.

galleys, usually by men rendered hopeless in the face of a long sentence at the oars. But at the same time, there was mediation of certain strategies of consensus, creating situations of tolerance difficult to transfer to other contexts under the Hispanic Monarchy: a degree of freedom aboard and on shore, the ability to live as a Muslim. For these and many other reasons, the galley squadrons formed the smallest and most distinctive Mediterranean viceroyalties under the rule of the Hapsburgs.

Bibliography

Abreu Bertonado, José A. *Colección de Tratados de Paz de España. Reynado de Phelipe III*. Madrid: Diego Peralta, Antonio Marín y Juan de Zúñiga, 1740.

Alonso Acero, Beatriz. *Orán-Mazalquivir, 1589–1639. Una sociedad española en la frontera de Berbería*. Madrid: CSIC, 2000.

Alonso Molina, María Paz. *El proceso penal en Castilla, siglos XIII–XVIII*. Salamanca: Universidad de Salamanca, 1982.

Andújar Castillo, Francisco. "Los rescates de cautivos en las dos orillas del Mediterráneo y en el mar (Alafías) en el siglo XVI." In *Le commerce des captifs. Les intermédiaires dans l'échange et le rachat des prisonniers en Méditerranée, XVe–XVIIIe siècle*, edited by Wolfgang Kaiser, 135–64. Rome: École Française, 2008.

Andújar Castillo, Francisco. "Sobre las condiciones de vida de los esclavos en la España moderna. Una revisión crítica." *Chronica Nova* 26 (1999): 7–36.

Aymard, Maurice. "Chiourmes et galères dans la Méditerranée du XVI siècle." In *Mélanges en l'honneur de Fernand Braudel*, 1:49–64. Toulouse: Privat, 1972.

Azpilcueta, Martín de. *Manual de confessores y penitentes, que clara y brevemente contiene la universal y particular decisión de quasi todas las dudas que en las confessiones suelen occurrir de los pecados, absoluciones, restituciones, censuras & irregularidades*. Antwerp: Viuda y herederos de Juan Steelsio, 1568.

Bamford, Paul W. *Fighting Ships and Prisons: Mediterranean Galleys of France in the Age of Louis XIV*. Minneapolis: University of Minnesota Press, 1973.

Baños de Velasco y Acevedo, Juan. 1680. *Política militar de príncipes*. Edited by Manuel-Reyes García Hurtado. Madrid: Ministerio de Defensa, 2011.

Barbero, Alessandro. *La battaglia dei tre imperi*. Rome: Edizioni Laterza, 2012.

Barroso, Bernardino. 1628. *Teoría, práctica y ejemplos*. Milan: Malatesta. Edited by Antonio Espino López. Madrid: Ministerio de Defensa, 2004.

Bennassar, Bartolomé and Lucile. *Les chrétiens d'Allah*. Paris: Perrin, 1989.

Benítez Sánchez-Blanco, Rafael. *Heroicas decisiones. La Monarquía Católica y los moriscos valencianos*. Valencia: Institució Alfons el Magnànim, 2001.

Benítez Sánchez-Blanco, Rafael. *Tríptico de la expulsión de los moriscos. El triunfo de la razón de estado*. Montpellier: PULM, 2012.

Ben Yessef Garfia, Yasmina R. "Perfiles de nobleza en la Monarquía Hispánica. La familia genovesa de los Serra entre Castila, Nápoles y Génova (s. XVII)." In *Estrategias culturales y circulación de la nueva nobleza en Europa (1570–1707)*, edited by Giovanni Muto and Antonio Terrasa Lozano, 187–212. Madrid: Doce Calles, 2015.

Berbouche, Alain. *Marine et justice. La justice criminelle de la Marine Française sous l'Ancien Régime*. Rennes: Presses Universitaires de Rennes, 2010.

Bertrand, Michel, and Natividad Planas. *Les sociétés de frontière. De la Méditerranée à l'Atlantique (XVIe–XVIIIe siècle)*. Madrid: Casa de Velázquez, 2011.

Bethencourt, Francisco. *La Inquisición en la época moderna. España, Portugal, Italia, siglos XV–XIX.* Madrid: Akal, 1997.

Bono, Salvatore. "Achat d'esclaves turcs pour les galères pontificales (XVIe–XVIIIe siècle)." *Revue de l'Occident musulman et de la Méditerranée* 38 (1985): 79–92.

Boyer, Pierre. "La chiourme turque des galères de France de 1685 à 1687." *Revue de l'Occident musulman et de la Méditerranée* 6 (1969): 53–74.

Braudel, Fernand. *La Méditerranée et le monde méditerranéen à l'époque de Phillipe II.* Paris: Librairie Armand Colin, 1949.

Bresc, Henri. "La piété des gens de mer en Méditerranée occidentale aux derniers siècles du Moyen-Âge." In *Le genti del mare Mediterraneo*, edited by Rosalda Ragosta, 427–44. Naples: Lucio Pironte, 1981.

Brogini, Anne. *Malte, Frontière de Chrétienté (1530–1670)*. Rome: École Française de Rome, 2006.

Bromley, J.S. *Corsairs and Navies (1660–1760)*. London: The Hambledon Press, 1987.

Bunes Ibarra, Miguel Ángel. "Felipe III y la defensa del Mediterráneo. La conquista de Argel." In *Guerra y sociedad en la Monarquía Hispánica (1500–1700)*, edited by Enrique García Hernán and Davide Maffi, 1:921–45. Madrid: Laberinto, 2006.

Bunes Ibarra, Miguel Ángel. "El marco ideológico de la expansión española por el norte de África." *Aldaba: Revista del Centro Asociado a la UNED de Melilla* 25 (1995): 113–34.

Bunes Ibarra, Miguel Ángel. "Relaciones económicas entre la Monarquía Hispánica y el Islam en la época de Cervantes." *Revista de Historia Económica. Journal of Iberian and Latin American Economic History* 23-Extra 1 (2005): 161–80.

Cabanous, Alain. *La mer et les hommes. Pêcheurs et matelots dunkerquois de Louis XIV à la Révolution*. Dunkirk: Westhoek-Editions, 1980.

Cabrera de Córdoba, Luis. *Relaciones de las cosas sucedidas en la Corte de España desde 1599 a 1614*. Salamanca: Junta de Castilla y León, 1997.

Calafat, Guillaume. "Premessa." *Quaderni Storici* 143, no. 2 (2013): 311–17.

Calderón Ortega, José Manuel. *El almirantazgo de Castilla. Historia de una institución conflictiva (1250–1560)*. Alcalá de Henares: Universidad de Alcalá de Henares, Servicio de Publicaciones, 2003.

Candiani, Guido. "Galere forzate o galere di libertà: una comparazione tra la marina veneziana e quella spagnola all'indomani della contessa dell'interdetto (1607)." In *Guerra y Sociedad en la Monarquía Hispánica (1500–1700)*, edited by Enrique García Hernán and Davide Maffi, 2:947–64. Madrid: Laberinto, 2006.

Capdeferro i Pla, Josep. *Ciència i experiència. El jurista Fontanella (1575–1649) i les seves cartes*. Barcelona: Fundació Noguera, 2012.

Capmany i Monpalau, José. *Memorias históricas sobre la marina, comercio y artes de la antigua ciudad de Barcelona*. Barcelona: Cámara Oficial de Comercio y Navegación, 1963.

Carpentier, Bastien, and Jean-Philippe Priotti. "La forge inestable d'une domination. Les Doria, Gênes et la monarchie hispanique (1560–1606)." In *Identités et territoires dans les mondes hispaniques (XVIe–Xxe siècle)*, edited by Philippe Priotti, 75–96. Rennes: Presses Universitaires de Rennes, 2015.

Carpentier, Bastien, and Jean-Philippe Priotti. "Philippe II, Giovanni Andrea Doria et le contrôle militaire de la Méditerranée à la fin du XVIe siècle." In *Circulations maritimes. L'Espagne et son empire (XVIe–XVIIIe siècles)*, edited by Michel Bertrand and Jean-Philippe Priotti, 159–83. Rennes: Presses Universitaires de Rennes, 2011.

Casado Moreno, José. "Las ordenanzas de Alejandro Farnesio de 1587." *Anuario de Historia del Derecho Español* 31 (1961): 431–58.

Catalá Sanz, Jorge, and Sergio Urzainqui Sánchez. *La conjura morisca de 1570. La tentativa de alzamiento en Valencia*. Valencia: Biblioteca Valenciana, 2009.

Chaline, Olivier. *Les armées du Roi. Le grand chantier, XVIIe–XVIIIe siècle*. Paris: Armand Colin, 2016.

Civale, Gianclaudio. *Guerrieri di Cristo. Inquisitori, gesuiti e soldati alla battaglia di Lepanto*. Milan: Edizioni Unicopli, 2009.

Covarrubias, Sebastián de. *Tesoro de la lengua castellana*. Madrid: Luis Sánchez, 1611.

Covarrubias y Leiva, Diego de. *Regulae, peccatum, De regulis iuris lib. 6, relectio*. Salamanca: Dominici a Portonarijs, 1571.

Croce, Benedetto. "La vita infernale delle galere." In *Varietà di storia letteraria e civile*, Serie seconda, 83–92. Bari: Laterza, 1949.

De Benedictis, Angela. *Politica, governo e istituzioni nell'Europa moderna. Una sintesi originale e innovativa di storia istituzionale fra XV e XVIII secolo*. Il Mulino, 2001.

Dessert, Daniel. *La Royale. Vaisseaux et marins du roi-soleil*. Paris: Fayard, 1987.

Édouard, Sylvène. "*Argo*, la galera real de Don Juan de Austria en Lepanto." *Reales Sitios: Revista de Patrimonio nacional* 44, no. 172 (2007): 4–27.

Eguiluz, Martín de. 1592. *Discurso y regla militar*. Edited by Francisco Andújar Castillo. Madrid: Ministerio de Defensa, 2001.

Enciso Alonso-Muñumer, Isabel. *Nobleza, poder y mecenazgo en tiempos de Felipe III. Nápoles y el Conde de Lemos*. Madrid: Actas, 2007.

Escribano Páez, José Miguel. "Los actores de la diplomacia hispano-maghrebí a comienzos de la Edad Moderna." In *Embajadores culturales. Transferencias y lealtades de la Diplomacia española en la Edad Moderna*, edited by Diana Carrió-Invernizzi, 37–52. Madrid: UNED, 2016.

Escribano Páez, José Miguel. "Juan Rena and the Construction of the Hispanic Monarchy (1500–1540)." Unpublished doctoral dissertation, European University Institute, Florence, 2016.

Favarò, Valentina. *Gobernar con prudencia. Los Lemos, estrategias familiares y servicio al rey (siglo XVII)*. Murcia: Edit.um-Red Columnaria, 2016.

Favarò, Valentina. *La modernizzazione militare nella Sicilia di Filippo II*. Quaderni Mediterranea. Ricerche storiche 10. Palermo: Associazione Mediterranea, 2009.

Fenicia, Giulio. *Il Regno di Napoli e la difesa del Mediterraneo nell'età di Filippo II (1556–1598). Organizzazione e finanziamento*. Bari: Cacucci, 2003.

Fernández Duro, Cesáreo. *Historia de la Armada española desde la unión de Castilla y de Aragón*, 1903. 9 vols. Madrid: Museo Naval, 1972.

Ferrer Valls, Teresa. "Las fiestas públicas en la Monarquía de Felipe II y Felipe III." In *Glorias efímeras. Exequias florentinas por Felipe III y Margarita de Austria*, 43–53. Madrid: Sociedad Estatal para la conmemoración de los centenarios de Felipe II y Carlos V, 1999.

Filioli Uranio, Fabrizio. *La squadra navale pontificia nella Repubblica internazionale delle galere. Secoli XVI–XVII*. Rome: Aracne Editrice, 2016.

Fiume, Giovanna. *Schiavitù mediterranee. Corsari, rinnegati e santi di età moderna*. Milan: Bruno Mondadori, 2009.

Fontenay, Michel. "L'esclave galérien dans la Méditerranée des Temps modernes." In *Figures de l'esclave au Moyen-Âge et dans le monde moderne*, edited by Henri Bresc, 115–43. Paris: L'Harmattan, 1996.

Fontenay, Michel. "Los fenómenos corsarios en la 'periferización' del Mediterráneo en el siglo XVII." In *Desigualdad y dependencia. La periferización del Mediterráneo occidental (s. XII–XIX)*, edited by María Teresa Pérez Picazo, Guy Lemeunier, and Pedro Segura, 116–21. Murcia: Universidad de Murcia, 1984.

Fontenay, Michel. "La place de la course dans l'économie portuaire. L'exemple de Malte et des ports barbaresques." *Annales: Économies, Sociétés, Civilisations* 43, no. 6 (1988): 1321–47.

Fontenay, Michel. *La Méditerranée entre la croix et le croissant. Navigation, commerce, course et piraterie (XVIe–XIXe siècle)*. Paris: Classiques Garnier, 2010.

Foti, Rita Loredana. *Guidici e corsari. Il tribunale delle prede di Sicilia 1808–1813*. Palermo: Istituto Poligrafico Europeo, 2016.

Fusco, Idamaria. "Istituzioni, movimenti di uomini ed epidemie: il caso della peste del 1656 nel Regno di Napoli." In *Identità mediterranea ed Europa. Mobilità, migrazioni, relazioni interculturali*, edited by Maria Rosaria Carli, Gioia Di Cristofaro Longo, and Idamaria Fusco, 81–112. Naples: Istituto di Studi sulle Società del Mediterraneo (Consiglio Nazionale delle Ricerche), 2009.

García Arias, Luis. "Estudio preliminar." In Hugo Grocio, *De la libertad de los mares*, 13–42. Madrid: Instituto de Estudios Políticos, 1956.

García Bernal, José Jaime. *El fasto público en la España de los Austrias*. Seville: Universidad de Sevilla, 2006.

Gelabert González, Juan. "Entre 'embargo general' y 'libre comercio.' Las relaciones mercantiles entre Francia y España de 1598 a 1609." *Obradoiro de Historia Moderna* 16 (2007): 65–90.

Gil Pujol, Francisco Xavier. "Más sobre revueltas y revoluciones del siglo XVII y sobre su ausencia." In *La crisis de la monarquía de Felipe IV*, coordinated by Geoffrey Parker, 351–92. Barcelona: Crítica, 2006.

Gilabert Tomàs. "La defensa contra el cors musulmà: l'esquadra de galeres de la Generalitat de Catalunya (1599–1623)." *Drassana: Revista del Museu Marítim* 21 (2013): 98–128.

Glete, Jan. *War and the State in Early Modern Europe: Spain, the Dutch Republic and Sweden as Fiscal-military States, 1500–1660*. London: Routledge, 2002.

González, Tomás. *Censo de población de las provincias y partidos de la Corona de Castilla en el siglo XVI*. Madrid: Imprenta Real, 1829.

González Cruz, David. "Las deserciones en las fuerzas armadas españolas y extranjeras durante la Guerra de Sucesión. Comportamientos y estrategias." In *Un estado militar. España, 1650–1820*, edited by Agustín González Enciso, 65–89. Madrid: Actas, 2012.

Gracia Rivas, Manuel. "La sanidad naval española. De Lepanto a Trafalgar." *Cuadernos de Historia Moderna. Anejo V: Armar y* marear *en los siglos modernos* (2006): 167–85.

Green, Molly. "Beyond the Northern Invasion: The Mediterranean in the Seventeenth Century." *Past and Present* 174 (2002): 42–71.

Greif, Avner. "Contract Enforcement and Institutions among the Maghribi Traders: Refuting Edwards and Ogilvie." SSRN Electronic Journal, February 2008. https://www.researchgate.net/publication/5002859.

Guglielmotti, Alberto. *Storia della Marina Pontificia*, 7. Rome: Tipografia Vaticana, 1892.

Guia Marín, Lluís. *Sardenya, una història pròxima. El regne sard a l'època moderna*. Valencia: Editorial Afers, 2012.

Guilmartin, John F. *Gunpowder and Galleys: Changing Technology and Mediterranean Warfare at Sea in the Sixteenth Century*. Cambridge: Cambridge University Press, 1974.

Haan, Bertrand. "La dernière paix catholique européenne. Édition et présentation du traité de Vervins (2 mai 1598)." In *La Paix de Vervins, 1598*, 9–63. Vervins: Fédération des Sociétés d'Histoire et d'Archéologie de l'Aisne, 1998.

Heras Santos, José Luis de las. "Los galeotes de la Monarquía Hispánica durante el Antiguo Régimen." *Studia Historica: Historia Moderna* 22 (2000): 283–300.

Heras Santos, José Luis de las. "Los galeotes de los Austrias. La penalidad al servicio de la Armada." *Historia Social* 6 (1990): 127–40.

Heras Santos, José Luis de las. *La justicia penal de los Austrias en la Corona de Castilla*. Salamanca: Ediciones de la Universidad de Salamanca, 1994.

Hernando Sánchez, Carlos José. *El reino de Nápoles en el Imperio de Carlos V. La consolidación de la conquista*. Madrid: Sociedad Estatal para la conmemoración de los centenarios de Felipe II y Carlos V, 2001.

Herrero Sánchez, Manuel. "La red genovesa Spínola y el entramado transnacional de los marqueses de los Balbases al servicio de la Monarquía Hispánica." In *Las redes del imperio. Élites sociales en la articulación de la Monarquía Hispánica 1492–1714*, edited by Bartolomé Yun Casalilla, 97–134. Madrid: Marcial Pons, 2009.

Hintze, Otto. "Organización militar y organización del Estado. Conferencia dictada el 17 de febrero de 1906 en Dresde." *Relaciones Internacionales* 5 (2006). https://dialnet.unirioja.es/servlet/revista?codigo=12666.

Jamieson, Alan G. *Lords of the Sea: A History of the Barbary Corsairs*. London: Reaktion Books, 2012.

Jiménez Estrella, Antonio. *Poder, ejército y gobierno en el siglo XVI. La Capitanía General del Reino de Granada y sus agentes*. Granada: Universidad de Granada, 2004.

Judde de Larivière, Claire. *Naviguer, commercer, gouverner. Économie maritime et pouvoirs à Venise (Xve–XVIe siècles)*. Leiden: Brill, 2008.

Kirk, Thomas A. *Genoa and the Sea: Policy and Power in an Early Modern Maritime Republic, 1559–1684*. Baltimore, MD: The Johns Hopkins University Press, 2005.

Ladero Quesada, Miguel Ángel. "El Almirantazgo de Castilla en la Edad Media. Siglos XIII al XV." In *La institución del Almirantazgo en España*, 57–82. Madrid: Instituto de Historia y Cultura Naval, 2003.

Ladero Quesada, Miguel Ángel. *La armada de Flandes. Un episodio en la política naval de los Reyes Católicos (1496–1497)*. Madrid: Real Academia de la Historia, 2003.

Lavenia, Vincenzo. *Il catecismo dei soldati. Guerra e cura d'anime in etıa moderna*. Bologna: EBD, 2014.

Le Flem, Jean-Paul. "L'Arithmétique navale de D. Pedro Giron duc d'Osuna, vice-roi de Naples et de Sicile (1611–1619)." In *État, Marine et Société. Hommage à Jean Mayer*, edited by Michel Vergé-Franceschi and André Zysberg, 239–49. Paris: PUPS, 1995.

León, Pedro de. *Grandeza y miseria en Andalucía. Testimonio de una encrucijada histórica (1578–1616)*, edited by Pedro Herrera Puga. Granada: Facultad de Teología, 1981.

Linde, Luis M. *Don Pedro Girón, duque de Osuna. La hegemonía española en Europa a comienzos del siglo XVII*. Madrid: Ediciones Encuentro, 2005.

Lomas Cortés, Manuel. "La armada de Felipe III. Gestión y logística de las escuadras de galeras permanentes del Rey Católico en la expulsión de los moriscos (1609–1610)." In *El mar en los siglos modernos*, edited by Manuel-Reyes García Hurtado, Domingo González Lopo, and Enrique Martínez Rodríguez, 2:265–77. Santiago de Compostela: Xunta de Galicia, 2009.

Lomas Cortés, Manuel. "L'esclave captif sur les Galères d'Espagne (XVI–XVII siècles)." *Cahiers de la Méditerranée* 87 (2013), 17–33.

Lomas Cortés, Manuel. "Las galeras de aprovisionamiento marítimo de Orán-Mazalquivir (1599–1621)." In *Orán. Historia de la Corte Chica*, edited by Miguel A. Bunes Ibarra and Beatriz Alonso Acero, 195–222. Madrid: Polifemo, 2011.

Lomas Cortés, Manuel. "Las Galeras de España en tiempos de Manuel Filiberto de Saboya. Dificultades financieras y proyectos de reforma." In *Identità e frontiere. Politica, economia e società nel Mediterraneo (secc. XIV–XVIII)*, edited by Lluís Guia Marín, Maria Grazia Mele, and Gianfranco Tore, 147–58. Milan: Franco Angeli, 2015.

Lomas Cortés, Manuel. "Les galériens du Roi Catholique: esclaves, forçats et rameurs salariés dans les escadres de Philippe III (1598–1621)." In *Des galères méditerranéennes aux rivages normands. Recueil d'études en hommage à André Zysberg*, edited by Gilles Désire dit Gosset, Bernard Garnier, Alain Hugon, Leila Maziane, and Élisabeth Ridel. *Cahiers des Annales de Normandie* 36 (2011): 103–14.

Lomas Cortés, Manuel. "Juan Andrea Doria y la cesión del Marquesado de Finale." In *En tierra de confluencias. Italia y la Monarquía de España*, edited by Cristina Bravo Lozano and Roberto Quirós Rosado, 111–27. Valencia: Albatros, 2013.

Lomas Cortés, Manuel. "Justicia y gobierno en las galeras de Felipe III." In *Tra Marte e Astrea. Giustizia e giurisdizione militare nell'Europa della prima età moderna (secc. XVI–XVIII)*, edited by Davide Maffi, 125–52. Milan: Franco Angeli, 2012.

Lomas Cortés, Manuel. "Patronazgo y servicio a la Corona en las escuadras de galeras del Mediterráneo. El caso del veedor general Martín de Quijano (1578–1606)." In *Cambios y resistencias sociales en la Edad Moderna. Un análisis comparativo entre el centro y la periferia mediterránea de la Monarquía Hispánica*, edited by Ricardo Franch Benavent, Andrés Robres Fernando, and Rafael Benítez Sánchez-Blanco, 435–43. Madrid: Sílex, 2014.

Lomas Cortés, Manuel. *El proceso de expulsión de los moriscos de España*. Valencia: PUV, 2011.

Lomas Cortés, Manuel. *El puerto de Dénia y el destierro morisco*. Valencia: PUV, 2009.

Lomas Cortés, Manuel. "Renovar el servicio a la Monarquía tras la muerte del rey. Juan Andrea Doria y el viaje de la reina Margarita (1598–1599)." In *Servir al rey en la Monarquía de los Austrias. Medios, fines y logros del servicio al soberano en los siglos XVI y XVII*, edited by Alicia Esteban Estríngana, 193–226. Madrid: Silex, 2012.

Lomas Cortés, Manuel, and Rafael Benítez Sánchez-Blanco. "La seconde Inquisition de la mer (1615–1621) face au problème morisque." In *Morisques (1501–1614). Une histoire si familière*, edited by Youssef El Alaoui, 65–85. Monts: PURH, 2017.

López de Coca Castañer, José Enrique. "El Reino de Granada como frontera. Organización de su defensa durante el reinado de los Reyes Católicos (1492–1516)." In *La organización militar en los siglos XV y XVI. Actas de las II Jornadas Nacionales de Historia Militar*, 93–110. Seville: Cátedra General Castaños, 1993.

López de Tovar, Gregorio. *Las Siete Partidas del sabio rey don Alonso el Nono, glosadas por el licenciado Gregorio López, del Consejo Real de Indias de S.M.* Madrid: Benito Cano, 1789.

Loriga, Sabina. *Soldats. Un laboratoire disciplinaire. L'armée piémontaise au XVIIIe siècle.* Paris: Mentha, 1991.

Lunenfeld, Marvin. *Los corregidores de Isabel la Católica.* Barcelona: Labor Universitaria, 1989.

Maffi, Davide. *Il baluardo della Corona. Esercito, finanze e società nella Lombardia seisentesca (1630–1660).* Florence: Le Monnier Università, 2007.

Maffi, Davide. *En defensa del Imperio. Los ejércitos de Felipe IV y la guerra por la hegemonía en Europa (1635–1659).* Madrid: Actas, 2014.

Manconi, Francesco. *Castigo de Dios. La grande peste barocca nella Sardegna di Filippo IV.* Rome: Donzelli Editore, 1994.

Marañón, Gregorio. "La vida en las galeras en tiempos de Felipe II." In *Vida e Historia*, 94–124. Madrid: Espasa Calpe, 1941.

Marchena Giménez, José Manuel. "La vida y los hombres de las galeras de España (siglos XVI–XVII)." Unpublished doctoral dissertation, Universidad Complutense, Madrid, 2010.

Maréchaux, Benoît. "Instituciones navales y finanzas internacionales en el Mediterráneo de la época moderna. Los asentistas de galeras genoveses al servicio de la Monarquía Hispánica (1500–1650)." Unpublished doctoral dissertation, Universidad Carlos III, Madrid, 2017.

Maréchaux, Benoît. "Le réseau entrepreneurial de l'*asentista de galeras* Marco Centurione. Organisation, financement et négotiation politique en Méditerranée Occidentale (1610–1620)." Presentation given at the Colloque international. Une république marchande européenne (Xve–XVIIIe siècle)? Mobilités, échanges, identités, Paris, 9–10 April 2015.

Martín Casares, Aurelia. "Repensar la esclavitud en el mundo hispano. Reflexiones y propuestas metodológicas desde la antropología histórica." In *Esclavitudes hispánicas (siglos XV–XXI). Horizontes socioculturales*, 11–40. Granada: EUG, 2015.

Martín Corrales, Eloy. "De cómo el comercio se impuso a la razzia en las relaciones hispano-musulmanas en tiempos del Quijote. Hacia la normalización del comercio con el norte de África y el Levante otomano a caballo de los siglos XVI y XVII." *Revista de Historia Económica: Journal of Iberian and Latin American Economic History* 23-Extra 1 (2005): 139–60.

Martínez Martínez, Manuel. *Los forzados de marina en la España del siglo XVIII.* Almería: Editorial Universidad de Almería, 2011.

Martínez Martínez, Manuel. "Los gitanos en el reinado de Felipe II (1556–1598). El fracaso de una integración." *Chronica Nova* 30 (2003–4): 401–30.

Martínez Ruiz, Enrique. "Legislación y fuero militar." In *Guerra y sociedad en la Monarquía Hispánica. Política, estrategia y cultura en la Europa Moderna (1500–1700)*, edited by Enrique García Hernán and Davide Maffi, 2:11–32. Madrid: MAPFRE—Laberinto —CSIC, 2006.

Martínez Ruiz, Enrique. *Los soldados del rey. Los ejércitos de la Monarquía hispánica (1480–1700)*. Madrid: Actas, 2008.

Masson, Paul. *Les galères de France (1481–1781). Marseille, port de guerre*. Paris: Hachette, 1938.

Mathiex, Jean. "Trafic et prix de l'homme en Méditerranée aux XVIIe et XVIIIe siècles." *Annales: Économies, Sociétés, Civilisations* 9, no. 2 (1954): 157–64.

Mattone, Antonello. "L'amministrazione delle galere nella Sardegna spagnola." *Società e Storia* 49 (1990): 514–45.

Mémain, René. *Matelots et soldats des vaisseaux du roi. Levées d'hommes au département de Rochefort (1661–1690)*. Paris: Hachette, 1937.

Merrien, Jean. *La vie quotidienne des marins au temps du Roi Soleil*. Paris: Famot, 1979.

Millán Garrido, Antonio. *Justicia militar*. Madrid: Ariel, 2012.

Mira Caballos, Esteban. "La Armada del Reino de Granada (1492–1550). Apuntes para su historia." *Revista de Historia Naval* 68 (2000): 35–54.

Molina Heredia, José María. "Las Galeras de España a fines del reinado de Felipe II. Un instrumento de poder y defensa en el Mediterráneo." In *V Jornadas Nacionales de Historia Militar*, 599–612. Seville: Cátedra General Castaños, 1997.

Moliné i Brassés, Ernest (ed.). *Les costums marítimes de Barcelona universalment conegudes per Llibre del Consolat de mar*. Barcelona: Estampa d'Henich y Cia., 1914.

Mora Casado, Carlos. "Las milicias en el Mediterráneo occidental. Valencia y Cerdeña en la época de los Austrias." Unpublished doctoral dissertation, Cagliari-Valencia, 2016.

Moreno Casado, José. "Las ordenanzas de Alejandro Farnesio de 1587." *Anuario de Historia del Derecho Español* 31 (1961): 431–58.

Mosquera de Figueroa, Cristóbal. *Comentario en breve compendio de disciplina militar, en que se escribe la jornada de la islas de los Açores*. Madrid: Luis Sánchez, 1596.

Mouline, Nabile. *Le califat imaginaire d'Ahmad al-Mansur*. Paris: PUF, 2009.

Muñoz Altabert, María Luisa. *Les Corts valencianes de Felip III*. Valencia: Universitat de Valencia-PUV, 2005.

Navarro Sorní, Miquel. *Calixto III Borja y Alfonso el Magnánimo frente a la Cruzada*. Valencia: Ayuntamiento de Valencia, 2003.

Olesa Muñido, Francisco-Felipe. *La galera en la navegación y el combate*, 2 vols. Barcelona: Junta Ejecutiva del IV Centenario de la Batalla de Lepanto, 1971.

Olesa Muñido, Francisco-Felipe. *La organización naval de los estados mediterráneos y en especial España durante los siglos XVI–XVII*. Madrid: Editorial Naval, 1968.

Oliver Asín, Jaime. *Vida de don Felipe de África, príncipe de Fez y de Marruecos (1566–1621)*. Introduction by Miguel A. Bunes Ibarra and Beatriz Alonso Acero. Granada: UEG, 2008.

Pacini, Arturo. *La Genova di Andrea Doria nell'Imperio di Carlo V*. Florence: Leo S. Olschki, 1999.

Pantera, Pantero, *Armata navale del capitan Pantero Pantera, gentil'huomo comasco & cavalliero dell'habito di Cristo, divisa in doi libri nei quali si ragiona del modo che si ha à tenere per formare, ordinare & conservare un'armata maritima*. Rome: Egidio Spada, 1614.

Panzac, Daniel. *La marine ottomane. De l'apogée à la chute de l'Empire*. Paris: CNRS, 2012.

Pardo Molero, Juan Francisco. "*Per terra e no per mar*. La actividad naval en la defensa del Reino de Valencia en tiempos de Carlos I." *Estudis: Revista de Historia Moderna* 21 (1995): 61–97.

Pardo Molero, Juan Francisco. "Los usos de Roma. Ideas y recursos políticos en la Monarquía Hispánica." In *L'*imperium Romanum *en perspective. Les savoirs d'empire dans la République romaine et leur heritage dans l'Europe médiévale et moderne*, edited by Julien Dubouloz, Silvia Pittia, and Gaetano Sabatini, 389–409. Besançon: Presses Universitaires du Franche-Comté, 2014.

Pardo Molero, Juan Francisco, and Manuel Lomas Cortés. *Oficiales reales. Los ministros de la Monarquía Católica (siglos XVI–XVII)*. Valencia: Universitat de València, 2012.

Parrot, David. *Richelieu's Army: War, Government and Society in France, 1624–1642*. Cambridge: Cambridge University Press, 2001.

Pelorson, Jean-Marc. *Los* letrados *juristas castellanos bajo Felipe III. Investigaciones sobre su puesto en la sociedad, la cultura y el Estado*. Valladolid: Junta de Castilla y León, 2008.

Peñera, Luciano. "Estudio introductorio. La tesis de la Paz Dinámica." In *Francisco de Vitoria. Relectio de Iure Belli o Paz Dinámica. Escuela Española de la Paz. Primera generación 1526–1560*, edited by L. Peñera, V. Abril, C. Baciero, A. García and F. Maseda, 127–33. Madrid: CSIC, 1981.

Pérez Embid, Florentino. *El Almirantazgo de Castilla hasta las capitulaciones de Santa Fe*. Seville: CSIC, 1944.

Phillips, Carla Rahn. *Seis galeones para el Rey de España. La defensa imperial a principios del siglo XVII*. Madrid: Alianza Editorial, 1991.

Portugués, José Antonio. *Colección general de las ordenanzas militares*, 1. Madrid: Antonio Marín, 1764.

Puddu, Raffaele. *El soldado gentilhombre*. Barcelona: Argos Vergara, 1984.

Quatrefages, René. "La *proveeduría* des *armadas*. De l'expedition de Tunis (1535) à celle d'Alger (1541)." *Mélanges de la Casa de Velázquez* 14 (1978), 215–47.

Quatrefages, René. *La revolución militar moderna. El crisol Español*. Madrid: Ministerio de Defensa, 1996.

Rambert, Gaston. *Nicolas Arnoul. Intendant des Galères à Marseille (1665–1674). Ses lettres et mémoires relatifs à l'agrandissement de la ville et à l'entretien du port*. Marseille: Provincia, 1931.

Redondo, Agustín. "La lucha contra el Turco del III duque de Osuna según las relaciones de sucesos (1611–1620)." In *Cultura della Guerra e arti della Pace. Il III Duca di Osuna in Sicilia e a Napoli (1611–1620)*, edited by Encarnación Sánchez García and Caterina Ruta, 395–416. Tulio Pironte, 2012.

Renzi, Salvatore de. *Napoli nell'anno 1656 ovvero documenti della pestilenza che desolò Napoli nell'anno 1656, preceduti dalla storia di quella tremenda sventura narrata*. Naples: Tipografia Domenico di Pascuale, 1867.

Rivero Rodríguez, Manuel. *La Batalla de Lepanto. Cruzada, guerra santa e identidad confesional*. Madrid: Silex, 2008.

Rivero Rodríguez, Manuel. *La edad de oro de los virreyes. El virreinato en la Monarquía Hispánica durante los siglos XVI y XVII*. Madrid: Akal, 2011.

Rodrigo Alfonso, José. "Un hospital real de los militares de Mesina (1679–1713). La sanidad militar en la monarquía Hispánica." *Estudis: Revista de Historia Moderna* 36 (2010): 295–313.

Rodríguez de Fonseca, Bartolomé Agustín. *Digesto teórico-práctico o recopilación de los derechos común, real y canónico, por los libros y títulos del Digesto*. Madrid: Imprenta Real, 1791.

Rodríguez Hernández, Antonio José. *Los tambores de Marte. El reclutamiento en Castilla durante la segunda mitad del siglo XVII (1648–1700)*. Valladolid: Castilla Ediciones, 2011.

Rodríguez Jouliá Saint-Cyr, Carlos. *Felipe III y el rey de Cuco*. Madrid: Instituto de Estudios Africanos, 1951.

Ruiz Ibáñez, José Javier. "Los juegos de azar en los cuerpos de guardia (Murcia 1580–1640)." In *Actas del II Congreso de jóvenes historiadores y geógrafos*, 301–9. Valencia: CSIC, 1992.

Ruiz Ibáñez, José Javier (coord.). *Las milicias del rey de España. Sociedad, política e identidad en las Monarquías Ibéricas*. Madrid: Fondo de Cultura Económica, 2009.

Ruiz Ibáñez, José Javier, and Vicente Montojo Montojo. *Entre el lucro y la defensa. Las relaciones entre la Monarquía y la sociedad mercantil cartagenera (comerciantes y corsarios en el siglo XVII)*. Murcia: Real Academia Alfonso X el Sabio, 1998.

Saavedra Vázquez, María Carmen. "La formación de armadas y sus efectos a nivel territorial. El ejemplo de Galicia, 1580–1640." *Cuadernos de Historia Moderna. Anejo V: Armar y Marear en los Siglos Modernos* (2006): 55–76.

San Ruperto Albert, Josep. "Emprenedors transnacionals. Les trajectòries econòmiques i d'ascens social des Cernezzi i Odescalchi a la Mediterrània occidental (ca. 1590–1689)." Unpublished doctoral dissertation, Universitat de València, 2017.

Sanz Ayán, Carmen. "El abastecimiento de pertrechos navales a la Monarquía durante el siglo XVII." In *Estado, monarquía y finanzas. Estudios de Historia financiera en tiempos de los Austrias*, 79–103. Madrid: CEPC, 2004.

Schaub, Jean-Frédéric. *Le Portugal au temps du Comte-Duc d'Olivares (1621–1640)*. Madrid: Casa de Velázquez, 2001.

Serra i Puig, Eva. "Galeres catalanes, forçats i moriscos." *Pedralbes* 28 (2008): 411–44.

Sicking, Louis. *El Almirantazgo y la Armada de los Países Bajos durante los reinados de Felipe I y Carlos V.* Santander: Ediciones Universidad de Cantabria, 2017.

Sirago, María. *La città e il mare. Economia, politica portuale ed identità culturale dei centri costieri del Mezzogiorno moderno.* Naples: Edizioni Scientifiche Italiane, 2004.

Sirago, María. "La flotta napoletana nel viceregno spagnolo (1507–1598)." *Frontera d'Europa: Società, economia, istituzioni, diritto del mezzogiorno d'Italia: Rivista Storica Semestrale* 1 (1999): 111–72.

Sirago, María. "La trasformazione dei porti e degli arsenali del regno di Napoli nel passaggio dalla propulsione remica a quella velica." In *II Convegno Nazionale di Storia dell'Ingegneria, Napoli 7–9 aprile 2008*, edited by S. D'Agostino, 1017–27. Naples, 2008.

Soto, Domingo de. *Controversias entre Bartolomé de Las Casas (obispo que fue de Chiapas) y Ginés de Sepúlveda (cronista del Emperador).* Valladolid: Editorial Maxtor, 2006.

Soto, Domingo de. *De iustitia et iure*, 5. Paris: Bartolomé Honorato, 1582.

Storrs, Christopher. "Health, Sickness and Medical Services in Spain's Armed Forces c. 1665–1700." *Medical History* 50, no. 3 (2006): 325–50.

Suárez Fernández, Luis. *Política internacional de Isabel la Católica. Estudio y documentos.* Valladolid: Instituto Universitario de Historia de Simancas, 2002.

Szmolka Clares, José Antonio. "Las fuerzas navales del Reino de Granada. Una excepción en la organización militar española de comienzos del quinientos." In *La organización militar en los siglos XV y XVI. Actas de las II Jornadas Nacionales de Historia Militar*, 115–20. Seville: Cátedra General Castaños, 1993.

Tarruell, Cecilia. "Circulations entre Chrétienté et Islam. Captivité et esclavage des serviteurs de la Monarchie hispanique (ca. 1574–1609)." Unpublished doctoral dissertation, Universidad Autónoma de Madrid, 2015.

Thompson, I.A.A. "Las galeras en la política militar española en el Mediterráneo durante el siglo XVI." *Manuscrits* 24 (2006): 95–124.

Thompson, I.A.A. *War and Government in Hapsburg Spain 1560–1620.* London: University of London, 1976.

Tierney, Brian. *Religion, Law, and the Growth of Constitutional Thought.* Cambridge: Cambridge University Press, 1983.

Varachaud, Marie-Christine, Michel Vergé-Franceschi, and A. Zysberg. "Qui étaient les capitaines de vaisseau du Roi-Soleil?" *Revue Historique* 582 (1992): 311–38.

Vargas-Hidalgo, Rafael. *Guerra y diplomacia en el Mediterráneo. Correspondencia inédita de Felipe II con Andrea y Juan Andrea Doria.* Madrid: Polifemo, 2002.

Vicens Vives, Jaime. "Estructura administrativa estatal en los siglos XVI–XVII." In *Coyuntura económica y reformismo burgués*, 101–41. 4th ed. Barcelona: Ariel, 1974.

Vincent, Bernard. "Les esclaves des galères napolitaines en 1585." In *Hacer historia desde Simancas. Homenaje a José Luis Rodríguez de Diego*, edited by Alberto Marcos Martín, 837–45. Valladolid: Junta de Castilla y León, 2011.

Vincent, Bernard. "Procédures et réseaux de rachats de captifs dans l'Espagne des XVIe–XVIIe siècle." In *Le commerce des captifs. Les intermédiaires dans l'échange et le rachat des prisonniers en Méditerranée, XVe–XVIIIe siècle*, edited by Wolfgang Kaiser, 123–34. Rome: École Française, 2008.

Visceglia, Maria Antonietta. *La città rituale. Roma e le sue ceremonie in età moderna.* Rome: Viella, 2002.

Wettinger, Godfrey. *Slavery in the Islands of Malta and Gozo (ca. 1000–1812)*. Malta: Publishers Enterprises Group, 2002.

Wheat, David. "Mediterranean Slavery, New World Transformations: Galley Slaves in the Spanish Caribbean, 1578–1635." *Slavery and Abolition* 31, no. 3 (2010): 327–44.

Williams, Philip. *Empire and Holy War in the Mediterranean: The Galley and Maritime Conflict Between the Habsburg and Ottoman Empires*. London: I.B. Tauris, 2014.

Williams, Philip. "Past and Present: The Forms and Limits of Spanish Naval Power in the Mediterranean, 1590–1620." In *Le Forze del Principe. Recursos humanos, instrumentos y límites en la práctica del poder soberano en los territorios de la Monarquía Hispánica*, edited by Mario Rizzo, José J. Ruiz Ibáñez, and Gaetano Sabatini, 237–78. Murcia: Universidad de Murcia, 2003.

Williams, Philip. "The Strategy of Galley Warfare in the Mediterranean (1560–1620)." In *Guerra y Sociedad en la Monarquía Hispánica (1500–1700)*, edited by Enrique García Hernán and Davide Maffi, 1:891–920. Madrid: CSIC-MAPFRE-Laberinto, 2006.

Zysberg, André. "Les galères de France sous le règne de Louis XIV. Essai de comptabilité globale." In *Les marines de guerre européennes (XVIIe–XVIIIe siècles)*, edited by Martine Acerra, José Merino, and Jean Meyer, 415–44. Paris: Presses de l'Université de Paris-Sorbonne, 1998.

Zysberg, André. *Les galériens. Vies et destins de 60000 forçats sur les galères de France, 1680–1748*. Paris: Éditions du Seuil, 1987.

Index

Abraham, Lorenzo 89
Aceñas de la Cartuja 113
Acevedo, Juan Baños de 52
Acosta, Domingo de 140
Acosta, Fransciso de 62
Acuña, Juan de 102–103, 105–106
Adana, family 106
Adelantado *see* Santa Gadea, count of
Admiral of the fleet 19–20
Aduna, Francisco de 164
Aguirre, Mateo de 130
Aguirre, Tomás de 102, 105–106
Agustín, Antón 148
Agustín, Juan 148
Alarcón, family 107
Alba, duke of 27
Albariel, Juan 135
Alberto, Manuel 152
Alcácer, slave 120, 124
Alcázar 85
Alcázar, licenciate 149
Alcoholado, Juan de 85
Alessandria 146
Alfenio, Antonio 147
Algarve 69, 151
Algiers 22, 61, 77, 87–90, 101, 125, 130–131, 133–134
Alí, slave 66
Alicante 69
Almazán, marquis of 59
Almirante mayor see High Admiral
Almodóvar del Campo 122
Alonso Acero, B., *historian* 61, 90
Alonso Romero, M. P., *historian* 71
Alphonse x the Wise 15, 42, 81
Alva, Andrés de 161
Alvarado, Juan de 161
Alzate, Bartolomé de 65
Alzate, Carlos de 65
Amar, slave 85
Amarexo, slave 89
Amsterdam 73
Amuza, slave 88
Andalusia 49, 103, 111, 154
Angelo, convict 128–129
Angulo, Tomás de 112
Antequera 151
Antolín, Pedro 142
Antonio, Giovani di 138
Apostolic Tribunal of the Roman Rota 46
Aquinas, Thomas 82
Aragon 7, 86, 90, 95, 166
Aragon, Admiralty of 16
Aragon, Crown of 16, 18, 44
Aristotle 170
Armada of the Ocean Sea 67, 73, 80–81, 91, 93–94
Armenta, Pedro de 75
Armijo, Catalina de 86
Aroztegui, Antonio 139, 150
Arreaga, Martín de 94
Arregoçes, Lucas 162
Arriarán, Garci López de 15
Arriola, Francisco 110
Arteta, Íñigo 14
Asistente of Seville 55
Austria, Albert, archduke of 72, 96
Austria, John of 18, 21–22, 25
Austria, Marguerite of, queen of the Hispanic Monarchy 34, 126, 152
Austria, María of, empress 95
Avellino, prince of 136
Avellino, prince of *see* Caracciolo, Marino
Ayamonte 66, 69
Aymard, M., *historian* 1, 5–6
Azambalí, slave 85
Azán, slave 87
Azores, islands 22, 46
Azpilcueta, Martín de 91

Baeza 86
Balabene, convict 138
Baños de Velasco, Juan 55
Barbarroja, brothers 18
Barbero, A., *historian* 6
Barbero, David 71
Barca, slave 87
Barcelona 34, 40, 42, 50, 59, 62, 77, 87, 89, 93, 100–102, 121, 135, 153, 155–156
Baretta, Anibal 138

Barrena, Diego de 104
Barrile, Domenico 62
Barroso, Bernardino 55
Bautista, Juan 147
Bazán II, Álvaro de 63, 86, 142, 145, 149, 168
Bazán, Álvaro de 19, 22, 39, 46–47, 51, 80, 164
Bazán, María de 63
Béjar, duke of 96
Belem 73
Bellido, Miguel 135
Beltrán, Pedro 146–147
Ben Aze, Mohamete 90
Ben Buxareb, Mahomete 90
Ben Yessef Garfia, Y. R., *historian* 4
Benamar, Alí 131
Benamar, Mahamet 131
Benavente, count of 131
Benavente, countess of 96
Benítez Sánchez-Blanco, R., *historian* 165
Bennassar, B., *historian* 6
Bennassar, L., *historian* 6
Berbouche, A., *historian* 8
Berdina, Guillermo 100
Beretta, Gaspar 139
Bermúdez, captain 153–154
Bizerte 134, 152–153
Bolin, Rocher 75
Bône 85–86
Boni, Antonio 159
Bono, S., *historian* 6
Borghese, cardinal 53
Borja, Melchor de 146
Botija, slave 88
Boyer, P., *historian* 6
Brabant, chancellor of *see* Damant, Nicholas
Bracciano, dukes of *see* Orsini, family
Braudel, F., *historian* 1
Bressae, Fray Juan 77
Brochero, Diego 48
Brochero, Francisco 144
Brogini, A., *historian* 5
Buenaboyas 5, 35, 146–148
Bunes Ibarra, M. A., *historian* 83, 85, 92
Buona voglia see buenaboya
Buoncompagni, Giacomo 30
Buriel, Gregorio 142
Butar, Ramon 76
Caballero, Juan 140
Caballero, Juan 140
Cabia, Antonio 140
Cabrera, Juan 140
Cáceres 122
Cáceres, Diego de 159–160
Cádiz 65–66, 69, 72, 74, 77, 101, 104–105, 107, 111, 113, 115, 121, 131, 149
Calais 79
Calderón, J. M., *historian* 14
Calvin 163
Camera della Sommaria 97–98
Candiani, G., *historian* 3
Canoli, Napoleón 90
Capitán Mayor del Mar 13–15, 19
Capitanía General de la Armada *see* *Captaincy General of the Fleet*
Capmany I Monpalau, *historian* 156
Captaincy General of the Fleet 17
Captive 7, 61, 87, 89, 93, 126, 152
Caracciolo, Marino 50
Caraffa, cardinal 153
Carcano, Cristoforo 124
Caribbean, sea 6
Carpentier, B., *historian* 3
Cartagena 33, 61–62, 65, 69, 77–78, 91, 97–98, 101, 106, 121, 131, 154–155
Cascaes 72
Castile 7, 12–14, 16–17, 26, 43, 59, 71, 76, 86, 90, 95, 99–100, 131–132, 134, 151
Castile, Admiralty of 14–16, 42
Castile, Council of 46
Castile, Crown of 19, 44
Castile, Guards of 44
Castro, count of 27
Catalano, Pietro 126–130, 159
Catalonia 21, 23, 49–50
Catalonia, *Cortes* of 23
Catalonia, Galleys of 6, 59–60, 65, 68, 82, 125, 135, 140
Catalonia, *Generalitat* of 59–60
Catholicism 8
Centurione, Carlo 162
Centurione, family 4
Centurione, Vincenzo 87
Cerón, Juan de 100
Chaline, O., *historian* 3
Charles V 3, 8, 17–19, 21, 44, 83
Chaves, Gabriel de 61–62

Chaves, Hernando de 159–160
Chaves, Pedro de 152–153
Chelva 136
Chercell 134
Chiva 138
Christendom 6, 84
Civale, G., *historian* 6, 34
Civitavecchia 27, 30–34, 37, 54
Claudio, convict 126, 128
Cobos, Jerónimo de los 66
Colonna, Marcantonio 29
Comes, Pere Joan 156
Commissioner General of the Crusade 64
Company of Jesus 153, 164
Consiglio Collaterale of Naples 97
Constable of Castile *see* Fernández de Velasco, Juan
Contador see purser or quartermaster
Convicts 5–7, 35, 41, 69, 88–89, 120–140, 149–152, 159–160, 171
Cornejo, Alonso 115
Covarrubias, Diego de 83
Covarrubias, Sebastián de 42, 45–46
Croce, B., *historian* 4
Cuenca, Gaspar de 56
Cuerda, licenciate 89
Curtis, Leonardo 109
Cusano, marquis of 138

Damant, Nicholas 152
Dançer, Simón 81
Danzig 77
Dávalos, Francisco 125
De Baudio, Claudio 140
De la Fuente, Guillermo 162
De la Serna, Francisco 100
De la Serna, Juan 97–98
De las Casas, Bartolomé 82–83
De las Heras, J. L., *historian* 5
De Lofredo, Juanelo 140
De Vicenti, Domenico 135
Del Castillo, Pedro 123
Del Castillo, Pedro 146
Del Mancino, Vincenzo 139
Del Valle, Luis 161
Denia 131, 149
Denia, Galleys of 61, 102, 125, 146, 148
Dessert, D., *historian* 3, 106
Digby, John 76
Djerba 134
Domingo, Juan 126, 128
Dominguillo, buenaboya 146
Dondano, Anselmo 136
Doria, Andrea 3, 17, 19, 22
Doria, Carlo 22, 33, 98, 100–101, 135, 141, 144–145, 149, 158
Doria, family 3, 68
Doria, Gian Andrea 3, 22, 31, 34, 35, 48, 50, 54, 81, 87, 89, 95–102, 106, 123–124, 126–127, 129–130, 133–136, 138, 145, 148–149, 152, 158, 162, 164, 171
Doria, Giannettino 28
Drake, Francis 105
Duarte, Xacome 105
Dunkirk 72–73
Durango, Martín de 65, 102, 106, 110, 149

Eguera, Pedro de 145
El Puerto de Santa María 62, 65–66, 72, 74, 76, 78, 89, 94, 102, 105, 107–117, 121–122, 144–145, 147, 157, 160, 168, 171
El Puerto *see* El Puerto de Santa María
Elba 146
Elda, count of 75, 94, 130
Endem 72
England 83
English Channel 150
Enríquez, family 13
Enríquez, Hernando 19
Escribano Páez, J. M., *historian* 2

Fajardo, Luis 81–84, 95
Falces, Juan de 140
Farnese, Alessandro 44, 47–48, 143, 168–169
Farnesio, Alejandro *see* Farnese, Alessandro
Favarò, V., *historian* 2
Felipe, Domingo 77
Fenicia, G., *historian* 2
Ferdinand II, king of Aragon 12, 15–17, 43
Feria, duke of 62
Fernández de Córdoba, Gonzalo 16–17
Fernández de Velasco, Juan 96
Fernández de Villegas 63, 106, 122, 140
Fernández, Francisco 135
Ferrer, Jerónimo 50
Ferrero, Ruggiero 125
Fez 134

Fiertempach, Cristóbal 96
Figueroa, Juan de 140
Filioli Uranio, F., *historian* 2
Finale 96
Fiume, G., *historian* 86
Flanders 15, 30, 32, 44, 69, 139, 150, 164, 168
Flanders, Council of 152
Flanders, Galleys of 23, 106, 150
Florence 84, 96
Fontanet, Cristóbal 140
Fontenay, M., *historian* 5
Fornal, Juan 86
Foti, R. L., *historian* 79
Fox, Juan 86
France 8, 67, 77, 84, 134
France, Galleys of 3, 6
Fuengirola 63

Gabriel, Antonio 144
Gabrietti, Juan Bautista 141
Galicia 69, 72
Gallardo, Catalina 89
Garbaransen, Juan 75
García, Juan 146
García, Pedro 125
García, Pedro 135
García, Sebastián 140
Garguillo, Leonardo 75
Garibaldo, Nicola 101–102, 135
Gaspar, Andrés 125
Gata, cape of 66
Gattinara, Mercurino 18
Gegrory XV 27
Genoa, Galleys of 33, 96, 99, 101, 133, 136, 138, 140, 148, 152
Genoa, port of 3, 27, 36, 50, 95, 97–98, 101–102, 126, 136–137, 139, 145, 148, 155
Genoa, Republic of 3, 31, 50, 96
Genovés, Bartolomé 162
Gentil, Nicolás 140
Gibraltar 62, 94, 104, 155
Gibraltar, straits of 12, 61, 72–73, 80, 93
Gil Pujol, X., *historian* 132
Gionta, Marco 126, 128–129
Girón, family. 153
Glete, J., *historian* 2, 8
Gómez, Francisco 94
Gómez, Juan 140
Gondomar, count of 76
Gonzáez, Blas 89
Gonzales, Miguel 87, 140
Granada 12, 15, 21, 76, 123, 162
Granada, Kingdom of 15
Grand Captain of the Sea *see Capitán Mayor del Mar*
Grand Turk 84
Grattapane, convict 126–130, 158
Gregory XIII 31
Griego, Juan 140
Griego, Niqueta 162
Grimaldo, Juan 165
Grotius, Hugo 79
Guadalete, river 107, 113, 116
Guadalquivir, river 31
Guatordio, Mario 139
Guillermo, Pablo 71
Guilmartin, J. F., *historian* 1
Guipúzcoa 69
Guise, duke of 136

Hamete, slave 66
Hamete, slave 88
Hapsburg, family 14, 45, 96, 172
Havre-de-Grâce 72, 77
Hermosa, Vicente de 7–9
Hernández, Ana 140
Hernández, Andrés 67, 86
Hernández, Sebastián 140
Herrero Sánchez, M., *historian* 4
Hintze, O., *historian* 2
Hispanic Monarchy 4, 7–9, 12, 17, 19, 21, 25–27, 29, 33, 38, 40, 43, 49, 59–61, 68, 79, 82–83, 85, 129, 141, 151, 166, 170–172
Holland 77
Holy League 34
Holy Office *see* Inquisition
Holy See 54
Hostilius, Tullus 55
Howards, corsair 81
Huelva 71
Hurtado, Juan 144, 168, 170

Iberian Peninsula 7, 10, 18, 26, 61, 85
Indies 61, 111, 150
Inicia, Alejandro de 138
Inquisition, Suprem Council of 7–8, 135, 161
Inquisition, tribunal 6, 160–167

Inspector general 42, 69, 72, 99, 105, 106, 135, 140, 144–145
Isabella I, queen of Castile 12, 15, 17, 43
Islam 6–7, 82, 165–166
Istanbul 134
Isuf, slave 87
Italy 10, 26, 44, 62, 100, 106, 134, 154
Italy, Council of 141

Jaén, Juan de 114
James I, king of England 76
Jerez de la Frontera 107, 111, 121–122
Jerusalem 29
Jiménez Estrella, A., *historian* 15
Joanna, princess of Castile 15
Jordán, Francisco 160
Juan, Diego 71
Judde de Larivière, C., *historian* 3, 7
Justinian, emperor 43

Kara Uthman Dey 81–84
Kirk Thomas A., *historian* 3

Ladero Quesada, M. A., *historian* 13, 15
Larache 65, 85, 88, 94, 155–156, 160
Lauro, Antonio 140
Ledesma, Cristóbal 109
Leiva, Pedro de 100, 158
Lemos, count of 153–154
Lemos, countess of 96, 98
Lemos, duke of 28
León, Francisco Antonio de 140
León, Mateo de 148, 157
León, Pedro de 162
Leonés, Juan 142
Lepanto, battle of 6, 25, 29–30, 107, 155
Lerma, duke of 24, 97–98, 102, 133, 149
Lezama, Íñigo de 102, 105
Lezcano, Juan de 15
Lisbon 48, 69, 72, 78, 130, 132, 149
Livorno 52–54
London 75–76
London, Treaty of 75
Lone, Jean de 77
López de Coca, J. E., *historian* 15
López de Tovar, Gregorio 82
López de Zárate 105–106
López León, Pedro 102
López, Diego 114, 125, 130
López, Juan 75
López, Sancho 164
Loriga, S., *historian* 56
Los Alfaques 125
Louis XIII, king of France 3
Louis XIV, king of France 3, 106
Low Countries 8
Loyola, Ignatius of 153
Luca, Giovanni di 52–54, 159
Lucca 138–139
Luna, Alonso de 114
Luther 163

Madrid 4, 34, 76, 139
Madruzzo, cardinal 138
Maffi, D., *historian* 151
Magalotti, Cesare 171
Majorca 131
Málaga 2, 30, 62, 69, 73
Maldonado, Francisco 147
Malta 84
Malta, Galleys of 5
Manrique, Íñigo 17
Mantua, duke of 138
Maqueda, duke of 90, 98
Marañón, G., *historian* 4
Marbella 67
Marchena Giménez, M., *historian* 4, 125
Marchena, Juan 93–94
Maréchaux, B., *historian* 4
Marín, Juan 105
Marroquín, Joan 105, 113
Martín Casares, A., *historian* 89
Martín Corrales, E., *historian* 85, 91
Martín, Alonso 114
Martín, Álvaro 142
Martín, Francisco 124
Martínez, M., *historian* 5, 120
Massa, Cesare 149
Mathiex, J., *historian* 5
Mattei, Giuseppe 32
Mattone, A., *historian* 2
Maza, Francisco 140
Mazalquívir 36
Medici, family 53
Medina Sidonia, duke of 72, 93, 95, 101
Medina Sidonia, family 85
Medina Sinonia, ville of 121–122
Medinaceli, duke of 107–116, 157, 168, 171

Medinaceli, family 116
Mediterranean, sea 3, 5–6, 8, 10, 12, 17, 19, 21, 24, 27, 30, 31, 34, 48, 57, 81, 85, 118, 152
Melone, Antonio 125
Mendoza, Juan de 96
Merenda, Lelio 144
Messía de Prado, Rodrigo 100
Messina 28, 53, 87, 97, 99, 152
Milan 96, 100, 136, 146
Milan, Senate of 138–139, 141
Mira Caballos, E., *historian* 17
Miranda, countess of 97
Molina Heredia, *historian* 108
Molina, Juan Alfonso de 65–66
Moncada, Hugo de 18–19
Monreale 28
Montes, Pedro de 89
Morata, Miguel 139
Moreno, Rodrigo 150
Morisco 6–7, 61, 67, 86, 89, 91, 122–123, 125, 130–131, 135–136, 155, 162, 165–166
Morocco 89, 93–94
Moroni, Giovanni 31
Mosquera de Figueroa, Cristóbal 46–49, 51, 70, 74, 80, 169
Mosquera de Figueroa, Juan 113
Mostafá see Ribera, Juan de, slave
Mudejar 7
Muḥammad, prophet 89
Mulato, Pedro 89
Mulay al-Shaykh 85, 94–95
Murcia 86, 161–162, 165
Muruzábal, Pedro de 100
Mutio, Alessandro 148

Nájera, duchess of 98
Naples, Galleys of 6, 50, 97–98, 119, 129, 152, 164
Naples, port of 2, 24–25, 27, 29, 53–54, 96, 98, 100, 106, 153
Naples, *Vicaria* of 97, 138
Nasrid, kingdom 12, 133
Navarro, Pedro 17
Negroponte 134
Niebla, count of 65
Nigule, Dionis de 77
North Africa 12, 67, 72, 77, 80, 82, 84–85, 91, 93–95, 113, 117, 125, 130, 148, 170
Novar, Melchor de 99

Obregón, family 106
Obregón, Juan de 99
Ocampo, Juan 66
Olesa Muñido, F. F., *historian* 4
Oliva 149
Olivares, count of 54
Oporto 69
Oran 36, 52, 61, 90, 95, 104, 154
Orce 123
Oropesa 62
Orsini, family 27
Ortiz de Zárate, Juan 102
Ossorio, Juan 71
Osuna, duke of 25, 29, 153
Ottoman Empire 6, 21, 82
Ovideo, Miguel de 69–70, 99, 159
Oviedo, Martín de 124

Pacharo, Francisco 136
Pacini, A., *historian* 3
Pagador see Paymaster
Palermo 28, 97, 144
Palo, castle of 27
Palomero, Francisco 140
Pantera, Pantero 89, 120, 123–124, 170
Pardo, J. F., *historian* 45, 48
Parma and Plasencia, duke of *see* Farnese, Alessandro
Parma, duke of 138, 141
Parrot, D., *historian* 3
Pascual, Juan 91, 122
Pastrana, duke of 27
Paul V, pope 53
Paymaster 42, 63–64, 67, 88–91, 94, 102, 104, 106, 110, 113, 120, 122, 140, 140–141, 147
Pedro Cifuentes 142
Pegi 126, 128
Pelorson, J.M., *historian* 45
Peñíscola 62–63
Peñón de Vélez de la Gomera 94
Pérez, Jerónimo 149
Pérez, Juan 109
Philip I, king of Castile 8
Philip II, king of the Hispanic Monarchy 3, 21–23, 31, 46, 72, 91, 102, 105, 119
Philip III, king of the Hispanic Monarchy 22–25, 34, 49, 69, 76, 78, 80, 89, 91, 93, 149, 165
Philip IV, king of the Hispanic Monarchy 26

Phillips, C. R., *historian* 2
Piacenza 141
Piombino 138, 146
Pisa 93
Pius V, pope 34, 158
Ponz, captain 146
Porres, Felipe de 144
Porto Ercole 37
Portugal 66, 73, 79
Portugal, Conquest of 22, 46, 94
Portugal, Crown of 22
Portugal, Galleys of 23, 73, 75–76, 124, 130, 133, 139–141, 151
Portuondo, Rodrigo 19
Proveedor General see *Purveyor*
Purser 42, 65, 102, 105–106, 108, 110, 149, 164
Purveyor 69, 90, 95, 99, 102, 104, 106, 108, 111–114, 117, 144, 156

Quartermaster 102–103, 106, 113, 117, 148–149, 156–157
Quatrefages, R., *historian* 2, 43–44
Questa, Guiseppe 137
Questa, Lorenzo 137
Quijano, family 106
Quijano, María de 100
Quijano, Martín de 99, 102, 106, 107, 133, 145–146, 160, 164
Quincoces, Pedro de 100, 102, 105, 110

Ramadán, slave 87
Ransom 65–66, 84–85, 89, 93, 95, 117, 125, 134, 137–138, 141, 148, 151
Rebella, Jacome 62
Riambau, Juan 156
Ribera, Juan de, archbishop 136
Ribera, Juan de, slave 86–87
Riccardo, Pietro 136
Richelieu, cardinal 8
Rico, Sebastián. 140
Rida, Francisco 124
Rincón, Bartolomé 65
Riva, Antonio Francesco 141
Rivero, M., *historian* 6
Roberto, Francesco 145
Rodríguez, Gonzalo 103
Rodríguez, Sebastían 114
Roget, Pedro 166
Rojas, Pedro de 140
Románico, *cómitre* 149
Rome 29, 55, 83, 138
Ronda 122
Rosales, Antonio de 106
Rota 121
Ruiz de Arce, Juan 136
Ruiz, Juan 145

Saba', slave 148
Sáenz de Oyanguren, Juan 102, 104, 106
Sahara 12
Saint George, Bank of 97
Saint George, Republic of, *see* Genoa, Republic of 27
Saint Stephen, Galleys of 53
Saint Vincent, cape of 75
Salazar, count of 67
Salé 93
San Germán, marquis of 85–86
San Remo 31
Sánchez de Marchena, Diego 149
Sánchez, Cristóbal 85–86
Sánchez, Diego 150
Sánchez, Gabriel 100
Sancho, Lope de 135
Sanlúcar de Barrameda 69, 113, 115
Santa Cruz, marchioness of 155
Santa Cruz, marquis of *see* Bazán II, Álvaro de
Santa Gadea, count of 51–52, 66, 73, 93, 108, 111, 114–115, 149, 162–163
Santander 32
Santans, Gabriel de 49
Sanz Ayán, C., *historian* 2
Sanza, Gabriel 63
Saona 50
Sardinia 2, 23, 25, 68, 102
Savo, Gio Maria 139
Savona 146
Savona 159
Savoy 136
Savoy, Emmanuel Filibert 25, 28, 59–60, 64, 68, 76, 86, 87, 99, 142, 165–166
Schaub, J. F., *historian* 51
Scio, Juan Domenico 141
Sepúlveda, Ginés de 82
Serra, E., *historian* 6

Serra, family 4
Serra, Pietro 145
Serrano Aguilera, Juan 139
Sestri Levante 148
Seville 31, 55–56, 63–64, 72, 78, 101, 107, 112–113, 120–122, 131, 160–164
Sevo, Domenico 101
Sicily 2, 28, 81, 95, 98, 104
Sicily, Galleys of 48, 96, 100, 140, 158, 160
Sicily, Kingdom of 16–17
Sicking, L., *historian* 8
Silita, Antonio 142
Silva, Pedro de 140
Sixtus V, pope 52, 54
Slave 5–7, 29, 37, 41–42, 55, 60, 64–69, 85–89, 103, 108–109, 117, 119–124, 126, 130–132, 134, 138–141, 146, 148–149, 152, 155, 166, 171
Solimán, slave *see* Sánchez, Cristóbal
Solís, Gonzalo 150
Soto, Domingo de 83
Spagnolo, Gio 126, 128–129
Spain 4, 7, 12, 18, 32, 54, 83, 94, 96, 101, 168
Spain, Galleys of 6–7, 13–14, 17, 23, 33, 35, 39, 49, 51–52, 55, 60–65, 67–69, 73–74, 76, 78–80, 86–87, 90–91, 93–94, 99, 102, 107, 111, 116, 117, 122–123, 131, 140, 142, 144, 147–150, 154, 157, 159, 161–162, 165, 168
Spanish, squadrons of galleys 1–2, 6–7, 9–10
Spínola, family 4
Spínola, Federico 32, 150
Squarciafico, Vincenzo 64
State, Council of 93

Tangier 94, 105
Tarifa 66
Tarruell, C., *historian* 86
Terán, Juan 140
Terceira, battle of 46
Terceira, island 22, 55, 80
Tercio 44
Tétouan 61–62, 66, 85, 88, 134
Thompson, I.A.A., *historian* 2
Tierney, B., *historian* 57
Tocina 49
Toledo, García de 119–120, 132, 152, 155
Toledo, Pedro de 35, 62, 67, 155–156, 159–160
Torcello, bishop of 53
Torres, Ginés de 144
Torres, Luis de 151
Torres, Mateo 142
Torres, Melchor de 140
Tortona, bishop of 138
Toulouse 76
Tribunale di Regio Patrimonio 97
Tribunale di Regio Patrimonio 97
Tunis 81, 83, 87, 95
Tursi, duke of *see* Doria, Carlo
Tuscany, Grand Duke of 53

Utrera 121

Valencia 21, 23, 34, 59, 67, 76, 91, 131, 136, 141, 149, 152, 166
Valencia, Kingdom of 24, 155
Valivadra 87
Valladolid 74, 83, 100
Vargas-Hidalgo, R., *historian* 3
Vargas, Francisco de 140
Vázquez de Andrade, licenciate 168–169
Veart, Adam 72
Veedor general see Inspector general
Velasco, Alonso de 69, 144
Velasco, Juan 124
Vélez-Málaga 142
Venart, Thomas 77, 93
Venice, Galleys of 7
Venice, Republic of 3, 80
Vergara, Bartolomé 138
Verio, Juan de 146
Vervins, Peace of 75–76, 126
Vicens Vives, J., *historian* 2
Vilar, Miguel de 148
Villafranca, marquis of *see* Toledo, Pedro de
Vincens, Honoré 126, 130
Vincent, B., *historian* 6
Vincenzo, convict 138
Visceglia, M. A., *historian* 29
Vitoria, Francisco de 81–82
Vivanco, Martín de 166

Walpole, Richard 163
War, Council of 24, 36, 49, 51, 59, 65–66, 71–73, 76–78, 81, 86–87, 90, 102, 108, 118, 123, 130, 139–141, 150, 160
Wettinger, G., *historian* 5

Wheat, D., *historian* 6
Williams, P., *historian* 1, 6, 61

Xeque, Muley *see* Mulay al-Shaykh

Yzá, slave 87

Zani, Marco Antonio 30–31, 36–37
Zarzaña, Hamete 120, 123
Zufre, family 106
Zufre, Miguel de 102, 104–106, 149
Zúñiga, Pedro de 75
Zysberg, A., *historian* 5, 6

www.ingramcontent.com/pod-product-compliance
Lightning Source LLC
Chambersburg PA
CBHW071250180926
51613CB00002B/186
* 9 7 8 9 0 0 4 3 8 1 4 6 9 *